ORDEAL BY PLANNING

ORDEAL
BY PLANNING

BY

JOHN JEWKES

STANLEY JEVONS PROFESSOR OF POLITICAL ECONOMY
IN THE UNIVERSITY OF MANCHESTER

NEW YORK

THE MACMILLAN COMPANY

1948

CONTENTS

THE greatest tyranny has the smallest beginnings. From precedents overlooked, from remonstrances despised, from grievances treated with ridicule, from powerless men oppressed with impunity, and overbearing men tolerated with complacence, springs the tyrannical usage which generations of wise and good men may hereafter perceive and lament and resist in vain. At present, common minds no more see a crushing tyranny in a trivial unfairness or a ludicrous indignity, than the eye uninformed by reason can discern the oak in the acorn, or the utter desolation of winter in the first autumnal fall. Hence the necessity of denouncing with unwearied and even troublesome perseverance a single act of oppression. Let it alone and it stands on record. The country has allowed it and when it is at last provoked to a late indignation it finds itself gagged with the record of its own ill compulsion.

The Times, August 11, 1846

INTRODUCTION

I HAVE written this book reluctantly. I know that it will offend some of my friends and I fear it may hurt some of those with whom I worked in friendly co-operation during the war. But I had no option. For I believe that the recent melancholy decline of Great Britain is largely of our own making. The fall in our standard of living to a level which excites the pity and evokes the charity of many other richer countries, the progressive restrictions on individual liberties, the ever-widening destruction of respect for law, the steady sapping of our instinct for tolerance and compromise, the sharpening of class distinctions, our growing incapacity to play a rightful part in world affairs — these sad changes are not due to something that happened in the remote past. They are due to something which has happened in the past two years. At the root of our troubles lies the fallacy that the best way of ordering economic affairs is to place the responsibility for all crucial decisions in the hands of the State. It is a simple error, it is certainly an understandable error. But it is one which, driven to its logical conclusion, as it is now being driven by those who have been constitutionally put into power, can bring upon us untold miseries and humiliations of which the past two years have given us a foretaste. Holding these views, and knowing that basically the men and women of this country are of such a quality that they merit, and can indeed in the right environment command, a better fate than now seems to be in store for them, it would have been disloyal of me not to attempt to say my part.

There will be those who will dismiss this book as essentially negative and destructive. And so it is, if clearing a field of weeds before planting the new crop is negative and destructive, or trying to stop a horse running wildly down a crowded street is negative and destructive. I have devoted myself to an attack on the latter-day planners because I am convinced that, whatever may be the right ordering of society, economic regimentation of the kind to which we are now subject is the wrong answer to our problems and is an arrangement which, so soon as it unfolds its inevitable consequences, will be repugnant to everyone of liberal instincts. Unfortunately, by the time that the lesson is learned the hard way from bitter, accumulated experience, the right of choice may no longer be ours. For the trap is slowly closing even in Great Britain. Economic confusion is the breeding-ground of totalitarian ideas. Everyone recognises that. Sir Stafford Cripps, in his moving speech to the House of Commons on October 23, 1947, said :

Our struggle is to maintain the decent standards and the freedom that our ever-expanding democratic experience has taught us, in circumstances in which it is only too easy for more violent and totalitarian methods to prevail.

The tragedy is that the planned economy is, in itself, one of the main sources of the confusion which drives men into political mania. So the first task, as it seems to me, is to do what one can to bring about greater maturity in economic thinking so that, without suffering all the pains that it is capable of inflicting upon us, we may come to recognise the idea of a centrally planned economy for what it really is — an attempt to build another Tower of Babel. There is, indeed, urgent need for all of us to concern ourselves with what should be put in the place of the planned economy ; we have taken the basis of our liberal society far too much for granted since the beginning of this century. But the first thing is to prevent the imminent disintegration of what remains of our liberal traditions.

I should have found no purpose in writing this book if other earlier words, wiser and more scholarly than mine, had been sufficiently pondered over. Everything that I have to say here, and indeed much more, is to be found in Professor Hayek's masterly *Road to Serfdom*. Every planner, who believes in reason as the guide in social organisation, should read or re-read that book now and honestly ask himself whether events are or are not following the course against which Professor Hayek warned us three years ago. But since the British are not given to overmuch theorising and since they find it odd that anyone should suggest that their liberties could ever be filched away, a study of planning in practice, such as I have tried to provide in these pages, may help to rouse them to the mortal dangers which now beset them.

I have relied largely upon British experience in the past two years whilst trying to interpret those events against what I saw of central planning in war-time. This means that I have had to quote extensively from the words of present British Ministers because they happen to be running, and trying to expound to the public, the planned economy. I hope that nothing I have said will be taken as personal criticism of individuals — it certainly is not intended as such. I look upon the present supreme human agents for planning in this country as victims, in common with us all, of a system, all innocently introduced, which threatens to become our master — an evil genie released from a bottle. The controversy over planning runs right across the divisions between the ordinary political parties — there are certainly many members of the British Conservative Party whose views on this subject I find it difficult to distinguish from those of members of the Socialist Party. But it happens to be the socialists who are responsible for the current experiment in economic regimentation. It is, therefore, only fair to interpret what is occurring in terms of their ideas and their policies.

One preliminary word concerning definition. I have contrasted in these pages the centrally planned economy with the free economy. The dividing line between the two can never be sharp. The free economy presupposes the institution of private ownership in property (including property in the means of production) ; the sovereignty of the consumer ; the freedom of contracts of service between independent parties ; freedom in the choice of occupation (including the choice not to work at all) and free economic intercourse between nations. These are ends in themselves ; they are bound up with the rightful place of man in society. The free economy also implies, not as an end but as the only known means for maintaining economic freedoms, a free price mechanism. But freedom in this sense does not mean license. The free economy will vary from time to time and from one set of circumstances to another.

The centrally planned economy implies the State determination of investment and its distribution, of occupation, of consumer's choice. It involves progressively the destruction of private property and it leads to national self-sufficiency. It, too, may be operated through a price mechanism, but one which, as I have tried to show in the following pages, must be directed towards the wrong ends. I am sure it will be said that the British planned economy is not of this kind, that it is a mixed economy gaining the advantages of all systems, that there is no intention anywhere to deprive people of their right of choice in occupation, consumption or production. In brief, that I am arguing against something which does not and, in Great Britain at least, never will exist.

It is true that every sensible economy is a 'mixed' system. But everything turns on the mixture. The presence in 1935 in Moscow of half a dozen decrepit droshky drivers, working for private profit, did not disturb the general conclusion that there was a planned economy in Russia. There is a watershed in these matters where, vague as the flows may momentarily seem, the difference between east and west, north and south, liberty and slavery is being irrevocably determined. I submit that there is no doubt in which direction the current has started to flow for us. If we ask

about the Britain of the present day the following questions,
— are people entitled freely to choose and change their
occupation ? are consumers free to distribute their incomes
between different goods in the proportions they would wish ?
are producers free to seek out and satisfy the freely expressed
preferences of consumers ? are contracts of service a matter
for individuals ? is the economy being allowed to knit
naturally with the world economy ? — the answer in each
case is categorically no. There is a second test. Is the
present economic organisation one which is accepted by
anyone as a stable system which well serves our purpose, or
is it regarded by all as a kind of purgatory from which some
advocate escape in one direction and others urge escape in
the opposite ? Surely it is accepted by all that we cannot
stay where we are, that either we go forward to more planning or we go back to the free price mechanism and all that
is bound up with it. It is precisely because I am convinced
that the choice has to be made, once and for all, in the
immediate future that I have written this book.

It remains for me to thank all those to whom I owe a
heavy intellectual debt for assistance in formulating my
views. They are too numerous to mention individually.
But I must express my gratitude to Mr. E. Devons, Professor
M. Polanyi, Mr. R. Spann, and my wife, although none of
them must be assumed as accepting everything I have
written. I owe much to Miss Coop for her patient handling
of my manuscript. And I have to thank the editors and
publishers for permission to reproduce passages from articles
of mine which appeared in *Fortune* (Sept. 1947) and *The
Manchester School* (Jan. 1947).

JOHN JEWKES

UNIVERSITY OF MANCHESTER
November 1947

CHAPTER I

THE SPREAD OF THE FASHION

The people never give up their liberties but under some delusion.—EDMUND BURKE.

I

FASHIONS in economic thinking are notoriously infectious and fickle. They run through communities with the speed of forest fires, often dying down as quickly as they arise. Since the end of the first World War there has been a long string of these crazes of which little now remains except derelict societies and neglected literature. It is difficult to recall now the vehemence of the propaganda in favour of rationalisation, technocracy or guild socialism, or the enthusiasm with which bands of zealots have found the real secrets of economic and social progress, now in the United States, now in Russia, in Sweden or in Switzerland. Even the obsession in Great Britain in 1946 for indiscriminate industrial re-equipment and vast capital investment has been almost forgotten.

These fashions perhaps do little harm : their excesses finally evoke the appropriate resistances. Where, as so frequently happens, they centre on the part which the State should play in society they help to sharpen our social wits and thus contribute to a contemporary solution of the finest problem of all legislation — ' how to determine what the State ought to take upon itself to direct by public wisdom and what it ought to leave with as little interference as possible to individual exertion '.

The current mania for comprehensive economic planning by the State may well appear, half a century hence, as just another of the red herrings which fate throws across the forward march of free peoples. But looking at it close up, as we must now do, it presents some more than ordinarily disturbing features which ought to put democracies on their guard and rouse them to ask whether they are not confronted with ideas fundamentally incompatible with their cherished ways of living.

Central economic planning has gained such a firm grip that it is often forgotten how new an idea it is. The patient reader will find no reference to it in the works of Marx or of the Fabians. The histories of British socialism up to the end of the first World War make no reference to it. Indeed the conception of an economic system operated by the State as a manager might operate one factory runs directly counter to many interpretations of socialism.

It seems to have originated, as many evil ideas originated, in Germany in the war of 1914–18 when it was conceived of as a technique for war administration. It was seized upon between the wars by German intellectuals who saw in it an endlessly fascinating set of problems in complex administration and an irresistible opportunity of breaking individuals to the purpose of the State. It came to real life when Lenin, finding himself with power over a demoralised economy, cast round for some way of diverting the thoughts of his subjects from their present tribulations to the hopes of a terrestrial paradise. He found no help in the existing literature. He said :

> We knew when we took power into our hands that there were no ready forms of concrete reorganisation of the capitalist system into a socialist one. . . . I do not know of any socialist who has dealt with these problems.[1]

He invented a new will-o'-the-wisp, an apparently simple and practical idea which swiftly swept through the existing intellectual vacuum. In 1920 he wrote thus to Krzhizhanovsky :

> Couldn't you produce a plan (not a technical but a political scheme) which would be understood by the proletariat ? For

[1] Quoted from Carr, *Soviet Impact on the Western World*, p. 23.

instance, in 10 years (or 5 ?) we shall build 20 (or 30 or 50 ?) power stations covering the country with a network of such stations, each with a radius of operation of say 400 versts (or 200 if we are unable to achieve more). . . . We need such a plan at once to give the masses a shining unimpeded prospect to work for : and in 10 (or 20 ?) years we shall electrify Russia, the whole of it, both industrial and agricultural. We shall work up to God knows how many kilowatts or units of horse-power.[1]

This was the embryo of the idea, with its already well-established characteristics of political cynicism, slap-dash economics and obsessions with the spectacular, which has grown up so quickly and threatens to cause so much trouble in the world.

Young as it is, the idea has already travelled far and wide. In Russia the very knowledge of what constitutes a free economy has been stamped out completely. In many of the countries of Europe the State has taken over the industrial equipment in whole or in part. In democratic countries the bait is being gobbled without too much thought for the hook that may lie in it. The rulers in Great Britain claim to have a centrally planned economy, to be carrying out a social and economic revolution. Even in the United States many of the young intellectuals are beginning to yearn after the benefits of ' social engineering ' in a fashion which suggests that they, too, will soon be calling for a regimented society.

It is not only the speed and fury of this movement in democratic countries which is alarming. It is also the incipient evidence of totalitarian fervour for doing good to other people at whatever the cost to them. The prophets of the new age are beginning to reveal a testy intolerance to all who stand in their way.

The critics of planning are in these days regarded almost as engines of evil. Their motives are impugned, their feeling for humanity doubted. This restive impatience in the face of criticism is destructive of the tolerance upon which

[1] Quoted from Webb, *Soviet Communism: A New Civilisation?* p. 615.

democratic communities are founded. It should increase the sense of ultimate danger and lead the socially wary to prod carefully for the traps before they go forward into the promised land.

It is also disturbing that, in their controversy, the planners and anti-planners dispute over one point but are really concerned about something else much more vital. They dispute as to whether an economic system run by the State would make us richer or poorer than one operated in a free society, where each man can choose his occupation and use his capital as he wishes. But the disputants have at the back of their minds a deeper question : what kind of society will go along with the planned economy ? We have it on the authority of one of the most acute social observers [1] that

a society may be fully and truly socialist and yet be led by an absolute ruler or be organised in the most democratic of all possible ways ; it may be aristocratic or proletarian ; it may be a theocracy and hierarchic or atheist or indifferent as to religion ; it may be much more strictly disciplined than men are in a modern army or completely lacking in discipline ; energetic or slack ; . . . warlike and nationalist or peaceful and internationalist ; egalitarian or the opposite ; it may have the ethics of lords or the ethics of slaves. . . .

If this is true it is clearly important to know which of these states of society is the more likely to arise in a planned economy. For whatever may be said about a free economy, experience shows that it is not consistent with dictatorship, slavery or other forms of extreme tyranny.

The struggle between central planners and their opponents goes on, therefore, in terms of economics. But the stakes are moral and spiritual. If the issue were merely that of a little more or a little less wealth the fight would be of no moment. In fact the prizes are the ultimate prizes : room for the mind freely to follow its own courses ; room for society to enrich itself by the encouragement of diversity and the tolerance of eccentricity ; room for the growth of

---

[1] Schumpeter, *Capitalism, Socialism and Democracy*, p. 170.

dignity in human relations. Everything, indeed, that is bound up with the uniqueness of personality and with the Christian ethic.

It is, at first sight, strange that the new ideas regarding economic organisation should have gained so wide and ready an acceptance. Experience might have been expected to restrain the movement. The only centrally planned economies we have so far known, those of Russia, Germany and Italy, have been born into, or have finally produced societies in which terror, sadistic cruelty and constant insecurity have been the lot of all save the privileged few. In each the arts sickened, science withered, charity declined. Each found it necessary to cut itself off from all ordinary intercourse with the outside world, to restrict the movement of its people across the frontiers, to misrepresent abroad what was happening at home and to misrepresent at home what was happening abroad. Each has been the source of a feeling of world insecurity and of the possibility of war. It is often held that such associations are not inevitable, that there can be 'good' planning as well as 'bad' planning. But to the objective mind there should be food for thought and grounds for caution in the undisputed fact that, so far as experience goes, the depths of human wretchedness and a centrally planned economy have invariably gone together.

It is clear that there are powerful impulses making for this new tide in economic ideas. Some of them are undoubtedly old evils in somewhat new forms. Among the leaders of this new movement would undoubtedly be found a high proportion of morbid types. Men who itch after power to control their fellows. Men of little understanding and less restraint who would smash the existing economic institutions out of pure ignorance of their functions. Egomaniacs who can conceive of no standard of values but their own and strive, with Jesuitical fervour, to save the world despite itself. But the activities of all such cannot wholly explain the rapid growth of the popularity of planning.

Among the converts are many men of good will. Their conversion can only be understood on the assumption that they are following social aims for the attainment of which central economic planning is regarded as essential.

I suggest that there are at least six highly commendable human aspirations lying behind this movement.

There is, first, the desire to avoid in the future the mass unemployment which occurred between the wars in every system of free enterprise.[1] An economy which leaves a significant part of its producing power unutilised does not make sense. Up to now, free economies have suffered from the serious defect of running at something less than full steam. Not unnaturally the ordinary man contrasts this with the full employment in Russia and in Germany between the wars and with the shortage of labour in all countries during the war and deduces that State planning has made the difference. If the State could only grip economic activities tightly enough, surely, he concludes, the waste of idleness and the dislocating effects of industrial fluctuations could be prevented.

Second, there is the growing feeling that men must be masters of their economic destiny.[2] The search for ways of controlling human environment is, indeed, one of the underlying causes of all progress. In all politically mature countries the individual has created devices to safeguard himself against the arbitrary acts of other individuals or groups. But the worker or the employer may still find his livelihood destroyed overnight by some unpredictable and apparently

[1] Mr. Morrison, House of Commons, July 8, 1947, " The test of a modern economic policy is whether or not it keeps the economy running somewhere near full capacity ".

[2] Mr. Morrison, *Economic Planning* (1946), p. 14: " In a few years' time people looking back will be amazed to see . . . how little was understood of the part which planning could play in freeing employers and workers and farmers from the horrors of uncontrolled and unforeseen fluctuations ".

Sir Oliver Franks, *Central Planning and Control in War and Peace*, p. 37 : " The Government must so present its policy and programmes that they are accepted as the right answer in the circumstances for a nation that will be master of its fate ".

uncontrollable jerk of the economic machine. These bolts from the blue are not merely painful, they are humiliating. They outrage the sense of order and appear to leave men at the mercy of chance. And the State seems to be the most convenient agent for creating security and certainty.

Third, planning is associated with the extension of the scientific method. The great achievements of the natural sciences in the last thirty years have stirred the popular imagination. Through some unfortunate twist in the interpretation of the scientific method it has come to be assumed that the economic system cannot be scientific unless everything which happens in it is under the direct and conscious control of some individual. If a Government official decides what amounts of a commodity shall be produced, where they shall be produced, how they shall be distributed, that constitutes 'scientific' planning. The human mind has been brought to bear in a systematic fashion upon a specific problem, collective behaviour is controlled by a single master plan from above. But if production and distribution is allowed to take place through the operation of an impersonal price system, that is to say, through the free co-operation of independent individuals — even though much the same results are achieved — then there is not the same feeling of achievement. This is much as if the force of gravity were to fall into popular disrepute, because it was not the outcome of the conscious activity of a human mind, and industrial processes were consciously planned to the neglect of, or in defiance of, this force.

Fourth, the State is being called into economic affairs because it is believed that increase in wealth can thereby be speeded up, or even that it will be possible to get something for nothing. To the social scientist an economic system which can double real income per head every thirty or forty years, with an occasional bonus added when some especially fruitful technical improvement comes along, would appear to be justifying itself. But to the individual who is looking for an immediate increase of one-third in his own income (and most of us are in that position) the matter appears quite different. Broad economic progress of the kind which free economies have achieved in the past is largely irrelevant to his own immediate problems. The State is expected to resolve this difficulty, partly by redistributing wealth to the advantage of the under-privileged, partly by creating a more efficient economic society which will turn a 2 per cent annual increase in income per head into something much larger.

Fifth, there is a widespread insistence upon economic security. It is, indeed, paradoxical that in this century when life is held cheaper than during most other periods of history ; when within twenty-five years the people of the world could twice be brought to slaughter each other in unparalleled numbers ; when peace-time machines (particularly in transport) which maim and kill increasingly are accepted without demur, other forms of courage should seem to be dying out and there should be this firmly held attitude that, whatever the cost in terms of individual liberty, economic risks must be reduced. And since a system of free enterprise inevitably creates discontinuities and personal hardships, partly as a result of its rapid absorption of the fruits of technical progress, partly as a consequence of its tendency to move forward in jerks and starts, those seeking a quick solution for these evils not unnaturally turn to the State as a possible stabilising agency.

Finally, there is a growing economic humanitarianism which renders intolerable the inequalities of wealth associated in the past with a system of free enterprise. Absolute economic equality, if that were possible, would probably be obnoxious to the sense of justice, for it is widely recognised that people work with varying intensities and that greater natural aptitudes should bring some differential award. But the striking disparities between the richest one-tenth and the poorest one-tenth of the citizens in many countries in the past fifty years is something which the twentieth century cannot stomach. Here again the deduction is drawn that only the direct control of the economic system by the State can bring improvements.

It is the purpose of this book to show that these legitimate aspirations — to make a steady, continuous and full use of the community's powers of production, to dominate one's economic environment, to operate economic institutions scientifically, to provide all with higher material comforts, to avoid economic fluctuations disturbing to the individual, to mitigate the grosser forms of inequality — are completely and finally frustrated by central State planning. For central planning ultimately turns every individual into a cipher and every economic decision into blind fumbling, destroys the incentives through which economic progress arises, renders the economic system as unstable as the whims of the few who ultimately control it and creates a system of wire-pulling and privileges in which economic justice ceases to have any meaning.

There can be nothing but bitterness and ruin waiting for those who create, or suffer to be created, a centrally controlled economy. It is not a system which can be coolly experimented with and then dropped, if it fails, with no greater loss than a return to the *status quo*. There is no easy way back. For the more threatened it is by failure, the more savage will be the efforts to make it succeed at any cost. The more apparent becomes the insolubility of the intellectual problems it involves, the crazier and more irresponsible will become the efforts to solve them. Nor is it true, as some of the less confident planners are inclined to argue, that at the worst the planned system amounts simply to bartering some part of our liberty for increased wealth or increased security. There is no choice open to us between slavery with plenty and freedom with poverty. For the consumer is just as certain a victim of the planned economy as is the free man.

II

If all this is true, how does it come about that so many intelligent, sincere and well-meaning people have been brought to accept, for the attainment of their aims, methods which are worse than useless for the purpose ? How have they been fooled or been brought to fool themselves ? One might probe endlessly into those dark and deep recesses of the mind wherein myths and confusions, and apparently economic myths more than others, grow in such profusion. But some of the more important sources of the confusions of our times are easily to be recognised.

The most important is the habit of the planner of comparing his ideals — his blue-prints, the products of his drawing-board — with the actual working, with all its defects, of the system he wants to get rid of. He is nearly always anxious in these days to keep out of court the evidence of what has actually happened in Russia. That is ' bad ' planning as contrasted with the ' good ' planning which he is anxious to introduce. But he insists upon dragging into court the actual experience of the free economy in the past fifty years. Suggestions that some of the admitted weaknesses of a free economy are susceptible to simple and effective remedies are rejected as wishful thinking. All kinds of improbable changes in human nature are assumed in portraying what will happen in a planned economy [1] but none of them are permitted for the purpose of foretelling the future of a free economy. The unresolved, or unresolvable, snags in a planned system are evaded by assuming that people will be ' sensible and play the game '. But no one

---

[1] Thus Schumpeter, *Capitalism, Socialism and Democracy*, p. 211 : " The socialist order presumably will command that moral allegiance which is increasingly refused to capitalism. This, it need hardly be emphasised, will give the workman a healthier attitude towards his duties than he possibly can have under a system he has come to disapprove." If, as is not at all unlikely, many people look forward to a socialist State because it will mean that they will have to work less hard, it seems unreasonable to assume that, once the socialist State is established, they will be prepared to work harder than ever.

can be assumed to be sensible or reasonable or fair-minded in the free economy.

The great attraction, for the naïve or the unscrupulous, of building up human societies on the drawing-board is that the incentives to effort cannot be depicted and, therefore, can be ignored. There is no room in the organisation chart of the U.S.S.R. for the secret police. The clean, simple lines of responsibility leave no room for sketching in the motor which is to do the driving. Blue-prints omit black markets. The social engineer can always assume that he can bend, twist and plane his human material against the grain without resistance and fractures.

This unscrupulous dodging about between dual standards confuses judgment. There is point in comparing the Russia we know with the Great Britain or the United States we know. There may be point in contrasting a socialist blue-print with what could be made of a reformed free economy. But to make the comparison on different levels of objectivity really begs the question.

A second source of confusion is the failure to recognise that differences of degree can ultimately become differences in kind. It is precisely at this point that those who are most strongly convinced of the potential evils of growing State control find it most difficult to hold their position in discussion of detail. For there comes a point at which to argue each case on its merits really amounts to not arguing the case at all. If, for example, the State proposes to nationalise some relatively unimportant industry, the pros and cons of that particular case may be equally balanced. It may seem highly unrealistic, in the particular context, to raise major issues regarding liberty and the general efficiency of the economic system. And yet a multiplication of such cases may alter for the worse the whole character of the economic and social system. This difficulty, of course, confronts all democratic communities in dealing with totalitarian ideas and tactics. At what point, it has to be asked, should we dig in our heels and declare that further infiltration, however minor, will be resisted ? It is this dilemma which creates the class of appeasers. For the habits of compromise, of empiricism, of tolerance and of open-mindedness which alone make a free society possible are just the habits which render the democrat an almost sitting target for his totalitarian opponent. The planner prefers to have each case discussed on its merits, *i.e.* to have it discussed without relation to its wider implications. It should be the tactics of his opponent to discuss each case within a wider framework of principle. But he can only do this at the risk of being described as doctrinaire and unrealistic. In political affairs, the appeasers of the period between the two great wars now suffer the contempt they merit. But in economics the appeasers still hold the field as the men of balanced and judicial mind responsive to the changing needs of the time.[1] Yet no democratic community can exist save where its members understand the difference between having their hair cut short and having their scalps taken clean off, and recognise in the former the ever-growing dangers of the latter.

An extremely important case where differences of degree may ultimately become differences in kind lies in the field of administration. Everyone knows that it is possible to plan, with purpose and success, a small organisation, such as a reasonably sized business or local authority. If planning is desirable on this scale why not extend its scope and plan the working of a whole country, or indeed, as many would suggest, the whole world ? The simple answer is that this is administratively impossible, that what can be done on a small scale cannot always be done on a large. But in social and economic

---

[1] Thus *The Times* leader of September 25, 1946 : " In the General Election last year . . . the centre of gravity was set markedly nearer to a planned economy and further from laissez-faire. But, while the right degree of this adjustment is and will be a matter of strong domestic contention, there was no break in the continuous evolution of an approach to social and economic tasks which has led the people and successive Governments of this country to seek, step by step and stage by stage, that habitable half-way house for which a large part of the world is now seeking."

affairs it is an answer which rarely appears conclusive. It is thoroughly grasped in other branches of thought. We can never have a wasp as large as a tiger, since the mechanisms used in integrating the functions of the wasp do not stretch to that size. We can never have an elephant fifty times as large as the present size : its legs could not carry the weight or, if they were made strong enough to carry the weight, they would be so thick that the animal would not be able to move at all. But most people assume that you can increase an administrative organisation indefinitely in size and that it will continue to do its job with just the same success and speed as before. In fact, the crowding together of vital decisions at the top would mean that the organisation ultimately would cease to do anything at all.

This is so critical a point that it is worth asking why the right answer is reached in one set of instances and the wrong answer in others. It may, in part, be due to the rudimentary state of the science and art of administration ; there we are still in the stone age. It may, in part, be due to woolly thinking regarding the advantages of decentralisation. It is often argued that all these problems of administration, even in a complete centrally planned economy, can be solved by ' decentralisation '. And, of course, within limits, decentralisation does help. What is overlooked is that decentralisation creates administrative problems of its own : how to co-ordinate the decentralised units. That can only be carried on successfully within narrow limits. To go back to an illustration given above, we may reach the point at which the job to be carried out really requires an elephant fifty times bigger and stronger than the present type. We know such an elephant does not and cannot exist. We may argue that the right solution is decentralisation — fifty elephants of the present size instead of one fifty times larger. But we do not, thereby, dodge the problem. For the question now is : can we get fifty elephants to work together with the sensitivity and the automatic adjustment provided by the instinctive reactions between the brain and muscles of one elephant? Here there clearly is a limit. The failure to attribute to administrative limitations the crucial rôle they should play in social and economic organisation is mainly due to the fact that in administrative problems there can never be the precise and final answer which can be given in scientific problems. Men differ in their powers of administration. Some cannot control successfully a toffee shop. Some can control an organisation with (say) 20,000 workers. So it is assumed that because there is no definite limit to the growth of a successful administrative unit there is no limit at all. This is just as wrong, and just as dangerous, as if we were to argue that, since some men are five feet high and others six feet high, there is no reason why we should not have men fifty feet high and proceed to design all our machinery so that it could only be operated by such giants.

Planning, again, commends itself to many because it is felt that ' this is the way things are going ', that it is a part of the ' wave of the future ', that it is foolish to press against the rising irresistible tide of affairs. This attitude of resignation, paradoxically enough, runs right across the view, already examined, that planning will put us in a position to become masters of our own economic destiny. It is also highly unscientific because it assumes that when any social force has gained momentum it must inevitably continue until it dominates the whole of human activity.[1]

Finally, in the period following a victorious war the conditions are ripe for the growth of the planned economy. The people have been subject for a number of years to personal regimentation. The fact that the war has been won surrounds the economic organisation which contributed to success with an often quite unmerited prestige;[2] the

[1] G. K. Chesterton long ago saw through this fallacy when he twitted the experts who "when they see a pig in a litter larger than the other pigs, know that by an unalterable law of the Inscrutable it will some day be larger than an elephant".

[2] Thus Sir Stafford Cripps never wearies of describing the success of planning during the war in the Ministry of Aircraft Production.

failures, weaknesses, wastes and losses are forgotten, the achievements unduly magnified by time.[1] The shortages and poverty which follow war create a real need for some extraordinary controls. If planning brought us victory through its powers to produce agents of destruction, how much more potent it might be if employed in peace-time constructive purposes.

III

The case for planning, however, could hardly have made the progress it has made were it not for the current misrepresentations and pure ignorance regarding the nature of the economic system : ignorance of the working of the price system, of the part played by risk-taking and speculation in economic progress, of the need for freedom for those minds which must do the path-breaking for society, of the enormous economic progress made by free societies in the last half-century and of their power to defend themselves, in the last extremity, against the armed force of totalitarian States. The wildest ideas are abroad — that big organisations and institutions are inevitably more efficient than small ; that the State (*i.e.* Ministers and Civil Servants) can draw on a fund of wisdom and judgment that is not available to other men ; that the techniques of production nowadays are so spectacularly different from those of thirty or forty years ago that little that we have learnt from the past is relevant to present-day conditions ; that the competition between business men is inherently immoral ; that business men no longer compete but fleece the community by creating monopolies ; that profit-making is evil ; that business is now controlled by an administrative class not directly concerned with profit-making ; that competition creates enormous waste by driving thousands of firms into bankruptcy ; that competition no longer works in eliminating surplus capacity ;

[1] See E. Devons, 'Economic Planning in War and Peace', *The Manchester School*, January 1948.

that monopoly brings into existence huge corporations too large for efficiency ; that monopoly will usually mean that the output of a firm will be smaller than it would be under competition ; that the free economy stifles inventions ; that the free economy creates widespread technological unemployment — an endless list of assumptions many of which are mutually contradictory and most of which are without foundation in fact. When there is added to all this the savage misrepresentation that has surrounded the subject of planning in the past twenty years, the causes of confusion are only too obvious. In such confusion any and every view, however bizarre or improbable, will get a hearing and the chance that truth will prevail is remote.

The obstacles encountered in establishing economic facts and in creating an understanding of economic cause and effect may well lead to a cynical, if not completely fatalistic, attitude. Is there some queer defect in the human mind, some universal black insanity which will inevitably lead us to destroy those very social and moral values which we most cherish ? Is it the calamity of modern life that we cannot learn, or learn early enough, all the things which we must know for our survival ?

It seems to me far too early to fall prisoner to such pessimistic moods. Economic rationality has, in some recent cases, suddenly shot above the apparently barren ground in a most unexpected fashion. Who would have believed ten years ago that countries could wage major wars, as Great Britain and the United States have done, without falling into inflation ? Who could have forecast the growing knowledge in labour circles of the relation between price and wage movements, which led to the far-seeing and courageous restraint during the war by British trade unionists on the subject of wage policy ? Who would have anticipated in 1925 that, within twenty years, the Keynesian economic doctrines offering us a route towards the maintenance of full employment within a free society would have been so gener-

ally accepted ?   It may be that the realm of popular understanding will widen even more quickly in the future.   In the
past planned economies have operated under a veil of secrecy.
Now, however, we have in Great Britain an experiment in
central economic planning carried on in the open, subject
to public discussion and scrutiny by Parliament.   The lessons
to be drawn from that experiment, if they can be drawn
coolly and without bias, may well change the whole course
of economic thinking in the world.   For even those who
regret that such an experiment had to be carried out merely
to reveal what they regard as the inherent defects and dangers
in a planned economy, may console themselves with the
thought that, if such an experiment was inescapable, much
better it should be carried out in Great Britain, with its
instinct for justice, fair play and free speech, and its strong
social cohesion, rather than in some other community where
the lines of social cleavage were more marked and the traditional impediments to the practices of human slavery less in
evidence.

CHAPTER II

IS THE BUSINESS MAN OBSOLETE?

THOSE who are opposed to the conception of a centrally planned State economy will not be able to make much headway with their case unless they can dispose of the argument that there is really no alternative to a planned system. It is declared with increasing frequency that the business man, the important initiating agent in the free economy, is destined to lose his functions, his powers and even his interest in performing the services which, in the past, have justified his existence. If it is true that private individuals can no longer be found to undertake the functions of investment, of risk-taking, of management and of innovation, then either the community must resign itself to a return to the simplicity and poverty of peasant farming or the State must take over the responsibilities of the entrepreneurs.

From Marx onwards, the business man has often been counted out prematurely by his detractors. Much of this theorising has failed to stand the test of time. There are, however, some modern theories as to the inevitability of the decay of the entrepreneur which have greater internal consistency and which command more general support. The most devastating attack has been made in Professor Schumpeter's remarkable book *Capitalism, Socialism and Democracy*. If Professor Schumpeter is right, then those who resist the growing tide of economic regimentation are wasting their time.

He argues that the business man, and the economic and social system which grew around him, are inevitably doomed, not because they have failed in any special way to deliver the goods but for four other reasons :

(*a*) Capitalistic enterprise has shown such great achievement in making economic progress automatic that there is nothing left for it to do. It has destroyed its own function. It has performed once and for all a service which need not be repeated.

(*b*) The business man has failed to create defences against political attack on the free economy. On the one hand, he has inevitably destroyed the feudal and aristocratic elements in society which might have provided a guardian for him ; on the other, he has brought into existence and failed to control a group of intellectuals who, by their very nature, will turn to destroy him.

(*c*) The business man has really lost interest in behaving as a business man. His incentives have gone or are going. He no longer reveals the instinct of self-preservation.

(*d*) The system of capitalistic economy has created an almost universal hostility to its own social order. This hostility may be largely irrational but it persists because the case for the free economy is complex, is based upon long-range considerations and is essentially lacking in an appeal to the emotions.

Has the Free Economy served its Purpose ?

The first and third of these reasons are by far the most important. For whilst the other two are reasons why the business man may disappear (irrespective of whether this will be a good or a bad thing), reasons one and three, if they can be substantiated, are reasons why he should go. No one wishes to retain for the sake of old times social and economic instruments which have become blunt.

The first reason boils down to this : the fundamental task of the business man is that of forcing innovations into the system, of breaking down resistance to change. But, by now, we have all " become accustomed to economic change — best instanced by an incessant stream of new consumers' and producers' goods. . . . The resistance which comes from interests threatened by an innovation in the pro-

ductive process is not likely to die out so long as the capitalistic order persists. . . . But every other kind of resistance
— in particular, to a new kind of thing because it is new —
has vanished already.   Thus economic progress tends to become de-personalised and automised. . . . Innovation itself
is being reduced to routine." Bureaux, committees and teams
of technicians can now take the place of the personality, the
driving force, the will of the individual business man.

This argument implies that once the customer has
become accustomed to a steady stream of new things he will
accept this state of affairs as a matter of course and that the
consumers' expectation that the stream will flow on endlessly constitutes, in itself, one of the motors of economic
progress.   I do not believe this to be the case.   Consumers
have short memories.   Provided the change is not too rapid,
the standard of living can be reduced almost without the
consumer noticing it.   No clearer illustration of that could
be found than the experience of British people who travel
now, after years of austere living, to the United States or
Sweden.   Their clearest impression is that of suddenly *re-
membering* the consumer joys of the past.   The consumer up
to now has not been an initiator in the system, he is much
more of an arbitrator and arbitration is bound up with a
certain conservatism and passivity.   In any case there are
wide ranges of consumers' demand where the producer
has never yet succeeded, even under the most favourable
conditions, in breaking down the instinctive resistance to
change.   Perhaps the most interesting is that of housing in
many countries where the consumer stubbornly clings to
ways of living which are sadly archaic.

Neither does it seem to be true that " technological
progress is increasingly becoming the business of teams of
trained specialists who turn out what is required and make
it work in predictable ways ".   Surely the words ' what is
required ' robs this sentence of the meaning which Schumpeter intended it to have ?   The application to commercial

purposes of the progress of pure science is essentially a process of risk-taking and guessing. The early exploitation of the ' deep ' freezing of foods — which promises to revolutionise domestic economy — could certainly not be regarded as automatic. It was due to a commercial plunge by one firm in 1929. The development of the jet engine in Great Britain was the outcome of the confidence of a financial company at a time when the official attitude to the idea was wholly tepid. And there are many cases at the moment — such as television, the pressurisation of high-altitude aircraft, the use of welding in shipbuilding — where it is far from being a simple matter of telling the technicians what to do and then waiting for the inevitable solution. All such decisions call for acts of faith amidst a tangle of conflicting considerations of commercial production and technological possibilities. Left to themselves, and having no particular reasons for taking risks, teams of technicians will almost invariably bog themselves down without direction or purpose. The record of State aeronautical-research organisations in Great Britain is one very good illustration of this point. They have produced virtually nothing ; almost all technical development in war-time came from the private firms ; Government technical experts frowned on nearly every one of the crucial new devices for improving aeronautical performance until the persistence of the entrepreneur settled the dispute beyond a doubt. The history of the appalling delays in British tank development, even during the war, is another excellent illustration of what a technical bureaucracy is capable. Take away the motive force of innovation — the business man — and the cautious and conservative habits of the consumer and technician would roll back over us with deadening effect.

Indeed one can go much further than this and argue that the development of the entrepreneur's function in merchanting and production is still only at a very primitive stage and has still wide fields to conquer.

As standards of living improve, the consumer tends to

become more discriminating and the task of suiting him more delicate and more risky. There is a stage in the growth of consumer taste and discretion when it is sufficient for the entrepreneur simply to offer something new. The first white men on the American continent could dispose of beads, wire, brightly coloured cloth; anything that had not been seen before. But, at a later stage of consumer sophistication, novelty of itself ceases to have any attraction since new things have become unexciting in themselves. The consumer reaches further back to a more rational examination of the attraction of the new. Fresh fields for entrepreneurial activity are, thereby, opened up. In the past the entrepreneur has been able to carry out his functions with an absence of real finesse and has relied upon two crudities, both of which must progressively fail to satisfy: large-scale advertising and mass production. The latter gives the consumer the second-best — an article which satisfies nobody because it is made for the average man who does not exist. It will become increasingly unpopular as communities grow richer and less immature. The former seeks to deaden the growth of discrimination and can hardly fail to produce a final revolt, all the more decisive because it is likely to swing to the other extreme where people begin to believe nothing they read and fall back on their own tastes and inclinations in the exercise of their consumer judgments.

On the supply side, the rôle of the entrepreneur in giving direction to technological progress must also become more complex and difficult. For the more numerous the strands of scientific knowledge, the greater the number of combinations of such strands available for technological application, the more arduous the choice among the various possibilities for successful commercial application. It is true that the actual technical work is increasingly performed by salaried teams; it is equally true that *what* technical work should be done is increasingly a function of risk-taking and of market intuition — *i.e.* a function of the entrepreneur. Even under mass

production the crucial question has to be answered : which thing shall be mass-produced ? In more discriminating production this question crops up more frequently and is more difficult to answer. Compare, for example, the position of an entrepreneur in 1900 wondering whether he should make bicycles with that of an entrepreneur in 1946 considering whether he should make television sets. The second question opens up a vast range of technical, commercial and production issues almost wholly lacking in the former.

It is, of course, true that some industries may have periods of quietude in which the rôle of the entrepreneur becomes of less significance. But these periods may be limited. Thus the textile industries, after a comparatively long breathing-space, now seem to be set on quite revolutionary changes as the result of recent developments in artificial fibres and in methods of arranging these fibres to form fabrics. And the tinplate industry, after a long period of relatively simple methods of production, has suddenly shot forward with the invention of the continuous hot-strip system.

In this connection Professor Schumpeter's military analogy is very revealing. He argues that, until recently, " the technique of warfare and the structure of armies being what they were, the individual decision and driving power of the leading man . . . were essential elements in the strategical and tactical situations. . . . This is no longer so. Rationalised and specialised office-work will eventually blot out personality, the calculable result, ' the vision '." Can there ever have been a more compendious misunderstanding of the vital rôle played by personality and morale in the last war ? For the battle units were admittedly larger than heretofore, the processes more mechanised. But, time and again, one man made an enormous difference to the outcome of the struggle because he was able to drive his personality through the administrative machine to get at the vital thing which decided battles — the morale of the fighting individual. In fact, the larger the units engaged the more precious were these qualities of leadership and of intuition. Can there be any doubt that the turning-point in the last war was the personal clash of wits between Montgomery and Rommel, or the defence of Stalingrad, which had as little to do with office-work as did the result of the battle of Trafalgar ?

This conclusion regarding the continuing rôle of the entrepreneur would be more easily accepted were it not for the perversity of many writers in refusing to examine what is really happening to the structure of industry. If the entrepreneurial rôle is becoming more difficult, more complex, more important, that would inevitably exercise a restraining influence on the size of the business unit : the limit to administrative skill would be reached fairly early. But Professor Schumpeter, although he has some qualifications to make, finally concludes that " the perfectly bureaucratised giant industrial unit not only ousts the small or medium-sized firms and expropriates its owners but in the end it also ousts the entrepreneur ". It will be shown in the next chapter that this picture of the whole industry dominated by a few giant concerns is misleading. It was not true in the past. There is no reason to believe that it will occur in the future. In some industries, of course, the giant concern has advantages over the relatively small firm. In many other industries the opposite is true. A healthy and progressive free economic system will always be creating a place for the small firm. New industries are always springing up in which the small man gets his chance. Increased discrimination by the consumer is constantly creating needs which can, in fact, only be met by relatively small and flexible firms. If the State carries out its legitimate function of controlling monopoly, and the size of an industrial concern is strictly linked to its efficiency, the scope for the small firm will become even wider.

But, leaving on one side the statistics regarding the size of firms, is there any evidence that the work of the business man is becoming more automatic, more routine ? On the contrary, is it not the case that the head of every large concern in these days groans under the difficulties of exercising his will powerfully enough to keep his administration going ; that every large business seeks methods of decentralisation in order to stop the rot of routine and the slowing down of progress ; that the heads of the largest concerns are the most sceptical of the advantages of great size ? If the Schumpeter diagnosis were correct the business man would be showing the clearest indications of obsolescence in the United States, where innovations in consumer goods are most rapid and organised technical research most advanced. But it is precisely in the United States that his functions are most vigorously pursued and developed.

The entrepreneur may be doomed, but, if so, it is not because his activities have become superfluous in a progressive economy.[1]

The Political Defencelessness of the Business Man

There is, second, the argument that the business man has failed to qualify as a political animal ; that right to the end of the period of vital and intact capitalism he left the governing, particularly in England, to the aristocratic element which his rational system was bound to destroy. Apparently the bourgeois is incapable of ruling. " There is no trace of any mystic glamour about him which is what counts in the ruling of men. . . . A genius in the business office may be, and often is, utterly unable outside of it to say boo to a goose, both in the drawing-room and on the platform. Without protection the bourgeoisie is politically helpless and unable not only to lead its nation but even to take care of its own particular class interest, which amounts to saying that it needs a master."

[1] It seems difficult to square Schumpeter's conception of automatic progress through the activities of consumers and teams of technologists with his statement elsewhere (*Journal of Political Economy*, June 1946, p. 270) that " the principles of individual initiative and self-reliance are the principles of a very limited class. They mean nothing to the mass of the people who — no matter for what reason — are not up to the standard they imply."

On *a priori* grounds, it would seem surprising that such a sweeping generalisation could be made in this way about any large class. For governments have in the past been drawn from any and every class of society. And within a class as large as (say) the British bourgeoisie there must have been found many different types, aptitudes and gifts which might have been expected, even by the laws of chance, to produce some men equipped for political leadership. Schumpeter does not specify why the successful management of a business under competitive conditions is such a very different task from running a party, or a government or a cabinet. He admits that the bourgeois class have often been successful in city management but he dismisses this as irrelevant — " city management was akin to business management ". This still leaves the question why business management is so distinct from political management. He further admits the appearance of the great merchant republics and the successful bourgeois governments of the Low Countries but he says " the merchant republics failed in the great game of international poitics ". It would, indeed, be interesting to know why the game of international politics is so different from the game of business. On the surface they might seem to have much in common. And, of course, he has to admit the presence of a continuing bourgeois government in the United States.

Let us take the special case of England — on which Professor Schumpeter leans very heavily for his theory. How far is it true that the bourgeois element found itself incapable of ruling " right to the end of the period of intact and vital capitalism ".

Between 1900 and 1940 there were long periods of predominantly conservative Parliaments in which ' hard-faced business men ' were perhaps only too numerous.

Mr. Thomas [1] has made an analysis of the ' interests ' of the members of the House for each of the Parliaments

---

[1] *The House of Commons, 1832–1901.*

between 1868 and 1900. This shows that business interests were extremely powerful between these two dates.

PERCENTAGE DISTRIBUTION OF INTERESTS [1] IN PARLIAMENT
1868–1900

	1868	1880	1886	1895	1900
Landowners, Army and Navy	43·2	33·9	24·5	22·0	22·6
Business Interests . .	42·9	49·3	52·0	52·2	52·2
Lawyers . . .	8·0	9·0	10·9	11·7	10·4
Men of Letters and Academic . . .	3·1	4·1	5·3	6·1	5·6
Others	2·8	3·7	7·3	8·0	9·2
Total . .	100	100	100	100	100

It has to be recognised, on the other hand, that many of these business men were probably concerned more with finance than with manufacturing proper, that the business men who have gone to Parliament have probably not found their way into the Cabinets with the frequency appropriate to their numbers and that the business men in Parliament have probably not been the best business men (the best preferring to stick to their own jobs). But when every allowance is made for these points Schumpeter's picture is overdrawn.

Whilst, according to Schumpeter, the business man has been kicking from under himself the prop of the aristocratic and feudal element in society, he has been further embarrassed by an intellectual class which has devoted its powers of exposition, and apparently its malice, to the destructive criticism of the bourgeois society. Schumpeter's analysis of the intellectuals is, indeed, one of the most penetrating parts of his book. He defines this group as that which wields the power of the spoken and written word, which has no

[1] In compiling the table attention was paid not to the number of members returned but to the number of ' interests ' which those members possessed. Therefore, when a landowner who was also a director of a railway company was returned to the House, it was made to count as the election of two interests to Parliament.

direct experience of a responsibility for practical affairs, which " cannot help nibbling because it lives on criticism that stings ", criticism that passes from persons to institutions. This group of intellectuals is brought into existence by the rationalism and freedom of a bourgeois society ; its weapons are sharpened by the growth of education, by printing, by the popular press, by the radio. The rôle of the intellectual groups " consists primarily in stimulating, energising, verbalising and organising and only secondarily in adding to the general hostile atmosphere which surrounds the capitalist engine ".

This is a damaging attack upon the scribblers of the Left. No one can doubt that it faithfully portrays the character and functions of the group which in Great Britain, before the war, came to be known as the ' Bloomsbury set ' or the group which in Germany did much to open wide the gates of totalitarianism. It is, indeed, depressing that since the beginning of the century those who have been best equipped in knowledge and powers of exposition should, by their extraordinary lack of wisdom and their malicious desire to upset, have acted as a continually destabilising social influence. But it is seriously to be questioned whether their power is as great as Schumpeter would have us believe.

This iconoclastic group is, at least in Great Britain, only a section of those who possess the power of expression or the leisure for speculation. There are others who think differently. The Leftist intellectuals do not always have it their own way. Among the British scientists, recently, the attempt on the part of a few to propagate the principle of ' pure scientific research with a social purpose ' (i.e. the Moscow line) produced a quite violent reaction among other members of the profession. It is extremely doubtful whether the social scientists of Great Britain do take up the attitude to a free economy which Schumpeter seems to take for granted. In Great Britain in the last thirty or forty years the intellectual power of the community has been predominantly liberal.

The social defence of a society against the stridency of the intellectuals of the Left lies, of course, in those deeper intuitions of the community which are broadly described as common sense. Now the intellectuals by their own activities create popular distrust. They quarrel among themselves with the same lack of restraint as they quarrel outside. They set up as experts in fields where they do not even possess knowledge (as the scientists who overnight become experts in the social sciences). They have a high mental volatility and a low intellectual flash-point, so that they change their minds with great frequency (particularly where they keep an eye on the line of the Party). They are comically lacking in a sense of humour.[1] They find it difficult to conceal their ambitions as administrators. The general suspicions which are bred by their somewhat adolescent strutting bring discredit on ' experts ' as a group.[2]

The Loss of Incentives

Thirdly, Schumpeter alleges that the business man finds his own incentives weakening. The controllers of large businesses more and more become executives with the psychology of the paid employee as distinct from the owner-employers of yesterday. Business no longer revolves around a family — with its sense of continuity, its desire for accumulation, its attachment to property.

It is, however, much to be doubted whether these changes do weaken incentives to the degree suggested. The point has already been made that those who insist upon regarding

---

[1] Thus the solemnity of the Webbs' *Decay of Capitalist Civilisation*, p. 31 : " It is not too much to say that, in the Britain or the United States of today, the very existence, in any neighbourhood, of a non-producing rich family, even if it is what it calls well conducted, is by its evil example a blight on the whole district, lowering the standards, corrupting the morality and to that extent counteracting the work alike of the churches and the schools ".

[2] Incidentally, if Schumpeter is correct, the Leftist intellectuals are strangely indifferent to the fate of their own intellectual progeny. Thus he states that, in the socialist State, " intellectuals as a group will no longer be hostile and those individuals who are will be restrained by a society that once more believes in its own standards. Such a society will in particular be firm in its guidance of the young."

the industrial system as consisting of a few large, bureau-cratically controlled firms are, in fact, discussing a system which does not exist. It is a serious over-simplification to suppose that property accumulation is the only, or indeed the major, driving force behind the entrepreneur. There is a mixture of motives at play : the desire to exercise power, the desire for independence, the scientific interest in making an organisation work, the thrill of risk-taking, the loyalty to a group which has grown up under one's hands. In an in-dustrial system which is devoting itself to meeting the needs of the consumer and evolving the type of industrial structure called for, it is difficult to imagine most of these motives becoming weaker of themselves. The destruction of the close relation between family and business may well encour-age, rather than discourage, business incentive. For in the past the family business, with its nepotism, has often con-stituted one of the principal obstacles to the poor and ambi-tious young apprentice and has bred among those privileged by birth an enfeebling sense of security which has weakened progress.[1] It is important for economic progress that men should recognise the urgency of their task and be disinclined either to leave their most baffling problems to be solved, or the fruits of their labour to be too fully enjoyed, by their descendants, attitudes highly typical of the socialist adminis-trator.

The Unexplained and the Irrational Elements

There remain only those elements in the opposition to the free economy which are generally admitted to be irrational or purely emotional. It *is* true that the case for the free economy is complex, that it involves wide and long-range considerations. As has already been pointed out,[2] it is

---

[1] Dare I quote, on this subject, the Webbs' *Decay of Capitalist Civilisation*, p. 122 : " Sons reared in luxurious homes, and . . . not picked out for their profit-making ability, succeeded to their father's businesses, which gradually ceased to be marked by those qualities of initiative, discovery and enterprise which had served as a justification for the dictatorship of the capitalist " ?

[2] See p. 16.

possible for the public to grasp sound economic ideas and to act wisely in the light of them. Why should they be considered at the end of their capacity for learning ? It is true " that no one can become emotional about capitalism " whilst they obviously can get emotional about socialism. But this may well be the result of the meretricious attraction of what is new. It will be interesting to see what light the experience of Great Britain during the next few years will throw upon this point. There remains what Schumpeter describes as the " almost universal hostility to capitalism " which means that capitalism " stands its trial before judges who have the sentence of death in their pocket ". No one can doubt the presence of this combination of crusading and hysteria.[1] And because it is so completely irrational it is most difficult to deal with and, in the last analysis, most dangerous to any rational organisation of society.

The Nature of the Beast through Socialist Eyes

Schumpeter's analysis is so powerful and informed that it largely supersedes much that has been written on the same subject by socialists. The contrast between his apt technique and that of the Webbs [2] or of Professor Laski,[3] to take two outstanding socialists, is very striking. But it is worth while making a short comparison of the two groups if only to indicate how hazardous is much of the broad sociological theorising regarding the functions of classes.

These three writers reach the same conclusion which may be summarised by a quotation from the Webbs. " Our present capitalist civilisation . . . is dissolving before our eyes not only in that septic dissolution . . . brought upon

[1] The latest converts to the idea of planning reveal the greatest irritability when confronted by the traditional liberal economic doctrines. Presumably they are anxious to make up for lost time. When, for example, a group of the British Working Party on the Cotton Industry put forward a sober case for free enterprise in that industry the *Manchester Guardian* described this case as " petulant ". And *The Spectator* described it as " sentimental search for some Victorian elysium ".

[2] *The Decay of Capitalist Civilisation* (1923).

[3] *Liberty in the Modern State* (1937).

us by war . . . but in that slower changing of the epochs which war may hasten."

But beyond that the careful reader will begin to rub his eyes. For it immediately becomes clear that there are at least two kinds of business man. Professor Schumpeter's business man is down and out :

> Entrepreneurs cease to stand by their guns. . . . They talk and plead . . . snatch at every chance of compromise . . . are ever ready to give in . . . never put up a fight under the flag of their own ideals . . . the bourgeois order no longer makes sense to the bourgeoisie itself. . . . When all is said and done, it does not really care.

The Webb business man is a much fiercer animal :

> The energetic spirits [of capitalism] have for the most part vulgar ambitions, vulgar capacities and vulgar tastes in excitement. They are competitive rather than cooperative : they like success, which means money-making and the personal power and prestige that money-making leads to, and the gambling element in big business flavours it attractively for them.

Professor Laski's business man is a veritable bulldog :

> The great army of owners . . . believe they will win ; and they prefer conflict to the alternative of abdication. . . . Would it not be rather surprising that its members should refuse to abdicate when they believe they have the prospect of victory ? No such class in the past, at least, has voluntarily parted with the right to dominate the state power. We need not be moved by the argument that there is no evidence of a will to fight. . . .

For the Schumpeter business man the lure of consumers' property is evaporating :

> The amenities of the bourgeois home are becoming less obvious than are its burdens. . . . The average family of bourgeois standing tends to reduce the difficulties of running the big house and the big country place by substituting for it small and mechanised establishments plus a maximum of outside service and outside life.

The Webb business man moves in quite a different way :

> The [captain of industry] will return after his day's work to his well-appointed home — the appointment of which probably

consists essentially in avoiding all labour-saving appliances and making necessary a whole group of domestic servants — to eat an unwholesome dinner on which ten times as much labour has been expended as on the meat by which his labourers maintain their health, and to encourage his wife to crowd his house with indiscriminate articles of furniture and ornamentation which have no merit beyond the amount of labour that has been wasted on them. In good times, he will respond to every caprice of his wife and children, " Get it, it only costs money ".

The Schumpeter type " drifts into an anti-saving frame of mind ". The Webb type is " dominated by the desire for amassing more wealth, without any very nice discrimination between the different forms of production ". For Schumpeter the tragedy of the bourgeois is that he destroys the feudal and aristocratic classes. For the Webbs the calamity is that " the specially active men arising in the old families nowadays vie with the crowd of the newly enriched in the making of profit by the organisation and administration of the instruments of production ".

To Schumpeter the bourgeoisie is politically helpless, is incapable of ruling, requires a master. To the Webbs " this far-reaching coercive guidance of national and local government by the property owners and profit-makers, large and small, [is responsible for] the sudden and rapid decay of the confidence of the wage-earning class in these institutions ".

To Schumpeter the intellectuals are the inevitable foe of the bourgeois. To the Webbs

the lawyers, the engineers, the architects, the men of financial and administrative ability, the civil servants, the authors and journalists, the teachers . . . the whole class of managers, the inventors, even the artists and the men of science . . . are almost inevitably retained, consciously or unconsciously, in the maintenance of the existing social order, in which the private ownership of the instruments of production is the corner stone.

Laski describes the bourgeoisie as

a class which dominates the courts, the civil service, and the defence forces of the modern state. Overwhelmingly, also, it controls all the techniques for influencing opinion.

To sum up : the business class in Schumpeter's view is fated to die out because it lacks certain qualities and attitudes. In the view of the Webbs and of Laski, the business class is doomed because it possesses those same qualities and takes up those same attitudes.

.   .   .   .   .   .

What then is left of the arguments that the free economy, and with it the business man, have reached the end of their days ?   A mass of sociological forecasting that has already in part proved unsound ; a conflict between the experts as to the character of the capitalist system and the frailties of the business man ; unanimity on final conclusions based on mutually exclusive trains of reasoning.   But the fact that it has been thought fit to make a diagnosis in this way leads to three reflections.   The first is that it is probably quite unsound to talk of business men as a class as if they were cast in a mould like Prussian officers.   The motives which lead men to engage in business as entrepreneurs are so complex that it would be surprising if, in any significant way, they constituted a class.   Among the business men of the last fifty years — provided we are prepared to judge them in the round, and not merely by the few spectacular cases — will be found scholars and buccaneers, the impetuous and the calculating, the avaricious and the generous, the scientists and the empiricists, the law-breaking and the law-abiding, the publicists and the retiring, the politically minded and those without political interest, in just about the proportions in which they are found in the community as a whole.

The second is that the business man would be unwise to ignore the criticisms which are now falling upon him thick and fast.   There are reasons, much simpler than those of the socialist intellectuals, to explain the frequent silences of the business man in the face of attacks.   He is busy.   His job ought not to leave much time over for other activities.   He must, on many occasions, find the critics so patently ill-informed that it hardly seems worth while to engage in elementary education. So that when the young men with the Marxian dialectic, the mystifying talk of imperfect competition and social costs, and the terrible facility with figures and charts, reach conclusions which he knows to be absurd, he probably keeps quiet. But he does so at the peril of his own existence and that of the free economy. For the cult of planning has now gone so far that it certainly cannot be checked unless business men as a group take thought as to why the type of economic system which finds room for them has positive advantages over a centrally planned economy, understand thoroughly the nature of the free economy, and take time and trouble to rebut misrepresentations of it.

The third is that the business man should recognise that he is now very carefully watched and that he is not likely to be able to engage in practices which are inconsistent with his own rationale. He cannot, for instance, pass off monopoly practices as part of a free economy. He cannot blindly resist all forms of State intervention. He should be prepared to take the initiative and put his own house in order before someone else burns it down out of a mistaken belief that it is derelict.

CHAPTER III

MUST MONOPOLY DESTROY THE FREE ECONOMY?

I

THE second major charge against the free economy, and one which would be decisive if it could be fully substantiated, is that monopoly will inevitably make destructive inroads into the competitive system and leave us no choice except that between monopoly capitalism and a State-operated economy.

The dangers of monopoly capitalism are well recognised. Industrial groups may become little empires within the community and exercise uncontrolled powers over the consumer. They may seek to widen their powers and their privileges through pressure on the legislature. They will normally produce a bad distribution of the resources of the community: too many of some things will be produced, too few of others. They will endanger the successful operation of a policy of full employment. They may well stifle enterprise and impede progress.

Monopoly sectionalises the community. Any industry which has power to fix prices and restrict entry can, of course, improve its own position. It can raise prices to the level it regards as reasonable, stabilise output, although at a relatively low level, pay good wages and provide steady employment for a limited number of workers. It can, in brief, feather its own nest. But the whole community must then pay higher prices and consume less. Workers lose their jobs. Other industries must pay more for their raw materials or components. To all these aggrieved parties the monopolist can turn a blind eye. Employers frequently find it worth while to collaborate

36

with the workers in their industry to make conditions secure by limiting output and employment. The British coal and cotton industries have already provided striking instances of this kind of syndicalism. One lot of workers or one lot of employers conspire to throw another lot out of work.

Monopoly capitalism, therefore, is both anti-social and inefficient. And there can be no doubt that, given favourable conditions, monopolistic practices can become extensive. The present position in Great Britain is evidence enough of that. Before the war powerful monopoly control was found in many stages and branches of industry: in iron and steel, aluminium, heavy electrical equipment, electric lamps, motor-car components, industrial alcohol, chemicals, cables, linoleum, cement, flour-milling. The State itself had taken an active hand in conferring upon producers the power to control the market by one statutory scheme after another: coal, milk, hops, bacon, cotton, fish. The war has undoubtedly encouraged extended attempts at monopoly in private industry, apart from the large-scale statutory monopolies created in coal, transport, electricity and gas, and other industries. Little wonder that the White Paper on Employment Policy, cautiously worded as it is, should in 1944 reach the conclusion that " in recent years there has been a growing tendency towards combines and towards agreements, both national and international, by which manufacturers have sought to control prices and output, to divide markets and to fix conditions of sale ".[1]

It is, however, fantastic to claim, upon the basis of such facts, that we are living in a " world of monopolies ". Mr.

[1] One peculiarly revolting illustration of economic exploitation was that of the price rings among British manufacturers of building materials and among builders. Mr. Molson, speaking in the House of Commons on May 15, 1945, quoted from a letter by Sir George Burt, head of the well-known contracting firm of Mowlems : " I do not know of a material used in housing of which the selling price of manufacture is not controlled by a combine, ring or other selling arrangement and, generally speaking, its distribution as well. My personal view is that in too many cases the selling price has no proper relation to the cost of production."

Lewis [1] in the best recent estimate has shown that the mono-
polised trades of Great Britain accounted for rather less
than one-third of all employment before the war. He
further shows that in nearly two-thirds of British industry
the organisation is such that any kind of effective control
would be very difficult to create or maintain. There is an
economic and social problem here but not one which is insoluble within the free economy, provided the right methods
are adopted to deal with it.

II

Why is it asserted that, whatever may have been true of
the nineteenth century, monopoly in the twentieth century
is bound to infiltrate into the free economy and destroy it ?

The Economies of Large-scale Operation

It is often argued that bigger firms, because of their
superior efficiency, must inevitably replace the smaller and
that, in consequence, each market will be supplied by one
or a few producers. Must we either accept a growing degree
of monopoly control for this reason or be prepared to tolerate
a relatively inefficient economic system ?

On this subject the planners seem determined to take a
spectacular view of economic changes and to refuse to
examine the facts dispassionately. Many of them are prepared to admit that the free economy ' worked ' in the nineteenth century. But, they assert, industrial organisation has
changed in so striking and dramatic a fashion in the twentieth
century that all past experience is irrelevant.

The evidence does not support the view that the really
big firms in an industry are more efficient than the smaller.

[1] *Monopoly in British Industry*, p. 18. There is a very striking similarity
between this conclusion and that of Ralph Borsodi, who, working on American
material, has reached the conclusion that mass-producing and mass-distribut-
ing methods are technologically justified in about one-third of the total production of goods.

The existing information is scanty and the comparison of the 'efficiency' of firms of different size in the same industry difficult, but the results obtained up to 1946 in the United States have been fairly summarised as follows : [1]

1. In general, large companies are more efficient than small companies, but the largest companies are not more efficient (and are frequently less so) than the large companies.
2. The quantitative differences between average costs of companies of various sizes are relatively small after a moderate size is reached.

Another authority [2] has concluded, " In most of British industry economies of scale have not been a factor promoting monopoly, and are not likely to be so for many decades ".

Are big firms, in fact, sweeping away the smaller in a manner which might be expected if they showed greatly superior efficiency ? The answer is that no one knows. For there is no continuous information in any country of the changes which have taken place in the size of firms over the last thirty or forty years. It can, however, be said with complete confidence that, so far, there is no reason to believe that large firms are driving small firms pell-mell from the market. This conclusion is so strikingly opposed to common beliefs that the evidence must be quoted. In Great Britain we have the facts concerning the size of firms [3] and the size of ' units ',[4] in what roughly constitutes the manufacturing and extractive industries and services for the year 1935.[5]

---

[1] Stigler, *The Theory of Price*, p. 207. Writing in 1932 I myself reached the following conclusion after a close examination of the American evidence, " There is yet no definite proof that the largest concerns, or even concerns of a size which is becoming quite common in many industries, bring lower costs, when allowance has been made for invested capital, or lower prices than the moderate-sized firms ".

[2] Lewis, *Monopoly in British Industry*, p. 6.

[3] *I.e.* the aggregate of establishments trading under the same name.

[4] *I.e.* single firm or aggregate of firms owned or controlled by a single company and employing 500 persons or more, control being defined as ownership of more than half the capital (or voting power) of each firm.

[5] Leak and Maizels, ' The Structure of British Industry ', *Journal of the Royal Statistical Society*, Parts I-II, 1945.

The following table summarises them.

SIZE OF FIRMS

Size of Firm (Av. No. Employed)	No. of Firms		No. of Persons Employed	
	Absolute	%	Absolute	%
11–49	31,756	59·5	795,809	11·1
50–99	9,459	17·8	656,237	9·1
100–499	9,722	18·3	1,993,241	27·6
500–999	1,270	2·4	878,764	12·2
1,000–1,999	612	1·2	844,349	11·7
2,000–4,999	297	0·6	915,579	12·7
5,000–9,999	70	0·13	479,416	6·7
10,000 & over	31	0·06	639,662	8·9
Total	53,217	100	7,203,057	100

In 1935, therefore, the average number of workers per firm was about 140. More than nine-tenths of the firms employed less than 500 workers and accounted for 48 per cent of the total employment for the group. These conclusions are not significantly modified if we take 'units' instead of firms. In interpreting this table it has to be borne in mind that it excludes—

(a) all firms with less than 10 employees. Of these there were about 200,000 before the war ;

(b) the whole of distribution and agriculture where most of the units are small ;

(c) the whole of the professional services.

At a rough guess, therefore, perhaps one-third or one-quarter of the total occupied population in 1935 in Great Britain worked in business units employing more than 500 workers.

In the United States the same sort of picture presents itself. Nine-tenths of the total firms employ less than 20 workers and cover about a quarter of all employed workers.[1] The average number of workers per *establishment* was only 138 in 1937.

We do not know whether the distribution of firms by

[1] Final Report of the Executive Secretary of T.N.E.C. on ' Concentration of Economic Power ', p. 298.

size has changed significantly in the past thirty or forty years. But one conclusion seems inescapable. If there is a long-period tendency towards increasing size in the firm, then it must be going on very slowly since, before the war, it had produced only the results shown above. If, on the other hand, it is argued that there is a rapid movement towards bigger units, then it must have begun only very recently and we cannot be sure it represents a deep-seated tendency. But, until those who believe in the inevitability of spectacular concentration make up their minds which theory they hold and provide the evidence in support of it, it is safe to conclude that industry is not being forced into monopolistic forms in the search for efficiency.

Why then are the facts so commonly and so grossly misconceived ? [1] Leaving on one side the self-inflicted myopia of many of the doctrinaire planners, the reasons are three. First, there is the failure to distinguish between the concentration which arises naturally because bigger units are more efficient than smaller, and the concentration due to deliberate attempts at monopoly whether it means increasing efficiency or not. Second, there is the very dangerous habit of thinking in terms of a few special cases. Sweeping general-

---

[1] A detailed rebuttal of all such statements would take up a volume in itself. But Mr. Dobb's latest writing on this subject may be taken as typical, *Studies in the Development of Capitalism*, pp. 341-8. Mr. Dobb begins by saying that " the facts of industrial concentration in the modern world are almost too familiar to need much emphasis ". When he starts to look at the facts, however, his confidence in this conclusion begins to waver. He confesses ' surprise ' at the average size of firms in Great Britain and the United States, and he finally concludes, " it remains true that there persist to this day important elements of competition of the 19th-century type — even if here such competition is increasingly imperfect and at a good distance from the text-book type — both on the fringes and in the interstices of giant industry and also over some autonomous tracts of economic country that are by no means negligible in extent ". But, in order that the facts should not interfere with his theories, he puts forward two arguments. First, that where the small units persist monopolies of the cartel type have been prevalent. There is no evidence given for this statement and in the United States it is palpably incorrect. Second, that the small firms live under the surveillance and patronage of the giant firms in the industry. If Mr. Dobb will only continue his studies of industrial organisation he will find that, more often than not, the small firms, because of their efficiency, call the tune in the industry and that the giant firms are often the ' marginal ' firms.

isations are made about industry as a whole on the basis of second-hand information about electricity generation, and the iron and steel, chemical and railway transport industries. Equally striking cases of the persistence and superiority of small-scale operation could be quoted from the clothing and food trades, road and air transport, and various of the later stages of the iron and steel industry.[1] Thirdly, and most important, is the habit of thinking of industry as static. In fact, of course, new industries are constantly forcing themselves into the system or expanding relatively to others. These new industries, for the most part, come into existence in the shape of small firms and are, indeed, industries where the small unit is likely to be able to hold its own. The industries most frequently chosen to illustrate the growing concentration of industry tend to become relatively less important as the economic system expands and diversifies.

There are, in fact, no grounds for believing that the need for firms to operate at the most economical size will produce a world of giant firms or of industries in which one or two firms will effectively dominate the market. We are not really confronted with the awkward choice between monopoly and inefficiency.

In the past few years a variation of this argument has become popular which is open to the same objections. It is that industry is increasingly confronted with the problem of ' indivisible ' lumps of technical equipment. The case of the electricity generating station is quoted *ad nauseam*. In such cases, it is said, the concerns will operate at diminishing costs. Competition would force the concerns to operate at a loss. Competition then destroys itself. For, socially, the right policy would be to go on producing at a loss although no private firm would be prepared to do this. Mr. Dickinson's views are typical.

---

[1] It is significant to find that in the Working Party Reports on British Industries no case could be found for the large firm as against the small in the cotton, boot and shoe, pottery, furniture or jewellery industries.

In the early and middle period of capitalism, diminishing costs did not often occur . . . equilibrium was possible under competition. . . . But more recent times have seen the rapid growth of decreasing-cost industries. . . . What is needed, at any rate for the large-scale sector of the economy, is a system of production by public bodies . . . not obliged to make profits.[1]

The economic analysis may be impeccable : the policy based on it more than dubious. Where is the evidence in support of the view that 'indivisibilities' are of growing importance ? Mr. Dickinson quotes four cases: a steel plant, a line of railways, an electric generating plant, a synthetic ammonia plant. Now railways have existed for a hundred years, they are steadily giving way to other forms of transport which do not create the same indivisibility problems. An electricity generating plant is a fair instance, but it must not be overlooked that the increasing use of a public supply of electricity reduces the indivisibilities in the firms now making use of the electricity. Steel plants and synthetic ammonia plants are admittedly getting larger, but in any fair-sized market, say that of Great Britain, there is room for many such plants all operating at the optimum scale. When one further bears in mind the recent growth of many industries where the minimum technical unit is small as in the food, clothing and building industries, it is difficult to believe that indivisibilities do really create a new situation in industry which now makes inapplicable the general case for a free economy which Dickinson would admit for the conditions of the nineteenth century.

The Splintering of the Market

Where the market is small, the likelihood that one producer will be the sole or the dominant supplier becomes the greater. Producers may, therefore, attempt to break up markets so that they can gain a ' pull ' in one of the segments. For this purpose they can play upon the ignorance of the

[1] *Humanitas*, Autumn 1946.

consumer in various ways. They may induce him by advertising into buying a product at a higher price when the same,
less-advertised, product is on sale at a lower price. They
may attach him to their products by some purely meretricious
attraction. They may secure his custom by special personal
relations. The upshot is that consumers do not buy in the
cheapest market.

There have in recent years been brilliant advances in the
theoretical analysis of imperfect competition which has much
advanced our knowledge of the economic system. But it is
widely believed that because at last we have recognised and
analysed this phenomenon that the phenomenon has quite
recently made its appearance, that a world of monopolies
has suddenly sprung into existence. Just as if people started
to feel colder because somebody had invented the thermometer.

Can it be proved that the consumers' choice is more
widely distorted now than in the past ? It is true that advertising through press and radio is now practised on a larger
scale than heretofore.[1] But much advertising is simply
informative, it thereby increases the perfection of the market.
Increasing general education should surely do something to
decrease the gullibility of the public. Improved and cheap-
ened transport in itself improves the perfection of the market.
And it certainly cannot be assumed that all cases of differentia-
tion of products constitute evidence of sinister plots by the
producer : they may simply be cases of a more scrupulous
regard for the needs of the consumer.

Such imperfections are surely of secondary importance in
judging the case of the free economy. It is true that I may be
drawn by advertisement to buy one kind of cigarettes when
other unadvertised types would be just as good. It is also
true that, if I am rational, I may steer clear of such cigarettes
because I know that advertising costs money and I presum-

---

[1] Those who believe that ' double-crossing ' the consumer began with large-
scale advertising should read O. Henry's short stories.

ably am paying it. It is, in any case, probable that the advertising ties me to one type of cigarette by a very slender bond which would be snapped quickly if an attempt were made to raise the price of that product. And the growth of the large store specialising in the sale of unbranded goods will provide a salutary check to the power of the advertiser of branded goods where these have really nothing to commend them.

Indeed static economic analysis, in this as in so many other cases, is no secure basis for policy. It may be true that imperfect competition, at any one moment, results in the production of goods in the incorrect proportions. But the devices by which this is brought about — such as advertising — may be the very devices by which the whole system is kept in a dynamic condition. Through them an entrepreneur may take the risk of putting some entirely new product on the market which ultimately proves to be of wide acceptability to the public and through which a general sense of buoyancy is created in the economic system. And through them attempts on the part of producers to cash-in on their existing markets secured by advertisement will be frustrated by a crop of new products. It is not an accident that, in the United States, where the practices which make for imperfect competition are more widespread than elsewhere, the nearest approach has been made to a competitive system and the advantages of such a system have led to unparalleled increases in standards of living.

There seems, therefore, little need to start talking of economic and social revolutions because silly or uninformed people can be persuaded to buy branded aspirins at five times the price of unbranded. For if consumers are gullible or without knowledge then the right solution is to provide them with more information. And if producers prove unscrupulous in playing upon consumers' ignorance then it is perfectly practicable within the free economy to restrict and control these activities to whatever degree may be required.

Monopoly and Ruinous Competition

When an industry finds itself over-equipped, so that profits cannot be made on the whole of the existing capital, it will turn to monopoly as a way out of its difficulties. The history of British industry between the wars provides numerous illustrations. Where a firm, because of a shortage of demand, cannot keep all its machinery running it will cut prices and continue to do so until the prices it obtains cover simply its prime costs. Other firms may be forced to follow suit. The whole industry may thus be thrown into ' ruinous ' competition. No firm, or few firms, can make profits. Re-equipment is, therefore, out of the question. Sporadic working may become common and ' the long-drawn-out agony of competition ' may, in areas dependent upon one industry, lead to much suffering and social disintegration. No one who watched the Lancashire cotton industry in the toils between the wars would wish to deny the horror of such conditions.

In such circumstances, attempts to create monopolies are almost inevitable. If firms can get together, agree upon minimum prices or upon output quotas, then prices can be raised and a measure of monopoly stability restored, and it is hard to criticise such a policy. Hard but necessary. For such monopolies invariably intensify the problem they seek to cure.

When demand falls off in one industry the consequential price changes tend to bring about the necessary readjustment. Prices fall and this tends to keep up demand ; wages are reduced which helps to divert surplus labour to other industries ; the marginal firms tend to be driven out which raises the level of efficiency in the industry ; capital ceases to flow to the industry because already there is too much equipment there. Surely these are the sensible steps to take ? Yet many would argue that that is not the whole of the story. Depression of this kind, they would say, operates with a snowball effect, pushing the industry further down into distress than it should go. The absence of resources for re-equipment and the reluctance of able young men to risk their careers in the industry, prevent it from dealing with its troubles by increasing efficiency and lowering costs. The psychology of depression becomes morbid. In any case, it is added, " competition does not work ", the marginal firms do not disappear, they hang on indefinitely so that the re-adjustment implied in economic theory never happens. Inevitably the familiar cries arise that " the house must be put in order ", that " the dead wood must be cut out ", " a bottom must be put into the market ". Employers and workers combine in putting this case and the State is under great pressure to connive in the setting up of a monopoly. It would be futile to suppose, given the kind of conditions which existed in the British cotton or coal-mining industries between the wars, that the State would ever be able to resist claims which, superficially, would seem to be based upon humanitarian and upon economic grounds.

The tragedy of such schemes is that they nearly always do more harm than good. For a long time they may be ineffective. It is difficult to enforce minimum prices or maximum output quotas in a buyers' market. The British cotton industry between the wars shows a long mournful series of price associations which ultimately broke down and which created greater instability than ever. When the State comes in to enforce legally the cartel arrangements, then, almost invariably, the arrangements keep in existence the less efficient firms, lead employers to rely upon raising prices rather than increasing efficiency as the way out of their troubles, reduce demand by so raising prices and thus increase unemployment. The melancholy story of the British coal-mining industry after the passing of the Coal Mines Act of 1930 — a story in which some of the costs of our past mistakes still remain to be paid — is sufficient proof of this.

It was the Coal Mines Act of 1930 which, under the guise

of "giving the industry a breathing-space", enabled both sides to evade the real causes of the trouble and made it possible for the State and the public to set on one side, although only temporarily, awkward decisions which sooner or later had to be faced. That Act consisted of two parts. Part I conferred upon the industry the power to set up regional organisations through which output would be controlled and compulsory minimum prices established. These privileges were to be conferred so that the industry should proceed under Part II of the Act to carry out wholesale reorganisation of the industry.

Nothing could be more definite than the temporary nature of the rights conferred under Part I. Mr. Ramsay MacDonald, speaking in the House of Commons on December 19, 1929, said, "when you have got amalgamations as we shall have, when royalties are nationalised as they must be, then the conditions which make Part I of this Bill necessary will have completely disappeared. . . . Therefore this scheme is bound to be temporary."

What in fact happened? The schemes for maintaining prices and controlling output became more deeply embedded with the passing of each year. More and more elaborate schemes were devised to milk the efficient firms in order to keep the inefficient in existence. The plans for reorganisation were stillborn. The Coal Mines Reorganisation Commission worked for nine years with no effect. The British coal-mining industry progressively fell behind the coal-mining industries of other countries in the improvement of technical methods. But was this really surprising? Was it not cause and effect? If an industry has monopoly conferred upon it by statute, is it likely that it will burn with energy to equip itself so that it can once again make an entry into the competitive world? Is it not virtually certain that, once the State has put a ring-fence around an industry in this way, then the employers and workers will naturally turn to methods which will safeguard their own position without any scrupulous regard for the economic interests of industry in general or the consumers as a body ? Now the coal-mining industry has been nationalised on the grounds that ' private enterprise has failed ' although the failure was that of short-sighted methods of stifling private enterprise.

Nor is it true, provided the State does not intervene positively to prevent it, that competition ' does not work ', does not bring about the necessary readjustment. Between 1930 and 1938 the spindles in the British cotton industry fell from 63 millions to 42 millions (33 per cent) and the looms from 700,000 to 495,000 (29 per cent).¹ Is that not readjustment ? Would anyone, standing in 1930 with a full knowledge of what would happen in the future, have dared to recommend a sudden reduction from the 1930 to the 1938 level with all the social upset that it would have caused ? And this decline in the industry went on despite the numerous attempts at price and output fixation which impeded normal readjustment. There is, in fact, great significance to be attached to a comparison of the rate of readjustment in Lancashire and the New England States of America. The economic problems were similar in the two countries but in New England, of course, price and output associations were illegal under the anti-trust laws. Between 1925 and 1935 spindles in New England declined by 50 per cent ; in Lancashire only by 30 per cent. The truth seems to be that competition can, if left free, be too sharp and savage, not too slow, in its working.

The crucial question is this. Will conditions of ruinous competition be frequent and widespread enough in countries such as Great Britain and the United States to force business men and governments to take desperate measures for restoring stability by the conferring of monopoly powers over large tracts of the economic system ? If so, then, of course, there is

¹ It is worth while noting that the readjustment in weaving went on at almost the same rate as in spinning although there was a special scheme in spinning, operated by the Surplus Spindles Board, by which spindles were bought up and destroyed by means of a levy which increased spinning costs.

no future for the kind of free economy for which this book is a plea.

It would be possible to examine the industrial structure of the different countries to try to ascertain whether there are many industries still left which, like the Lancashire cotton industry before the war, might receive a sudden deadly blow through the emergence of new forms of competition ; to speculate as to whether industries in the future will seriously over-equip themselves in boom periods and pay the price later on ; to examine the nature of technical changes to try to determine whether these are likely to leave some industries high and dry without much notice ; to scrutinise the nature of consumers' demand to try to ascertain whether fluctuations in it in future would dislocate industrial expectations. I suspect that such enquiries would be interesting but inconclusive, although it seems that never again, perhaps, will any country find itself in so vulnerable a position as did Great Britain after the first World War with its high dependence upon exports in a limited range of goods, its concentration of the export trades in a few areas of the country and the dependence of those areas upon exports.

The answer, however, to these queries depends almost wholly upon the answer to another, prior, question : are we to assume that we shall be successful in avoiding, by policy, the conditions of mass unemployment which afflicted us before the war ? If we can, then it is reasonable to assume that monopolies designed to prevent ruinous competition will be few and far between. It is only if we fail in maintaining a general high rate of employment that we need have fear that the free economy would be wrecked by the multiplication of defensive monopolies.

An economic system suffering chronically from a high general rate of unemployment is a fertile breeding-ground for restrictive policies. For no obvious remedies then exist for dealing with the problems of an industry where demand has fallen off seriously and probably permanently. In such industries it is easy enough to talk about readjustment. But where are the surplus workers to go ? Mobility of labour will be low. Employers will be able to force wage cuts without running serious dangers of losing their workers, which prolongs and delays the necessary readjustment. Entrepreneurs in the depressed industry find it difficult to discover alternative and more profitable lines for their energies and their capital. At such times any policy which appears to bring immediate relief, however frustrating it may be in the long run, will find its supporters. And monopoly is one obvious way out. In this sense the futile policies pursued in the British coal-mining, cotton and other depressed industries between the wars were just as much the consequence of the failure to maintain a high general demand for labour, through the maintenance of a sufficient level of national expenditure, as the consequence of the depressing factors peculiar to these industries.

The political and social pressures in favour of sectional monopoly cannot be resisted where the State has failed to maintain general expenditure and the demand for labour at a high level. But where the State does not fail in that essential function [1] then everything becomes different. For if one industry suffers a decline, whilst the general demand for labour is brisk, readjustment would go on much more quickly. If men are thrown out of work in the one industry, they will find it easy to get jobs elsewhere ; if the employers try to cut wages they will the more rapidly encourage their workers to seek employment in other industries where wages have not been reduced ; the marginal firms in the depressed industries will be eliminated more quickly ; the business men there will more swiftly find other profitable outlets for their work. We need no longer fear that, like a man with haemophilia, the economic system will bleed to death from any minor cut : the buoyancy of the system will provide a natural remedy for the minor disturbance. And we need,

[1] See Chapter IV.

therefore, no longer tolerate panic restrictionist measures as a cure.

The Predatory Habits of the Business Man

There remains the argument that, since the business man is engaged in essentially predatory activities, he will seek after monopoly for its own sake and that the free economy, therefore, contains the seeds of its own destruction.

The most effective way of evoking economic effort from any group is to create a system in which the average return is low but in which a few large prizes exist for exceptional achievement, prizes after which all may strain but which few can achieve. In a free economy that is the position in which the business man finds himself. Competition under relatively stable conditions will gradually force down the rate of profit. The average rate of profit has never been high over long periods if account is taken of failures and successes. The large prizes obtained by those of exceptional energy are offset by the modest returns or losses of the remainder. A sensibly conceived economic system should sweat the business man.

Such arrangements are not pleasant for him. Nor should they be. It is not pleasant to dig coal, to nurse the sick, to drive a locomotive or an aircraft year in and year out, to teach the young, or to engage in the million and one necessary activities of a complex society. We need shed no tears for the business man in his tribulations. Brisk competition may be a strain. But nobody forces anyone to be a business man.

Like everybody else he will normally seek the line of least resistance. And the creation of a monopoly is one obvious way in which he can do it. It cannot be denied that, through history, there have been cases, many cases, where the cornering of the market has been due to the activities of men who sought power for its own sake, the counterpart in the economic system to the great dictators in the political order. But they are the exceptions. For the most part predatory monopoly is the result of the activities of men, with no greater evil in them than in the majority of us, who wish to make life a little less strenuous and who naturally are inclined to minimise the advantages to the community of the steady pressure of competition. In any economy where monopoly is not controlled, it will become prevalent.

One cannot, however, deduce from this that the free economy stands condemned or that the activities of the entrepreneur are so inherently anti-social that they should be swept away. The power of the business man must be properly harnessed. This is by no means a novel doctrine. There are, indeed, many forces in the social system which uncontrolled are destructive but controlled are of enormous value. Individual freedom itself, if wholly uncurbed, would be highly disruptive of organised society. In the political field we recognise that those who reach the head of their parties will probably be men of more than ordinary ambition and belief in their own wisdom with temperaments out of which dictators are made. We consequently surround them with all the curbs and safeguards of a democratic constitution. It would be a bad day for us all if we appointed as our political rulers men consumed with philosophic doubts, almost as bad as if we placed in charge of business those indifferent to their own interests. In the physical field there are other analogies. We lay on gas and electricity to our houses for our own comfort although, improperly controlled, the one can suffocate and the other electrocute us. We swallow, to our benefit, drugs in controlled quantities which could poison us. We ride about at high speeds in vehicles which could, without guidance, smash us to pieces. It is a namby-pamby approach to life to argue that we must get rid of the business man because, in the wrong social environment, he can and would do harm.

It ought to be a comparatively simple matter to maintain a competitive system. The monopolist is, in ordinary circumstances, on the defensive. He is not master of the market ; that power resides with the consumer. If the price is raised the purchaser will buy less, and other producers will be tempted to enter the industry. The competition from substitute products, from imported goods, from non-profit-seeking organisations — such as local authorities or co-operative societies — can never be wholly eliminated. Nobody loves a monopolist and, recognising this, he must be at pains to avoid public suspicion which might fatally damage his market. In fact, there are very few monopolies which have been able to resist successfully the inroads of competition unless they were encouraged, supported or created by the State, or unless they were based on the possession of the sole sources of supply of some limited natural raw material.

Indeed, in a progressive economic society, the scales are weighted against the monopolist in two crucial ways. First, the laboratory is fighting against him. New methods of meeting the same demand are constantly being invented. Coal, gas, electricity and fuel oil compete as methods of heat. Houses may be constructed of brick, cement, aluminium or steel. Containers may be made of paper, glass, tin, aluminium or plastics. As scientific knowledge and technical adaptation spread like the branches of a great tree the costs and risks of creating a monopoly become the greater, the gains smaller and more precarious. Second, the steadily improving standard of living is fighting against him. For, as the standard rises, a higher proportion of the consumers' expenditure is devoted to the wide range of non-essential articles and services where the consumer can easily change the direction of his demand. If the price of the cinema seat rises, he will switch to the purchase of more chocolate, more tobacco, more frequent attendance at football or cricket matches, more wireless sets, more motor cycles and so on. Monopoly under such circumstances becomes highly elusive.

So that a progressive economy is not without its natural defences against monopoly. But they should be supported by two other forms of control.

It is just as much a normal part of the function of the State to curb monopoly as to formulate and enforce traffic rules. A sound anti-monopoly policy would have many facets. On the negative side, and perhaps most important of all, the State should itself refrain from creating or conniving at the creation of monopolies. On the positive side it should encourage those conditions and institutions which widen and strengthen the field of competition : free trade, consumers' co-operative societies, local authority trading, the operation of State factories in unsubsidised competition with the free sector, are all important ways of doing this. Further, there should be a code of rules designed to prevent the obvious abuses of monopoly and to maintain a competitive economy : some practices should be definitely proscribed, others should be kept under constant surveillance. A Government research body should be engaged continuously in the study of changes in industrial organisation so that the public may be kept informed of those changes, and industries given proper and timely warning of practices which threaten the free economy.

This technique has been highly developed during more than half a century in the United States. No one would claim that the hopes of those who drafted the first anti-trust laws in that country have been fully realised. Much monopoly still exists,[1] it may indeed be that the methods of control must always be somewhat imperfect. Some would go further, indeed, and claim that the whole experiment in monopoly control has been a failure, so complete as to deter any other country from following the same path. That surely is a short-sighted view. For it must not be overlooked that the control of monopoly in the United States has been surrounded by quite exceptional difficulties : the vastness of the territory to be controlled ; the traditional protectionist policy of the country ; the double jurisdiction of State and

---

[1] See *The Concentration of Economic Power*, David Lynch, and the voluminous reports of the Temporary National Economic Committee.

Federal government ; the phenomenal expansion of industry ; the unparalleled achievements in mass production which call for large manufacturing units ; the frequent voltefaces in policy with the changes in government. All these have rendered the United States probably the most unsuitable environment in the whole world for a successful policy of anti-trust control. Despite all this there would be few who would recommend the repeal of the present anti-trust legislation or who would deny that many abuses have been remedied or prevented by it. The facts are that the United States is the scene of the most ambitious experiment in monopoly control and is also the country which most closely approximates to a free economy. The presumption must be that these are, at least in part, cause and effect.

In Great Britain, certainly, there is much that the State could do to revivify the competitive process. For more than a quarter of a century after the first World War no British Government recognised that it had any responsibility whatsoever in this field. On the contrary every Government contributed to the establishment of monopolies in agriculture, transport, coal-mining and cotton. The courts, naturally enough, reflected this growing public tolerance of economic restriction so that the law regarding restraint of trade ceased to provide any protection for the consumer. The tide of opinion now, however, seems to be turning. The Coalition Government in its White Paper on Employment Policy in 1944 declared itself in favour of monopoly control. All three political parties in Great Britain have indicated their opposition to restrictive practices and their determination to set up machinery to discover and to curb it.[1] If they prove

[1] Mr. Churchill, Conservative Party Conference, 1946 : " It is an essential principle of Conservative policy to defend the public against abuses by monopolies and against restraints on trade and enterprise, whether these evils come from private corporatiɔns, from the mischievous plans of doctrinaire governments or from the incompetence and arbitrariness of departments of State ".

Mr. Attlee, October 10, 1946 : " To match the economics of full employment we need the ethics of full employment. . . . Restrictive practices on either side . . . are out of place today."

as good as their word something may be done to reverse the dangerous drift towards restriction.

Business men, themselves, have a responsibility in this matter which they can ignore only at the peril of their own survival. They must recognise that nobody can defend, on rational grounds, a system of monopoly capitalism — least of all those who are concerned to defend the free economy. They must learn to take the rough of the competitive system with the smooth. It should be the business man who clamours for legislation and administrative machinery for the control of monopoly. Only in that way can he forestall the socialist who advocates nationalisation as the cure for private monopoly.

Yet there is still extant much special pleading for monopoly. A Cotton Yarn Spinners' Association has been formed in Lancashire, one of the objects of which is to resume control of selling prices by the trade when control by the Government is eventually withdrawn, in order to guarantee that " the earning power of the industry is sufficient to provide for its constant and continuous equipment ".[1] Similar organisations are being discussed in weaving and doubling. The Committee set up by the Ministry of Works on the Welsh slate industry openly recommended monopoly : " the true interest of the slate producers lies in uniting against [other roofing materials] to secure an equitable share of the roofing available and to avoid a policy of price cutting ".[2] The Working Party on Linoleum[3] made light of the monopoly practices in the linoleum industry although it was admitted that, before the war, prices were fixed by an Association which had no knowledge of actual costs, that the costs of production of the least efficient firms were between 20 and 30 per cent above those of the most efficient firms, and that the British industry was a member of a strong international cartel which

---

[1] *Manchester Guardian*, January 7, 1947.
[2] *The Welsh Slate Industry* (1947), p. 25.
[3] *Linoleum* (1947), chap. v.

divided markets. The Committee on Cement Costs [1]
reported that the Cement Makers' Federation had fixed
prices and quotas, taken action to discourage new entrants,
operated a deferred rebate system and organised a basing
point price system. It is known that the costs of the different
firms vary considerably. Despite all this the Committee
restricted itself to a few mild recommendations which would
have left the power of the Federation intact. In the middle
of 1947, in a period of acute food shortage, the Scottish
Herring Producers' Association, representing the majority
of East Coast fishermen, refused to sell surplus herrings for
reduction at a low price and were dumping them into the sea. [2]
This kind of reasoning by business men is as dangerous
to their survival as would be the drinking of salt water by
men in an open boat far out at sea.

[1] ' Cement Costs ', Report by the Committee appointed by the Minister of
Works, 1947.
[2] House of Commons, July 7, 1947.

CHAPTER IV

IS MASS UNEMPLOYMENT INEVITABLE IN THE FREE ECONOMY?

I

THE third major charge against the free economy is that it results in mass unemployment.[1] No one would wish to deny that, in the past, private enterprise has been the cause of heavy and prolonged unemployment. The first forty years of this century will go down as the period when the fear of being without a job was as intense and widespread as the terrors which accompanied some of the great epidemics of the past. It is also indisputable that if mass unemployment recurs then the liberal society will perish as it perished in Germany between the wars. For general unemployment is a scourge which wastes economic resources, fosters restrictions of every kind and destroys the belief in the rationality of society.

But what was true of the past need not necessarily be true of the future. In the past twenty years the work of Lord Keynes has revolutionised [2] our thinking about the operation of the economic system, has isolated the flaw

[1] By mass unemployment I mean a chronic general shortage of jobs as distinct from temporary and localised unemployment due to workers changing their jobs, to seasonal factors, to switches in consumers' demand or to changes in the methods of production.

[2] How swift and complete has been the revolution is indicated by the following quotations. In 1929 in his Budget Speech the Chancellor of the Exchequer (Mr. Winston Churchill) had declared, " It is the orthodox Treasury dogma steadfastly held that, whatever might be the political and social advantages, very little additional employment and no permanent additional employment can, in fact, and as a general rule, be created by State borrowing and State expenditure ". In 1944 in its White Paper on Employment Policy the Coalition Government declared, " The Government accepts as one of its primary aims and responsibilities the maintenance of a high and stable level of employment ".

which may lead the free economy to run at less than its full power and has pointed clearly to the methods to be adopted to remedy the defect. There need never be mass unemployment again. On that there is very general agreement. The only question at issue is just how far the State must intervene in the working of the economic system to prevent it. This chapter is, therefore, concerned with two questions.

(a) Can a full employment policy, based on the Keynesian diagnosis, be operated without dealing a mortal blow at the market economy in which consumer and producer have sufficient freedom to preserve a sound foundation for a liberal society ? If so, what conditions must be satisfied if we are to obtain the best of both worlds, steady adequate employment and individual freedom ?

(b) Can the wholly planned economy give us full employment and, if so, what price must we pay for it ?

II

There is no need to go into detail regarding the Keynesian employment theory. It has been much written about elsewhere.[1] But from the point of view of practical policy it may be summarised thus. Mass unemployment is due to a deficiency of demand for goods and services. If this kind of unemployment threatens, it is the responsibility of the State to intervene and either to spend more money itself or to put its citizens in the way of spending more. So, as the total national expenditure increases, more goods are called for and more people are employed in making them. The threatened unemployment is avoided.

The State can spend more money itself : it can undertake the building of extra roads, bridges, houses, etc., and thus provide more employment. The wages of those so employed are spent on food and other consumer goods and create

[1] For the general reader the best exposition of it is perhaps to be found in Boulding, *Economics of Peace*.

further employment. This, however, will only happen if the State spends more by methods which do not automatically reduce what the private individual spends. For example, if the State spends more on roads by increasing taxation, the citizens will now have less to spend and there may be no net increase in expenditure. Or the State can, on the appropriate occasions, create the conditions under which the public will spend more. It might reduce taxation (without reducing its own expenditure) ; the public will then have more money to spend. Or it might increase family allowances or decrease the rate of contribution to the Social Insurance Fund which would have the same effect.

In one way or another the State must see to it that total national expenditure is kept at a high enough level to create a demand for goods and services which will keep in a job everybody who wants a job. And, in the last resort, the instrument of the State is that of spending, when necessary, more than the taxes it collects, of running an ' unbalanced ' budget. How can it find this additional money without first collecting it in taxes ? From two sources. First, it might borrow from the citizens and spend money which they would not spend anyway. Second, it might simply print the additional money and either spend this money itself or hand it out in some predetermined way to the public.

All this implies, of course, a new and highly important rôle for the State. But no one need be alarmed about that. The government must, of course, always intervene where it can be shown that individuals, acting in what appear to be their own self-interest, will not only frustrate their own purposes but also the aims of all other members of the public who are seeking to act rationally in their own interest. State employment policy satisfies this test. The point can be simply explained. If general unemployment threatens it could always be avoided if people would react to the threat by spending more : by the consumer buying more goods, or by

the business man buying more machines or erecting new
factories.   But the instinctive reaction of the prudent individual consumer or business man would, in the face of an
anticipated depression, be in precisely the opposite direction.
For if the ordinary worker anticipates unemployment it seems
wise for him personally to save more and spend less in order to
have something to fall back upon if he is thrown out of work.
And if the business man expects a decline in trade it would
seem to him just the wrong time to spend more money on
new capital equipment.   The more actively individuals seek
to protect themselves the more certain it is that the combined
effect of their actions will bring upon all the evils they seek
to avoid.   Only action by the State will be sufficient to reverse
the trend and to bring about the correct volume of expenditure.

The same point can be illustrated in another way.   A
community cannot maintain a condition of full employment
unless, once having reached that position, it spends in total
(either on consumer goods or capital equipment) the whole
of its income.   Some people will wish to save, of course.
That does not matter so long as somebody else is prepared
to spend these savings.   In practice this means roughly that
some members of the public will buy less consumer goods
than they might but they will lend their savings to manufacturers who will spend on capital equipment.   So long as
the manufacturer spends in this way as much as the public
saves then all is well.   But a community, by saving, may
be cutting its own throat.   It may be bringing upon itself
a deficient total of national expenditure, unemployment,
depression and a fall in national income.   Now individual
saving is not an ignoble practice.   It may spring out of
entirely laudable social habits and the deeper human gener-
osities : the desire to be independent in case of misfortune,
the desire to engage in the work of one's choice.   Yet if the
volume of savings arising in this way exceeds the volume of
spending on equipment which the employer finds it worth

while to incur, the community is digging the ground from under its own feet. Only the State can repair this deficiency in expenditure.

III

How far does this added rôle of the State involve the destruction of the market economy ? We may first allow the author of the new economic doctrine to speak for himself. Keynes has said : [1]

The result of filling in the gaps in the classical theory is not to dispose of the " Manchester System ", but to indicate the nature of the environment which the free play of economic forces requires if it is to realise the full potentialities of production. The central controls necessary to ensure full employment will, of course, involve a large extension of the traditional functions of government. . . . Within this field the traditional advantages of individualism will still hold good.

When the master has spoken thus, it is time for those who seek to twist his doctrines to their own political ends to take notice.

The precise methods by which the increased spending necessary for maintaining employment is to be created, and the respective parts to be played by State and private expenditure, or by expenditure on consumer goods and on capital equipment, would, of course, have to be worked out by experience and would vary from one set of conditions to another. But two possible schemes have already been outlined either of which, as it seems to me, would operate successfully without biting into the sphere of individual initiative which must remain inviolate if there is to be a free society.

The first is that laid down, in its White Paper on Employment Policy, by the British Coalition Government in 1946.[2] In that document it is declared that the Government must accept responsibility for the maintenance of a high and

[1] *The General Theory of Employment*, p. 379.
[2] Cmd. 6527.

stable level of employment. The procedure outlined there was that of estimating for a period ahead the probable total national expenditure, assuming that the Government itself pursued a normal financial course. If this total appeared to be insufficient to maintain the requisite level of employment then the Government should intervene to increase expenditure by bringing forward public works, carefully prepared and organised beforehand ; by increasing consumption through a cut in contributions to the Social Insurance Fund and (although this method was suggested more tentatively) by remission of taxation. It was laid down that the Budget should not necessarily be balanced each year, although it was argued that the case for balancing over a period was strong.

The essence of this programme, however, was that of allowing the market economy to run without hindrance or interference unless private and normal Government expenditure seemed likely to be inadequate. The Government action would be sufficiently tentative and its weapons sufficiently flexible to enable it to adjust its own activities if its estimates of ' normal ' national expenditure proved unsound. There is nothing here of programmes for individual firms or industries, nothing of the establishment of social priorities which would bind the consumer or producer, nothing, in fact, of what is normally understood as comprehensive planning by the modern socialist. The policy is one of trying to control the economic climate rather than of telling each citizen when he should put up and down his umbrella, when he should don and doff his overcoat.

The second group of proposals are those which have been put forward by Professor Lerner.[1] He rejects " both the dogma of the Left that 100 per cent collectivism is necessarily in the social interest and the dogma of the Right that the government of a country must keep to the fiscal principles appropriate to a grocery store ". The subtlety and elegance of Lerner's analysis cannot possibly be compressed into one

[1] *Economics of Control* : in particular chap. 24.

paragraph. Briefly his theory is that the Government should increase or decrease taxation,[1] increase or decrease its borrowing, not for the purpose of meeting its own needs, but for the purpose of increasing or decreasing national expenditure in order to maintain the requisite employment level. A reduction of taxation will increase spending, a raising of taxation will decrease it. A reduction of borrowing by the Government (*i.e.* by reducing the National Debt) will cause a fall in the rate of interest and encourage expenditure on capital equipment ; increased borrowing by the Government will raise the rate of interest and discourage spending on capital equipment. The State must tax and borrow so that what is spent on consumer goods plus what is spent on capital equipment will add up to a total national expenditure sufficient to bring about a demand for goods which will keep everybody in a job.

Lerner's words read paradoxically and few would claim that the economic mechanism is as simple as he sometimes, rather perversely to my mind, suggests. But here, at least, is a logical theoretical framework for State action in the central field of finance which puts the responsibility upon the State for maintaining employment. But it involves nothing of what the planner conceives of as comprehensive planning. It leaves a very broad field for the operation of competitive industry. It leaves the consumer sovereign over the disposition of his income and over the activities of the producer. Lerner, indeed, claims that his system would reduce the complexity of regulation due to " piece-meal legislation with some relatively small problem in mind each time ".

Until weightier objections than have yet been advanced can be found to either of these two techniques, the presumption must be that a full employment policy can be

[1] Lerner, of course, would also use taxation as a method of encouraging or discouraging the consumption of certain goods and for the purpose of redistributing income within the community. But this is not directly relevant to the argument.

carried out without the detailed control of industry and the consumer and within a self-regulating price mechanism acting as a non-personal, neutral guide to individual action.

IV

The planners, however, with their one-track minds, have seized upon the general dread of unemployment and the work of Keynes to push hard their own particular gospel and to insist that an employment policy must be one of detailed central control of the minutiae of economic activity. Sometimes the attitude arises through pure ignorance.[1] Sometimes it is to be feared that it is a trick, by those who really know better, to rivet upon us controls as the only alternative to unemployment.[2] Certainly the vague conception of planning is a heaven-sent opportunity for every humbug to slip in his own particular nostrum as a part of the essential order of things.

Now it is true that an economy, planned to its limits, can prevent unemployment and normally will do so. Nobody need ever be technically unemployed in an army, in a prison or in a slave camp. But full employment, in this sense, is not a worth-while aim. It is important that the work performed should also be *effective* : effective in the sense that the worker is free to balance the satisfaction (or dissatisfaction) he derives from his work against what the consumer is prepared to pay for the job and to make his decisions accordingly about what work he will do.

[1] A close reading of the speeches of Mr. Morrison and Sir Stafford Cripps certainly suggests that they regard their tangle of nationalisation schemes, detailed control of raw materials and labour and rationing as essentially a part of full employment policy. Thus Sir Stafford Cripps in *Democracy Alive*, p. 19: " We are convinced . . . that it is impossible under modern circumstances to provide the opportunity of full employment . . . without that sort of planning and control which has brought us such large dividends of production during two world wars ".

[2] One of the most ardent among the intellectual planners has been heard to remark that " planning is such fun ". The individual sufferer from this ' fun ' might well groan, " As flies to wanton boys, are we to the gods ; they kill us for their sport ".

In this sense the planned economy is unlikely to provide effective employment at a high level. For, as will be pointed out in a later chapter, it will inevitably generate its own internal crises as the planners, from time to time, discover their errors and jolt the system round on to a new tack. The workers, indeed, during the resultant confusion may continue to stand by their machines as technically employed persons, or they may go on producing unwanted goods, or they may be moved about under compulsion. But all this amounts to waste of labour, concealed unemployment.

If the planned economy has not yet reached its logical limit by controlling and directing all labour then the waste of labour will be particularly serious. For then the economy will be planned in terms of something other than labour (for example, raw materials) and it is extremely unlikely that raw materials and labour will come together at the right times in the right proportions. That is why in Great Britain, from 1945 to 1947, industries could be divided into two groups : those in which there was plenty of raw materials and insufficient labour and those in which there was plenty of labour and inadequate raw materials. In those industries where shortages of raw materials led to part-time working (notably in the building and rubber-tyre industries) the Government had no remedy except to call for higher productivity from workers whose output was low because of planning blunders. Disequilibrium of this kind plays into the hands of vested interests which gain from, and naturally wish to perpetuate, the existing shortages. There seems little doubt, for instance, that the British coal-miners were, throughout 1946 and 1947, very conscious of the power which they wielded over the community through the shortage of coal and were not anxious to see a rapid increase of the labour force in the coal-mines, such as might have been brought about by the introduction of foreign labour.

On the other hand if the planned economy has finally taken full powers of direction then the vested interests may be overridden, provided they are not too powerful for the Government to tackle, but only by sacrificing a fundamental prop in individual freedom.

It is, indeed, dangerous to seek to combine policy for the maintenance of employment with other social and economic purposes, however attractive on the surface those purposes appear, for they must nearly always set out to make a better society and finish up by creating a worse. A striking illustration of this is provided by Sir William Beveridge's scheme as described in his book *Full Employment in the Free Society*. No one is more conscious of the claims of the individual against the State.[1] No one has written more forcibly and movingly on that subject. Yet he falls into the trap. It is important to understand how he has done so.

His diagnosis of the causes of general unemployment is that which is now generally accepted. His prescription in broad outline is consistent with that of the White Paper on Employment Policy or with that of Professor Lerner. " Total expenditure on all items must be sufficient for full employment. This is a categorical imperative, taking precedence over all other rules, and overriding them if they are in conflict with it." He believes that it is, if possible, preferable to do this without incurring a Budget deficit, although he is prepared to sacrifice the balancing of the Budget if this is necessary. He considers that " full employment could be secured in peace . . . while leaving the major part of industry to private enterprise " and that " the basic proposals of this Report are neither socialism nor an alternative to socialism : they are required and will work under capitalism and socialism alike ".

But Sir William draws into his scheme two other ideas which, as it seems to me, would undermine the essentials of a free society.

[1] In this particular book, Sir William insists throughout on the need for preserving all essential citizen liberties. He specifically " excludes the totalitarian solution of full employment in a society completely planned and regimented by an irremovable dictator ".

(1) In order to maintain stability in the expenditure on capital investment by private firms he would set up a National Investment Board which would have the power to control in detail all private investment.

(2) Bound up with this, and largely carried out through the work of the Investment Board, he would impose social priorities so that "first things should be produced first".

Both measures would inevitably draw the economy into State regimentation.

Sir William's policy involves the stabilisation not merely of total expenditure but of each main section of expenditure.[1] Private investment, therefore, must be stabilised. This is the function of the National Investment Board, " to plan investment as a whole, using powers of control and loan and taxation policy. . . ." " Assistance would take the form of ensuring, by a Government guarantee, a lower rate on investments for approved purposes . . ." (this fits in with the scheme for social priorities on the demand side). " For . . . the stabilisation of private investment the Board would have some power, suitably safeguarded, of direct control of investment — that is to say, power to stop or reduce by order a proposed private investment plan." This seems to envisage the examination by the Board of the investment plans of every firm.

Sir William underestimates the formidable, not to say insuperable, difficulties of any such scheme. Let us take first the case where private investment is flagging and must be raised : suppose, for instance, shipping companies find that due to a decline in world trade they need fewer new ships and unemployment is appearing in the shipbuilding industry. What is to be done ? Only two remedies are mentioned. The rate of interest might be lowered: But this might be quite useless. Experience indicates that at such times the rate of interest would have to be much less than nothing to

[1] *Ibid.* pp. 178 and 271.

encourage the business man to embark upon expansion in a time of falling demand. The other remedy is " that if private owners of business undertakings . . . fail, with all the help of the State, and in an expanding economy, to stabilise the process of investment, the private owners cannot be long left in their own ownership ". In other words, nationalise. But if this is put into action, does the State then proceed to build ships which nobody wants ?

Take now the other case where it is necessary to damp down private enterprise because it threatens to push total expenditure to the point where inflation will occur. It is easy to apply a *general* brake to private investment : the rate of interest courageously and opportunely employed will do this. But, of course, we do not need a National Investment Board, controlling in detail the flow of capital to every industry, in order to raise the rate of interest. Sir William has a more selective process in mind. He has his eye upon the social priorities. He would presumably discriminate between the investment plans of private firms : this to be allowed to go forward because it fits the master plan ; this to be retarded because it is outside it.

Discrimination of this kind would lead to the most formidable obstacles in logic and administration. In the first place, a great part of new industrial investment takes place, not through the public capital market, but by the ploughing back of profits into the firm. Is this internal financing to be controlled ? If so, it could only be done properly by controlling the supply of labour and raw materials to that firm and we should need a system of controls as complete as those of war-time. The number of firms, mainly small, which would be expanding at any one time would be enormous. How could any Investment Board acquaint itself with the details of each case sufficiently to make prompt and wise decisions ?

Sir William is apparently aware of that difficulty for he mentions (page 177) that " probably not more than 25 per cent of the total national investment will be accounted for by private manufacturing industry, and half of this 25 per cent is controlled by about 3000 firms, numbering less than 2 per cent of all firms ". But an attempt to simplify the problem by confining control to the 3000 firms above a given size would create even more serious difficulties than it disposes of. For suppose that in a given industry there were 20 firms altogether and that 5 of these firms were in the group of the 3000 large firms and 15 firms were smaller. The industry is expanding. The National Investment Board decides that this is not in the social interest. A curb is put on the 5 large firms. The 15 smaller firms continue to expand even more rapidly because they recognise that their larger competitors are hamstrung. The 15 firms might then all become large firms. The net result would be, either that the Investment Board would have to control the investment of all firms, 200,000 of them, or this industry would expand : and the expansion might be among the less efficient firms. Meanwhile the danger of the creation of surplus capacity, with all the possibilities of instability of operation, would be increased.

But, administrative difficulties apart, the problem Sir William sets himself is insoluble. Upon what principles would any Investment Board decide that one firm has stronger claims to be allowed to expand than another ? Upon what principles would a Board pick out the small firms which might expand and encourage them ? Who was to know that a small cycle shop in Oxford was the seed from which the largest motor-car factory in Great Britain would grow ? By what devices could the Investment Board trace through the reactions of its own decisions ? If it agrees that a chocolate firm should expand, does it then seek out and approve, or even encourage, the firms who will make what is needed in the shape of the additional machinery, bricks, cement, nuts and bolts, and so on ? Hopelessly caught in a labyrinth of detail, of conflicting claims for resources, of rival claims by competing consumers, it would finally be driven either to a type of totalitarian dictatorship, or to a feeble fumbling towards a limited number of decisions of a purely arbitrary kind, or to an acceptance of complete defeat in the tasks laid upon it.

Looked at from the side of demand, the principle of social priorities carries with it the most dangerous implications. It may be wrong or it may be right (I would think it right) that we should as a community seek to ensure that people had enough good food, clothing and housing before they spent money on unnecessary luxuries. But it is not directly relevant to the task of keeping people in work. Ignorance or indifference may mean that some people spend their incomes in ways which appear short-sighted to others. This, as far as possible, should be remedied not by compulsion but by propaganda and education. By and large, the best person to decide how his income can best be spent is that person himself. Certainly the State has only the most limited knowledge and facilities for assisting in this delicate process of adjustment of incomes to individual tastes and inclinations. Pushed beyond a certain point, therefore, the social priorities established by the State which Sir William has in mind would wreck individual priorities and create within the State a group of officials who ostensibly would be concerned with deciding what food, clothing and furniture we like but really would be deciding either what the officials liked or what the officials thought we *should* like. The rôle of the State in the determination of public taste is a matter of considerable controversy : it should not be confused with the rôle of the State in maintaining employment, on which there is now such encouraging unanimity.

If a system of social priorities is to be built up it should be done gradually, with every case being examined on its merits and against the background of the incontestable fact that individuals know what they like much better than anybody else. This is a branch of social welfare far removed from the technique of maintaining full employment. It must be kept separate.

V

General unemployment can be avoided in a free society by using central financial devices which still leave the decisions regarding production and consumption widely diffused throughout the community. The full employment of a planned economy means, at best, concealed unemployment or, at worst, universal forced labour. But the full fruits of the great intellectual victory of Keynes cannot be gathered and theory faithfully applied to policy unless certain conditions are scrupulously observed. Those conditions can be boiled down to four words : inflation must be avoided.

As the State increases national expenditure the demand for goods and services is enlarged and employment expands. This process has only one limit — the available supply of labour. Once the position of full employment is reached any further increase in expenditure is self-frustrating, for if no additional labour is available no additional goods can be produced. The extra expenditure will simply force up the price of goods. If the public then lose confidence in money, if they begin to believe that a one-pound note will buy less tomorrow than it would today, if in consequence they all seek as quickly as possible to turn money into goods, then prices of goods will soar and there is no natural end to this process until confidence is once again re-established in money.

Uncontrolled price inflations of this kind are destructive of economic efficiency and social stability. They destroy savings and stimulate violent speculation and thus undermine the incentive to work and to accumulate which is the mainspring of economic progress. They bring about a rapid redistribution of income and wealth in which there is neither sense nor reason. They create a fever in which all are forced to live only for the moment. War and uncontrolled inflation

are the two great disrupters of economic advance; in their
wake may follow political hysteria and reaction.

The world has had sufficient experience of these wild
price inflations to understand, to dread and to avoid them if
it is at all possible. But since the end of the second World
War another form of inflation—repressed inflation—has made
its appearance, which in the long run can be just as deadly.
If the public possess purchasing power the unfettered use of
which would bring about a rapid, and perhaps uncontrollable,
increase in prices the correct policy of the State is to withdraw some part of this purchasing power from the community by taxation. If the Government shrinks from such
an unpopular policy there remains another seductive, but in
the long run almost certainly ineffective, solution. The
State may try to prevent spending by rationing everyone and
by fixing maximum prices. Theoretically, the individual
consumer cannot then spend more than a certain sum of
money, he is forced to save some part of his income, because
the goods are just not there to buy. A part of his income is
immobilised; temporarily, at least, that part of his money has
no value at all.

In practice this policy must inevitably break down.
First, it encourages black markets. If too much money is
chasing too few goods the gains from illegal sales are high and
there will always be unscrupulous people in the community
prepared to take risks to seize them. Second, the rationing,
to be adequate, must cover virtually everything that can be
bought. If not, then the surplus purchasing power will be
compressed into the channel of the non-rationed articles and
will lead to an even more intense price rise. It is not administratively possible to ration everything. Transport, power,
heat and light, luxury articles, the whole range of second-
hand goods, housing: in all these cases the normal requirements of the individual vary so greatly and the diversity of
the product is so extensive that rationing on any equitable
basis is hopeless. Most important of all, inflation repressed

by rationing produces chaos in industry. If essential goods are rationed and other goods not rationed, the surplus purchasing power runs increasingly towards the inessential unrationed goods. Labour and raw materials are drawn off for their manufacture. The fantastic position is reached where the economic system is increasingly engaged in making things which people want less than others. Last things are produced first. Everything seems to be in short supply : the essential goods are rationed and, therefore, seem scarce. The whole weight of the surplus purchasing power impinges upon the inessential goods and makes them scarce too. The shops are always empty, for the goods are sucked out of them immediately. Behind this, the intense demand for finished goods results in raw materials being drawn through the industrial system at a rapid rate ; stocks fall to low levels ; every factory tends to be short of some essential raw material ; half-finished products lie strewn about everywhere and the reduced flow of completed goods adds to the inherent force of the inflation. The constant complaint of shortages leads the Government to take steps to cure the shortages by trying to arrange that first things must be produced first, by extending its control over the distribution of more and more raw materials and over labour.

In brief, therefore, the attempt on the part of the State to repress inflation, without cutting off the surplus purchasing power, is either incomplete, in which case it puts a premium on black markets, law-breaking and speculative gain, or it is complete, in which case it calls for complete State control over production, that is to say, it calls for a Plan of the kind which leads to administrative chaos. The experience of Great Britain after the end of the second World War puts this point beyond all doubt. At the end of the war the public had been deprived of a wide range of consumer goods for five years, and were hungry for goods. They had the money to buy these goods. They had patriotically saved hard between 1939 and 1945 and they were looking for means

of spending their savings.   In fact, the goods were not there
to buy.   The economic disruption of the world, the depletion
of capital equipment in Great Britain, the exhaustion of the
population and the disposition to go easy once the war was
over, the loss of foreign investments and the consequent need
to export on a larger scale — all these made it impossible to
restore immediately the full pre-war standard of living.

Times would have been hard in any case but the policy
of the Labour Government made them unnecessarily hard.
They shared the general fear that there might well be after
the war the same kind of price inflation which followed the
first World War.   They argued, and rightly, that this called
for the continuation of some economic controls in order to
bring about an orderly transition from war to peace.   But
they made the crucial blunder of intensifying the inflationary
pressure in four ways :

(1) By piling upon the existing surplus expenditure large-
    scale spending of their own for the social services, hous-
    ing, the armed forces and assistance to foreign countries.
(2) By supporting a campaign for indiscriminate and precipi-
    tate large-scale spending on re-equipment in industry.
(3) By forcing down the rate of interest which had the effect
    of placing large additional blocks of purchasing power in
    the hands of holders of shares which had risen sub-
    stantially in price.
(4) By failing to warn labour of the dangers of increased
    wages.   Wage rates rose by 34 per cent between June
    1945 and April 1947 whilst the cost-of-living index re-
    mained unchanged.

The controls which were needed after the war were those
which would exercise a strong anti-inflationary effect and
at the same time free and loosen-up industry so that production might increase to reduce the inflationary pressure.
But precisely the opposite policy was followed.   Until the
middle of 1947, when the balance of payments crisis forced

itself upon Great Britain, restriction of expenditure was widely advocated and universally ignored, most of all by the State. More serious still, the controls exercised were precisely those best calculated to delay the restoration of full working pace. When the Labour Government came to power in the middle of 1945 it found itself in possession of a complete set of detailed economic controls imposed for war-time purposes. This was, indeed, a gift from the gods. The doctrinaire belief in the planned economy made the Government reluctant to remove these controls however unsuitable they might be for peace-time purposes. But, in the absence of resolute attempts to deal with inflation directly, these controls had to be retained and even extended. As the maldistribution of resources increased, more and more detailed State intervention seemed to be justified in the day-to-day working of industry. The net output of finished goods from the labour and raw materials available was much lower than it would have been in a free market purged of the inflationary pressure. So that a controlled economy which had been accepted for political reasons now seemed to be essential on grim economic grounds.

The vicious circle was complete. Inflation unattended to ; controls over the distribution of resources to prevent price rises ; maldistribution of resources because of the inherent clumsiness of controls ; dwindling production intensifying the inflation ; more controls and so on, endlessly. Finally, in July 1947, the Government, having learnt and forgotten nothing, announced that the economic crisis called for direction of labour, tighter distribution of raw materials to cut out inessential work and more elaborate discrimination over capital expansion. In short, more of the old poison to cure the disease.[1]

Inflation, therefore, is the great confidence-trick which the State plays upon the public. Whenever inflation occurs

---

[1] Mr. Attlee, speaking on the economic crisis in the House of Commons on August 6, 1947, said, " It may well be that we have relaxed controls too soon ".

the full responsibility for curing it must be with the existing Government. The only proper way to prevent it is to neutralise some part of the existing purchasing power. If, through ignorance, timidity or political expediency, the Government does nothing, a large section of the people are robbed directly. If the Government attempts to deal with the problem by exercising physical control over the flows of raw materials, labour and capital, then the people are robbed indirectly and they further run the danger of finding their freedom swept away as the Plan inexorably proliferates.

VI

There is a very serious danger that the second half of the twentieth century may be the age of inflation just as the first half was the age of mass unemployment. We may, that is to say, jump from the frying-pan into the fire. For the prevention of general unemployment calls for the maintenance of national expenditure up to, but not beyond, the critical point at which inflation results.

If democratic communities are to use the technique for preventing unemployment with discretion and are not to throw away the important social values which distinguish them from the totalitarian states, they will be called upon to exercise their democratic virtues in the economic sphere as already they have revealed their power to exercise them in the political. In doing that the following rules will help.

The Target Level of Employment

The target of employment set should not be too high. In progressive communities, given the normal movement of workers from one job to another, natural seasonal fluctuations, the inevitable decline of some industries and the expansion of others, the temporary disturbances which technical change brings about and the presence of a certain proportion of sub-normal workers, it would be unwise to try to exceed, *by the use of this method of increasing national expenditure*, a level of about 94 or 95 per cent of employment, *i.e.* 5 or 6 per cent of unemployment. We cannot work to finer limits than that. Used beyond that point increasing national expenditure is almost certain to slip over the edge into inflation and everything it involves.[1] Unemployment of 5 or 6 per cent should not be a matter for concern. In a buoyant community a part of it would measure the efforts of workers to better themselves by changing their jobs, a part of it would consist of

[1] Sir William Beveridge's target of always having more vacancies than jobs and keeping the average unemployment rate below 3 per cent would almost certainly be violently inflationary.

Sir William asserts that the average unemployment percentage need not exceed 3 per cent ; he allows 1 per cent for seasonal unemployment, 1 per cent for the inevitable unemployment arising as men fall temporarily out of work in moving from one job to another and 1 per cent for unemployment due to unavoidable fluctuations in the export trade. Closely examined, his figures become even more optimistic. Six-sevenths of the employment in Great Britain is for the needs of the domestic market and not for export. It follows that in six-sevenths of British industry the average unemployment is to be reduced to 2 per cent. The overall average unemployment allowed for fluctuations in the export trades is 1 per cent ; since employment in exports is about one-seventh of total employment, this means that the average unemployment assumed in the export trades themselves will be 7 per cent. An average of 7 per cent unemployment might well cover fluctuations between (say) 5 per cent and 15 per cent. If unemployment is to fluctuate in this degree in the districts specialising in export trades there would, without doubt, be important secondary reactions upon domestic production in those areas and elsewhere. If cotton operatives are thrown out of work, even if only temporarily, they will buy less chocolate, attend less cinemas and so on. This makes the assumption of 2 per cent for all non-export employment still more unrealistic. As regards seasonal unemployment, it has been shown that before the war it amounted to 2 to 2½ per cent and that the industries suffering most heavily were those where fashion and natural phenomena played the greatest part in determining demand, such as tailoring, linen, cotton, building and coal-mining. It is difficult to see how, at a stroke, seasonal variations in such industries could be reduced to one-half as is suggested.

In the thirty years before the 1914–18 war average unemployment was about 6 per cent. Between the two great wars the average was about 14 per cent. There seems little reason to anticipate that in the future we can cut unemployment to one-half of what it was before 1914. On some grounds, indeed, one might expect the average unemployment rate to rise. The improvement in our system of social security, whatever its social and economic advantages in other directions, will lessen the immediate pressure upon the unemployed to find other work. The changing age-structure of our population, with a smaller proportion of juveniles, means that industries can less quickly than formerly change the number of workers attached to them through the reduction of new entrants. The shortage of houses from which we will undoubtedly suffer for many years after the war will reduce labour mobility. It is true there are countervailing factors. The wider dispersion of industry

workers who, for the moment, were anxious for a break in the routine of working life, a part of it would represent the normal dismissals which are inseparably bound up with maintenance of discipline. For those who are still hagridden by the pre-war dreads, 6 per cent unemployment may be a terrifying prospect. But the real curse of unemployment is not the loss of one job but the failure to find another. In a society where it was known that depression would never become epidemic and where the ordinary conscientious and hard-working person would always have a place, such a rate of unemployment would pass unremarked.[1]

The Need for Mobility

The target to be aimed at may be defined in another way. There are some forms of unemployment closely associated with changes in methods of production and with changes in the habits of the consumer which cannot be remedied, and for which remedy should not be sought, by the increase of national expenditure. If, for example, the public start to spend more money on cinemas and less on chocolate, the right remedy is a reshuffle of the labour force and not the pumping by the Government of additional expenditure into the system. If some invention reduces the labour required for a particular operation, the right solution is for the redundant labour to move elsewhere. It would be the task of the State to keep the general background of expenditure adequate so that other jobs could be found readily, but not to press total expenditure to the point at which inflation is threatened.

which is now being sought through Government policy should make it easier for displaced workers to find new posts. And the experience of the Ministry of Labour during the war in handling large transfers of workers may well mean that their placing activities will be more successful and on a larger scale than heretofore. Without further evidence, however, it would be an unwarranted assumption that we could reduce average unemployment to one-quarter of that which existed between the wars.

[1] In 1947 in the United States, where there was a general shortage of manpower and an unparalleled standard of living, unemployment was between 4 and 5 per cent.

Admittedly, the Government's task would not be an easy one when confronted with cases of this kind. If unemployment is tending to rise some answer must be found to this question : is this unemployment due to a general lack of expenditure such as can be cured by State action ; or is it some passing and minor fluctuation about which nothing need be done since the workers will reasonably quickly be re-absorbed in their old jobs ; or is this a permanent change in the structure of industry which calls for a redistribution of labour and capital ? The easy course is to make the first assumption or the second, for then no individual need be disturbed. The hard decision is the third, for it involves the uprooting of working lives, the recognition that economic progress calls for readjustment. If the first decision is made when the second or third is really appropriate, then there is danger of inflation. If the second decision is made when the third is really correct, chronically depressed industries or areas may result. If the third assumption is made when the first or second is the right answer, then unnecessary upset is caused to industries and persons. The third decision, as to the need for permanent readjustment, involves estimates of the future. No Government can be expected always to make such decisions without mistakes. All that can be hoped for, and this is essential for the success of a full employment policy in a democratic society, is that the Government should not, through ignorance or languor or political timidity, apply the policy of increasing national expenditure when mobility is called for. That would be tantamount to over-administering a general tonic when the patient really needs a first tooth extracted in order to make room for the second.

All this means that there must be mobility in the system and that restrictive practices, both by workers and employers, should be reduced to a minimum. The greater the mobility of labour and capital, the higher the target of employment which can be safely fixed and attained, without fear of inflation, by the method of increasing national expenditure.

Now there are two ways of attaining mobility. The planner would reach it by compulsion. Workers would be directed into industry, detailed control would be exercised over investment and the location of industry. In that sense it is certainly true that the more controls we are prepared to put up with, the lower would be the average level of unemployment. Dictators need never be short of work for other people to do. The democratic way of making these adjustments is to rely first on the price system. Wages will rise in the expanding trades and fall elsewhere. The temporarily unemployed must be maintained at a reasonable level of life. Beyond that the State has an important part to play in assisting and simplifying the decision of the individual, in reducing the personal inconvenience of moving from one job to another, in stimulating the growing points in industry and thus widening the choice of the worker displaced from a declining trade. It is one of the important functions of the State to improve knowledge of the local supply and demand for labour and to make that information more widely available, to build up a great system for enabling displaced workers to re-train themselves at the expense of the State for other jobs, to cover amply the personal costs of transfer. For the worker moving from a declining to an expanding industry is paying a part of the cost of economic progress which benefits the whole community. Mere equity demands that the whole community, through its taxes, should be prepared to take this cost from his shoulders as far as possible.

In Great Britain there is an altogether excessive pessimism regarding the possibilities of maintaining a sufficiently fluid movement of workers from one job to another. It is undoubtedly the product of our pre-war experience with its horror of the depressed areas and the long period when there was a surplus of labour everywhere so that the movement of labour seemed utterly futile. But if the general demand for labour can be kept brisk, and that the Keynesian theory makes possible, this attitude will quickly change. The desire for

an occasional change of occupation or place of work is by
no means rare. As an antidote to the inevitable routine of
much industrial work and the dangers of excessive parochial-
ism it should be encouraged. An expanding economy is
dependent upon mobility, but it is equally true that such an
economy stimulates mobility as experience in the United
States proves. A decade of full employment would completely obliterate the bogy of labour immobility. For the
moment, however, some special effort is needed to put behind
us the ancient fears.

The Level of Wages

A full employment policy, successfully pursued, places
greater powers, and therefore greater responsibilities, in the
hands of the workers. When the demand for labour is well
maintained then the bargaining power of labour is great and
wages may be pushed up to high levels. For a time the increases may be met by squeezing profits but ultimately they
will increase costs and bring about a rise in prices. The
rise in prices may lead to further wage demands and to the
spiral of inflation.

There are, here, three closely related issues. There is
first, that of the general level of wages ; is the wage bill so
large that it results in spending power on a scale which will
force up prices in a dangerous fashion ? Second, there is the
question of the rate at which wage levels are increased, for
that may turn a stable condition into one which is inflationary.
Third, there is the whole question of the relation between
wages in different industries, the mechanism by which labour
is redistributed between occupations.

On none of these points is it possible to provide from the
outside an answer which is demonstrably correct. The
bargaining of the market is, indeed, the only democratic way
of reaching working conclusions. But it cannot be overlooked that labour in all democratic countries is now strongly
organised and that the power which they have now drawn to

themselves can, if used without restraint, play havoc with the stability of the economy.

In practice the safeguards seem to me to be these :

(a) If the target of employment is not fixed too high, as discussed earlier, then much of the danger is avoided. For it is in a period of acute general shortage of labour that the combined effect of trade-union action to raise wages and competition between employers for more workers will invariably push wages out of line.

(b) If, nevertheless, it appears that the total wage bill has risen beyond the danger point, then the State must increase taxes on the ranges of incomes which will include the greater part of wages. This action may not prevent price increases, for the rise in wages is an increased cost to the manufacturer, who will therefore be under greater pressure to raise his selling prices. But it would serve to check the upward price trend.

(c) The method of payment by result should be widely adopted throughout industry so that some link is created between wage increases and increases in production. This again is no certain safeguard against inflation since the piece rates themselves may be too high. But it provides a safety-valve since there is now another channel through which earnings may rise without wage rates, or labour costs, increasing.

(d) Whilst a ' national wages policy ', in the sense of a pre-determination from the centre as to how each one of the multitudinous wage rates in the economy shall move over a given period, is administratively and politically impossible, trade-union leaders should regard it as one of their duties to bring before the whole of their movement the basic facts regarding productivity. No simple rule, such as that wages should rise with national productivity, would help in the determination of any specific wage rate. Yet the better the workers as a whole know the facts and understand the relation between their output and the real wages which can be paid to them, the greater the scope for trade-union leaders to exercise the statesmanship in industry they have frequently shown in the past.

(e) The assumption that, whilst wages may rise, they should never fall is a potential danger to the stable economy and to full employment. For wage disparities between different industries are a powerful lever to bring about, voluntarily, the requisite transfer of labour and to enable wage rates to rise at the growing points of industry without any undue swelling of the total wage bill.

The leadership of British labour has now for half a century been distinguished by a sense of responsibility and a disposition to face facts which has been as important an element as any other in building up the flair for compromise and the instinct for the middle of the road under which democracy flourishes. The achievement of trade unions in war-time and their steadying influence in the past two years does not suggest that, provided they are brought adequately into the deliberations of the State and equipped with the facts of the economic situation, they would fail in the future.

VII

When, therefore, the planners in Britain condemn the free economy by its past performance in the maintenance of employment their views are as obsolete as those of the early socialists who declared that capitalism meant the progressive impoverishment of the working classes, or those who asserted that Labour could never come to full political power without a bloody struggle with the bourgeoisie. They still wait wistfully for the economic smash in the United States which seems to them so exasperatingly overdue. They either ignore Keynes or misinterpret him for their own ends. And whilst they foretell for the free economies the horrors of the trade cycle, deflation, mass unemployment and a falling standard of living, they feverishly seek to find alibis and scapegoats for the very evident recurrent crises, misdirected production, reduced rations and dwindling liberties from which Great Britain suffers in its planned state.

CHAPTER V

CONFUSION AMONG THE PLANNERS

In an economy where the functions of the State are limited, economic relations are impersonal and individual decisions are made by reference to a framework of prices. A mechanism of this kind cannot be substantially influenced by any one individual. Its study is in the nature of a science. In a community subject to an ' overall economic plan ' economic analysis is more diffuse and less scientific. An overall plan implies that, in the last resort, one man, or a few, make the decisions for the many. The personal opinions, idiosyncrasies or even prejudices of the Supreme Planners may then become of great importance in determining the form and purpose of the economic system. There may be many different suggested plans since planners tend to be strongly individualistic.[1] The varying conceptions of the overall plan may thus lead, particularly in the early stages of its development, to significant conflicts of ideas.

Confusion is the more likely in the embryonic planned economy since the normal procedure is for the planners first to seize power and only later to consider what should be done with that power.[2] The upshot is that, so long as freedom

[1] Planners often complain that their opponents are discussing not their kind of planning but somebody else's. Mr. Durbin, in the *Economic Journal*, December 1945, takes Professor Hayek to task because the Professor bases his understanding of economic planning only upon modern references to students of government and sociology, and such socialist economists as Marx, Engels, Shaw and the Webbs, and ignores the writings of " those of us who are now both practising economists and also socialists ".

[2] It has been pointed out (p. 2) that this was the case in Russia. It was also the case in Great Britain. In the House of Commons on August 8, 1947, Mr. Morrison, in introducing the Supplies and Services (Transitional Powers) Bill, which gave the State vast powers over persons and property, said : " We have no preconceived notions as to precisely how we propose to utilise [the Bill]. What we need is the power to utilise it."

of speech remains, there will be a babel of voices each seeking
to provide the authoritative answer to the crucial question :
What is Planning ?

I

Experience in Great Britain between 1945 and 1947 is
extremely illuminating on this point. There seems little
doubt that the members of the British Government believed
that they had created, or were in the process of creating, a
centrally planned economy. They frequently spoke of the
social and economic revolution through which we were
passing. They contrasted the British type of economy with
that found in the United States. Mr. Attlee put this point
beyond doubt by his declaration that " in matters of economic
planning we agree with Soviet Russia ".[1] But there were
many conflicting strands of thought to be found among the
British Supreme Planners and, indeed, some Ministers
seemed to subscribe to a whole range of mutually exclusive
ideas. The classification which follows cannot, therefore,
be watertight. Indeed, the vocabulary of planning has now
become so opulent and varied as almost to defy the efforts
of the cataloguer.

Planning with a Purpose

Perhaps the most important question to ask about an
overall plan is this : does it express a purpose, something
which the planners intend to make happen ? Or is it something far less substantial than that, an estimate of what might
happen, a prayer for what ought to happen ? The fundamental difference between these two approaches has been
well put by Monsieur Stalin : [2]

Admittedly they [*i.e.* under the capitalistic system] too have
something akin to plans. But these plans are prognosis, guess
plans which bind nobody, and on the basis of which it is impos-

[1] House of Commons, November 18, 1946.
[2] Quoted from Baykov, *Soviet Economic System*, p. 424.

sible to direct a country's economy. Things are different with us. Our plans are not prognosis, guess plans, but instructions which are compulsory for all managements and which determine the future course of the economic development of our entire country. You see that this implies a difference of principle.

There were first, then, the British planners with a purpose. They believed, with Monsieur Stalin, that men are masters of their economic environment, that they can lay down in advance what should happen and then proceed to make it happen. Sir Stafford Cripps is perhaps the leading figure in this group. He has said,[1] " I was delighted with the general measure of agreement that we should plan, and having a plan that we should try to carry out the plan ". He is anxious to follow the Russian model and get the kind of results achieved in Russia. He employed the ' must ' technique for the first time when, in September 1947, he fixed export targets for the different industries, without prior consultation with those industries, at the same time indicating that " where particular firms or whole industries find themselves unable to sell abroad their export quota . . . labour will have to be withdrawn from that particular form of production ".

The significant point about planning with a purpose is that, once the plan has been set, then the Supreme Planners tend to fall into the frame of mind in which they are prepared to make any ' sacrifice ', or more exactly force any ' sacrifice ' on others, in order to achieve the plan. So that a plan laid out for promoting the interests of the consumers often leads to the deliberate and implacable sacrifice of those interests. This could only be regarded as logical if the attainment of the plan, independently of the economic consequences of fulfilling the plan, were regarded as an end in itself. Broadly speaking, any plan which calls for ' sacrifices ' should be subject to suspicion since the purpose of a plan (except perhaps in the case of war or threatened war) should be to

[1] House of Commons, February 28, 1946.

lessen sacrifices and not increase them. A pertinent illustration is provided by the campaign to raise British exports to
75 per cent over pre-war levels. That figure saw the light of
day as a rough estimate of the export target to be reached if
Great Britain were to enjoy the pre-war standard of living.
But in the minds of the planners with a purpose it rapidly
became a target to be reached for its own sake even if, in order
to attain it, the standard of living had to be cut down below
the level it might have reached with a lower level of exports.
A close analogy would be that of a relieving force which sets
out to bring food supplies to a besieged and starving garrison.
The relieving force meets unexpected difficulties and is
compelled to consume both its own food and that intended
for the garrison. But with blind courage the relieving force
presses forward and gloriously reaches its objective, but only,
of course, to add to the sufferings of the garrison by increasing
the number of people to be maintained on the garrison's
depleted resources.

Free Planning

Sharply contrasted with the planners with a purpose are
the free planners. This name is most suitable for the group
partly because they appear to contemplate the possibility
that the plan may leave room for some private enterprise,
partly because they emphasise the need for planning for
'freedom', and, most important, because they envisage a
procedure by which the plan will emerge, as the feeling of the
meeting emerges at a Quakers' conference, out of widespread
discussion of the plan at every level in the community.
Every fact must be assembled, every interest consulted and
the resultant plan thoroughly explained to the public. Mr.
Morrison has most clearly defined this attitude :

The idea of planning is by now over and above party politics.
There is only one basis on which planning can succeed in a democratic society and that is the conscious understanding by each

section of its place in the community as a whole and the deliberate acceptance of the resulting obligations and loyalties.[1]

In another place he has explained : [2]

> As we believe in a free society we must have the courage of our convictions and trust the people to achieve more by understanding and backing an agreed plan than other nations might achieve by carrying out under orders a plan dictated to them by their rulers.

This type of planning, however, has some serious defects. It is not possible to collect all the facts, particularly those relating to future events. And what is to happen if the people do not agree, or agree so slowly that by the time agreement is reached another plan is called for ? Moreover other Supreme Planners do not acccept this conception. Thus Mr. Dalton in the House of Commons on June 30, 1947, said :

> In a democracy such as ours in which differences of opinion are widely held and freely expressed there is no one economic policy which would unite the country.

Flexible Planning

The third group of flexible planners also have ideas which run counter to those of the ' must ' planners. They attach great importance to keeping the plan so flexible and altering it so swiftly that reality will never falsify the plan. Thus Mr. Dalton has said : [3]

> These plans must not be mere essays. They must be consistent with practical possibilities. They must not be too rigid or hidebound. They must be capable of continuous adjustment in the light of changing conditions. We shall never be able to sit back as some planners imagine and close our eyes and let the plan take charge, like one of the automatic pilots in an aeroplane. . . . Eternal vigilance is the price of successful planning.

[1] June 10, 1947.
[2] *Economic Planning*, p. 9.
[3] House of Commons, February 5, 1946.

Mr. Morrison, speaking on September 6, 1947, under the pressure of the balance of payments crisis, subscribed to the same idea.

We have had to modify our plans quickly. . . . The course of international politics, and economics, and even of Nature itself, has been far more unfavourable to us than could reasonably have been expected. . . . Earlier this summer the Government announced that it was working on a Four Year Plan. That plan is being modified to cut out the frills and concentrate on essentials. When it has been completed it will be announced. But it is unreasonable to ask the Government in a flash to produce a master plan to solve all the difficulties of a disorganised, uncertain world.

This type of planner may easily become a menace to logical thought because, if he is successful in changing his plans sufficiently quickly to fit the facts, then he comes to believe that he is controlling the economic system when he is really controlling only the statistics in his own plan. This wastes effort just as it would be wasted by a man who took great pains to keep his watch scrupulously correct so that the movements of the sun should not be held up.

Planning through Dislocation

There is, fourthly, a group of thinkers who would appear to push opportunism to the point at which they deny the very purpose of the overall plan. Whatever disagreement there may be on other points, most people would consider it axiomatic that an overall plan should strive so to distribute national resources that the efforts of the different co-ordinated pieces of the system would fit snugly together. The different flows of raw materials, labour and capacity should be adjusted so that the predetermined flow of consumer goods should issue without stoppages or wastage at any point. But some planners seem positively to welcome the waste of ' bottlenecks ' (*i.e.* of shortages of supply of one thing in relation to others) and indeed to consider that the plan makes this inevitable. Thus Mr. Morrison addressing the Labour Party Regional Council at Leeds on November 30, 1946, speaking of the many bottlenecks in the economic system, said :

> It is not at all my view that this array of bottlenecks is a cause for gloom or discouragement. On the contrary, the fact that we see so many bottlenecks is evidence that we are expanding our economy. Let us be realistic and recognise these bottlenecks not as reasons for alarm and inertia but as challenges to our resource and initiative. . . . In a full employment world where the bad old practice of wasting plant and labour and materials is frowned upon, we must expect that the higher level of demand and the fuller use of resources will constantly thrust this bottleneck problem upon us.

Planning on the bottlenecks was a method which was widely used in the urgency of war. But it confronts its operator with many problems of practice and logic. If, as is indicated above, the " bottleneck problem " is simply the problem of having to waste one lot of resources because they have not been properly matched in the plan with other sets of resources, then it would seem that there is little to choose between the bad old world and Mr. Morrison's brave new world.

This point can perhaps be made clearer by taking a parallel case in an ordinary business. If a business man planned his production, acquired his labour, machines and raw materials and then discovered that, unfortunately, he could not operate because he had forgotten to acquire a supply of lubricating oil, we should naturally consider this as a breakdown of his planning. Any attempt at robust blustering on his part that " this kind of thing is inevitable " would properly be looked upon as pure make-believe. But when national overall planners make such mistakes we are expected to welcome the dislocation as evidence of the expansionist *tempo*.

There is a second point in Mr. Morrison's statement which seems to defy the principles of elementary economic logic. A " bottleneck " is the item which ultimately is holding up everything else. That is to say, there cannot be several bottlenecks simultaneously because there cannot be several items all in shortest supply at the same time. A man who is mixing mortar cannot be shortest of cement and sand at the same time. When Mr. Morrison speaks of simultaneous bottlenecks in man-power of all kinds, raw materials, coal, electricity and gas, he can only mean either one of two things. Either that the plan has been drawn up in defiance of the facts upon which the plan should have been based, that the plan is far too large to be carried out. Or that whilst there is an adequate supply in total of (say) raw materials they have been distributed to the wrong points, *i.e.* that the distribution side of the plan has broken down. In neither case does there appear to be cause for self-congratulation.

Even, however, if the principle of the uniqueness of the bottleneck is accepted, difficulties arise in identifying the bottleneck. For when one bottleneck is cured (or opened, broken, released or whatever is the appropriate term) then another is automatically created. Much time is wasted in chasing the bottleneck. Thus, June 18, 1947, Mr. Morrison had said :

The shortage of steel had been threatening to replace the shortage of coal as " the most vexatious and crippling bottleneck ".

To which *The Times* was forced to reply a few days later :

Though it was recently stated by the Government that steel had replaced coal as the first limiting factor, the shortage of steel is itself largely due to insufficient supplies of coal, and freedom of coal supplies to the steel industry will quickly restore coal to its baleful pedestal.

It was perhaps this kind of fundamental difficulty which led Mr. Morrison at one stage to put up on the pedestal an entirely novel first limiting factor.

What is Britain's greatest shortage now ? Is it dollars, is it coal, is it man-power, is it food ? It is none of these things. It is Time. Time is running against us faster even than the drain of dollars.[1]

[1] August 23, 1947.

Guess Planning

The fifth group of planners, to employ Monsieur Stalin's phrase, are the guess planners.[1] They recognise that events will be determined by forces at least partly outside their control. They are interested in what is likely to happen in the future but they recognise the fallibility of economic forecasting. Mr. Attlee himself seems to fall into this group. He has said,[2] " Although we may have to plan without having all the data, it is better than having no plan at all. We must make some kind of economic forecast." So long as the guess planners do nothing which binds anyone, their activities are of no great significance. But the state of being a guess planner seems to be a highly transitional one. For if their prognosis is a gloomy one the guess planners are easily led on to try to avoid by positive action what they believe, rightly or wrongly, they see in the future. If their prognosis is favourable they will be tempted to try to bring about the desirable conditions much earlier than they could normally be expected. Indeed it seems to be a general working rule among many planners : " find out what is going to happen and then make it happen more quickly ". In both cases guess planning is transmuted into planning with a purpose.

There are many other forms of planning[3] but sufficient has perhaps been said to indicate the discordant character of the discussions during the early stages of the planned economy.

[1] Some authorities prefer to describe this as ' wish ' planning or even ' dream ' planning. Actually the most striking cases of wishful thinking are found not in Great Britain but in other countries. Thus in the French ' Monnet ' Plan enormous increases in productivity per head were wished into the plan. The Czechoslovakian Plan was based upon the unlikely assumption that very large foreign loans would be available. An interesting case of ' wish ' planning in Great Britain was revealed when Sir Stafford Cripps announced on January 13, 1947, that the allocations of coal to industries would be roughly halved but that this would not necessarily reduce the amount of coal which would actually be received since the old allocations had been on an ' unrealistic ' basis. Another case was when Sir Stafford announced in September 1947 that the steel control must be modified because there had been a serious ' inflation ' of steel allocations.

[2] House of Commons, February 26, 1946.

[3] ' Variety Among the Planners ', *The Manchester School*, January 1947.

II

Another bone of contention among the planners is the form that the plan should take. Most planners think of it as a very large document (similar to the fat volumes embodying the various five-year plans of the Soviet Union) which would lay down in detail the output of each commodity and would prescribe the allocations of raw materials, capacity and labour for each specific final commodity. This would go along with a group of physical controls exercised by the State which would steer resources into the correct channels. That is to say, there should be a plan continuously controlled in detail. Sir Stafford Cripps appears to hold this view.[1]

Our objective is to carry through a planned economy without compulsion of labour. The general idea is that we should use a number of controls in order to guide production into the necessary channels, according to the plan we have formulated. The principal controls will be financial, including price control and taxation, materials control, building control, machinery and exports control.

Sir Stafford, however, subsequently changed his ground somewhat, perhaps because of a growing realisation of the administrative impossibility of co-ordinating a mass of physical controls. On November 21, 1946, he said in the House of Commons :

. . . A great many controls have been removed. . . . This process is continually going on and will continue until we have been able to get rid of a great many in the future.

He placed increasing emphasis on the planning of the distribution of man-power as the fundamental instrument of planning.

The planning of the choice of products . . . carries with it the planning of the distribution of man-power.

If the central plan is to be based on a detailed man-power budget without labour compulsion, difficulties immediately arise. Is the plan to be based on the labour allocations which

[1] House of Commons, February 28, 1946.

the Supreme Planners regard as ideal ? Or is it to be based on labour allocations which are regarded as practicable in view of the ' stickiness ' of the labour supply. If the former, then the plan becomes a pious aspiration ; if the latter, then an estimate has to be made of the probable effect of Government propaganda. For example, if the Minister of Supply believes that another 20,000 foundry workers are vitally necessary, and he starts a drive to get these workers (without using the incentive of ' inducement-wages '), will the plan assume that he will or he will not get these workers for the foundries ? How are such estimates to be made ?

The chief drawback of planning through the distribution of labour is that, whatever the original intentions of the planners, compulsion of labour soon becomes inevitable. For how, otherwise, can labour be got into the appropriate jobs ? Thus Sir Stafford Cripps said in the House of Commons on February 28, 1946 :

> No country in the world, so far as I know, has yet succeeded in carrying through a planned economy without compulsion of labour. Our objective is to carry through a planned economy without compulsion of labour.

Yet, eighteen months later, direction of labour was introduced in Great Britain.[1]

Unfortunately just at the time when Great Britain was embarking upon an overall plan under the guidance of a group of thinkers who favoured a plan and the instrument of physical labour controls for carrying it through, another group, the real intellectuals of the planning movement, were cutting the ground from under the feet of the first by attacking the idea of *a* Plan, sometimes on the grounds that it will not work, sometimes because they fear the destruction of democratic liberties in the process. Mr. Durbin, for example, has stated quite specifically :

> Planning does not in the least imply the existence of a Plan —

[1] See p. 198 *et seq.*

in the sense of an arbitrary industrial budget which lays down in advance the volume of output for different industries.[1]

Other thinkers in this group such as Mr. Lerner [2] have swung even further from the old line and would seek to combine the benefits of the capitalist economy and the collectivist economy in a sort of ' mixed ' economy. But they all contemplate a system in which the State would make a few major economic decisions and, thenceforward, the distribution of production factors would be carried out by a socialist ' pricing system '.

Theoretically, many of the logical and administrative problems bound up with central planning can be avoided by the use of a price system operating within a framework of major economic decisions by the Supreme Planners. Progressively intricate discussions on this subject are now going on among the economic experts.[3] It is not to be assumed that they have yet reached agreement or that their findings prescribe practical measures for the running of a controlled economy. In particular, they appear to ignore, in their theoretical working models, most formidable problems associated with incentive. But they are all agreed, as far as I can understand them, on two points : first, that the price mechanism must be allowed to operate sufficiently extensively to leave to the individual a great mass of detailed decisions which the old-fashioned planners now in charge in Great Britain would leave to the State ; second, that the consumer must be free to distribute his income as he wishes and that the productive system must be free, within the framework of the major economic decisions, to adjust itself to the consumers' wishes. Whether the ingenuity of the academics will ever produce a scheme of thought which will provide a solid basis for practical policy only time can decide. We

---

[1] *Economic Journal*, December 1945.
[2] *Economics of Control*, p. 1.
[3] See Lerner, *Economics of Control* ; Meade, *Economic Journal*, April 1945 ; Wilson, *Economic Journal*, December 1945 ; Fleming, *The Manchester School*, September 1946.

certainly need not hasten to implement their findings until these have reached a more advanced stage of precision and are more widely accepted.

Even if they ever do reach final agreement, their ideas will be obstructed, first, by the inherent attraction of planning through the physical controls mentioned above, and second, by an almost pathological dread among many of the older type of planners of the working of the free price system.[1] This in itself is causing a great deal of confusion. The two main functions of price movements are to bring about necessary changes in supply and to distribute goods among potential consumers. But Mr. Strachey, the Minister of Food, for example, seemed to reject both these functions. On August 19, 1946, speaking of the Wheat Agreement with Canada, he is reported as having said :

He had been criticised on the ground that in two or three years the price of wheat might have dropped. Even if there was a great slump in wheat prices again, he said, quite frankly, that they could buy from the Canadian farmers too cheaply. If they got their wheat from them at the price of sawdust, the Canadian farmers were ruined, which was not a very nice or fraternal or good thing.

(Incidentally it may be noted that the Ministry of Food fixed prices for Danish agricultural produce at a level which, the Danes allege, involved losses for the Danish farmers.) Mr. Strachey further rejected the price mechanism as a device for rationing (without coupons, queues or black markets) the available goods between consumers. In the House of Commons on July 18, 1946, he described a rise in the price of bread as the traditional method of rationing such a commodity. He indignantly rejected the idea that the Govern-

---

[1] The head-on conflict of principle is perhaps seen most clearly in the application of the marginal principle. Thus the modern planners insist upon the importance of the rule that marginal cost should equal price, which, in cases of increasing returns, would imply that a concern as a whole would run at a loss. But the old-fashioned planners who were responsible for the Bill to nationalise the British transport industry will have none of this. They assert (Clause 3) that the enterprise must cover its total costs.

ment would resort to it. He is reported on October 27, 1946, referring to the varying consumption of meat, eggs, butter and milk by rich and poor people before the war, as saying :

that was rationing all right for the poor family. It was the most vicious, pernicious, vilely unfair kind of rationing that you can imagine — rationing in which the rich got three times as much as the poor. That is the kind of rationing to which we will never go back.

Now, unless Mr. Strachey had in mind a policy of completely equal distribution of income (which it is difficult to imagine is the case in view of Government policy regarding the salaries of Ministers, M.P.s, officials of Public Boards, etc.), this must mean that he regarded ' rationing by income ' as inconsistent with his conception of a planned economy. If this is really correct, those who are working on the possibility of a ' socialist price system ' are wasting their time.

III

These fundamental confusions naturally led in Great Britain after the war to anxiety, impatience and criticism among the planners themselves and tended to undermine public confidence. For in a society where some freedom of speech, thought and action still remains it is impossible for the community to be mobilised behind the plan unless a satisfying answer can be given to the crucial question : What is Planning ? The growing disillusionment passed through three stages.

First, the more robust believers in planning began to criticise the existing form of planning and to call for the introduction of their own particular ideas of planning. There was a cry that the planning should be ' positive ' instead of negative, ' real ' instead of unreal, ' good ' instead of bad.

What the nation urgently needs, and would respond to, is some real economic planning, some purposive direction of its affairs instead of the present hortatory, sloganised drifting.[1]

[1] *Economist*, August 30, 1947.

A new start was widely called for. But there was no agreement from which point the new start should be made. As a consequence of the failure of the Government to produce an overall plan which satisfied all planners, a large crop of planning schemes poured into the centre from the periphery. The sectional planners were anxious to put purpose into the overall plan. From their knowledge of their immediate economic environment they saw clearly that, as far as their own sections was concerned, the overall plan was defective. They concluded that the first step required was for the Central Government to put their section right and they could not understand why this should not be proceeded with forthwith. What they did not see was that their sectional plans might well conflict with other sectional plans or with the necessary character of the co-ordinating agency at the centre. On the other hand the central co-ordinating agency was not in a position to chop the sectional plans about in order to make them fit together, partly because it did not know enough to do so, partly because the number of possible permutations and combinations of sectional schemes was infinitely large. So whilst those at the centre pleaded patience, those outside cried forward. All this added to the original confusion.

The cleavage of purpose revealed itself even in Government documents. In the *Economic Survey for 1947* the conflicting views emerge sharply. In Section I it is said :

A democratic Government must conduct its economic planning in a manner which preserves the maximum possible freedom of choice to the individual citizen. . . . During the war, the Government could direct labour and was the direct purchaser of a large part of the nation's production. The Government's influence in peace-time must be exercised by other less drastic measures. . . . The task of directing by democratic methods an economic system as large and complex as ours is far beyond the power of any Governmental machine working by itself, however efficient it may be.

The remainder of the *Survey* is a description of the existing controls and proposed plans which involved the State in tasks which earlier had been declared administratively impossible.

> Those things which are fundamental to our national life must come first. . . . Planning the allocation of resources between the various national requirements is at present a task of deciding which out of a number of claimants must go short. . . . It is precisely the same problem, only on a national scale, as the house-wife has to solve every week.

As the year 1947 went on the Government imposed more and more controls, culminating finally in the control of labour.

The clamour in Great Britain for the real overall plan could not, however, be stilled. Each new plan was clearly obsolete, overrun by the speed of events as soon as published. There was a widespread demand for ' the real facts of the situation ' (although they were obvious) and for an even more supreme planning organisation, such as an inner Cabinet to devote itself wholly to planning. The Supreme Planners sought to recreate confidence by various stalling devices such as—

(a) declaring that a plan cannot be properly formed until much more information has been collected. Thus Sir Stafford Cripps : [1] " It is no good doing any more today because no plan can be any more than an approximation. The statistics do not exist yet " ;

(b) complaining that there is " a shortage of administrative talent " ;

(c) complaining that some members of the community are trying to obstruct the plan ;

(d) asserting, as did Mr. Morrison, [2] that it is " unreasonable to ask the Government to produce in a flash a master plan to solve all the difficulties of a disorganised, uncertain world ".

At this second stage, the Government was able to quieten some of the criticism and create the impression of real action

[1] House of Commons, February 28, 1946.
[2] September 6, 1947.

simply by taking on more powers for the State, imposing more controls and enlarging the planning bureaucracy. In the late summer of 1947 the Government established new forms of regimentation for labour and for industry. In July 1947 a new Economic Planning Board was set up to advise the country on the best use of the country's economic resources. In September 1947 Sir Stafford Cripps was appointed to take charge of the whole of the economic affairs of Great Britain. The paradoxical position was, therefore, reached in which liberally-minded citizens were urging on the Government to a swifter creation of a totalitarian regime.

The third stage, and the one which at present (September 1947) is not yet fully worked out, was the tug-of-war between the alleged advantages of the overall plan and the claim of the individual to elementary liberties. Freedom of choice of occupation has gone but freedom of speech still remains. And yet freedom of speech is highly injurious to central planning. It makes for confusion and destroys the homogeneity of communal purpose and the blind faith in the omnipotence and omniscience of the Supreme Planners so necessary for the success of the plan. The attack on personal liberty as antagonistic to the plan will, in the early stages, probably take the form of exhortations to the people to keep steady, not to bother too much about what is said in the newspapers, on the radio or by rival political factions, to trust their leaders, and so on.

After two years of so-called planning in Great Britain the fundamental obstacle still remained that no one could answer the question : What is Planning ? Experience suggested that planning was bound up with extreme confusion regarding the aims and methods of the economic system and that it meant personal restrictions on the individual both as consumer and producer. Beyond that all was darkness.

CHAPTER VI

PLANNERS AS A SPECIES

So soon as they are called upon to put their ideas into practice the overall planners break up into numerous factions so that no one conception of planning will enjoy a fair trial until one group has seized power and firmly suppressed all rival views. But up to that point the planners jointly subscribe to many economic articles of faith which constitute the breeding-ground for some of the major economic fallacies of our times.

The Craving for a New World

Most planners suffer from a turbulent craving for a new order of things. A pathological dread of becoming old-fashioned leads them to press for Utopias at almost any cost. They express their hopes for the future in ornate imagery, such as ' the wave of the future ', the ' shape of things to come ', ' social engineering '. The psychological causes of this exaggerated restlessness cannot be examined here. At the one extreme it may amount simply to a desire to be ostentatiously different. At the other, it may arise from infantile anxieties to escape from the implications of human mortality.

Whatever its cause, this impatience with the facts of life leads to much economic irresponsibility. It is, for instance, very surprising how many, otherwise rational, people will seriously argue in favour of central economic planning because ' something will always beat nothing ' or ' the clock cannot be put back ', as if it were never good to leave things alone and as if change were always preferable to rest. The disposition to ignore the continuity of human societies, the feeling that at any time the slate can be wiped clean and the writing started again, is bound to create a care-free indifference to the risks of change.

The itch for novelty goes far to explain two very common attitudes taken up by the economic planner. First, he is much more concerned with the distant future than with the present, and is prepared to make immediate sacrifices, and force these sacrifices on others, for some hypothetical gain in the future. The planned economy always promises 'jam tomorrow',[1] always calls for immediate sacrifices by the consumer, always occupies itself with capital investment on a large scale whatever the present poverty of the consumer. Second, the planner is prepared to go ahead with his schemes even if it means leaving all the difficult and unanswered questions to a wiser future, as if time itself could heal the wounds of ignorance. Much of the legislation framed by the present British Government for the purpose of carrying out socialisation has left all the really difficult questions to be solved, if soluble they are, to somebody else and to a later time.[2] The consequence is that those who embark upon socialist policies find unsuspected difficulties often when it is too late to draw back. Thus the Parliamentary Secretary to the Minister of Fuel and Power, as late as the Third Reading of the debate on the Coal Nationalisation Bill, said :

It is not for me to say, at this stage, although we might have a very interesting discussion on the matter on some future occasion, the precise criteria which should be applied to measure efficiency but it is a subject which would repay thought and some of us are thinking about it.

The Minister of Fuel and Power, November 22, 1945, said :

We are about to take over the mining industry. It is not so easy as it looks. I have been talking about nationalisation for 40

---

[1] Mr. Dalton, of ' song in my heart ' fame, in speaking on the Town and Country Planning Bill, a measure singularly well designed to damp down enterprise and change, said, quoting H. G. Wells, " ' For a moment I caught a vision of the coming City of mankind, more wonderful than all my dreams, full of life, full of youth, full of the spirit of creation.' That is the spirit of the Bill."

[2] This is particularly true of the National Health Scheme and of the scheme for nationalising Transport.

years but the implications of the transfer of property have never occurred to me.

And it is only too obvious that the British Labour Government in 1946 embarked upon a policy for destroying the free economy without having any clear idea of how, in the absence of a price system, labour could be properly distributed.

The Over-simplification of the Economic Problem

Most planners, until they really have to operate their plan, have a remarkably over-simplified conception of the task which lies before them. They believe, for instance, that the world is, or could easily be made, very rich ; that there is some little trick of technique or of administration which will suddenly unloose an unlimited flood of wealth. Just round the corner lies the end of the economic quest. Hence the popularity of such terms as ' the problem of production is solved ' or ' poverty in the midst of plenty '. It is easy to understand the exasperation, of those who hold such views, at any delay in establishing the Utopia.[1]

The facts are quite otherwise. The world, judged even by the standards of living which have been attained in a few places such as the United States or Great Britain, is deplorably poor. Pre-war international comparisons of income per head,[2] however rough they may be, reveal an enormous range of incomes per head between the different countries. Three-fifths of the world's income before the war was found in the United States, Great Britain, Germany, France and the U.S.S.R. which account for only one-quarter of the world's population. Perhaps three-quarters of the population of the world had an average pre-war income per head lower even than that in Great Britain. Improvement can be, and

---

[1] Aldous Huxley, *Science, Liberty and Peace*, p. 27, has pointed out that " faith in the bigger and better future is one of the most potent enemies to present liberty ; for rulers feel themselves justified in imposing the most monstrous tyrannies on their subjects for the sake of the wholly imaginary fruits which these tyrannies are expected to bear some time in the distant future ".

[2] Colin Clark, *The Conditions of Economic Progress*.

has been made steadily, but it will always be relatively slow. No one denies that, in the past, the free economy, under appropriate conditions, has proved the most powerful instrument for increasing national income. Yet, even in their best periods, the United States and Great Britain have not been able to increase real income per head by more than about 2 per cent per annum. The economic problem of the world is poverty. There are no spectacular cures for it. Nothing but frustration can come from the view that the vast world economic engine can suddenly be made to run twice as fast as before.

Spectacular results are always expected from the installation of new capital equipment. No one would wish to minimise the importance of new technical and mechanical ideas in improving the standard of living, in reducing human drudgery and in thus enhancing human dignity. It can be confidently expected that, as science and technology develop, economic progress will become more rapid. But the planner sees this process in the wrong light. He is over-much concerned with dramatic developments — such as electrification [1] and wholesale schemes for rationalisation. Yet by far the most important progress comes from the million and one tiny improvements in transport, distribution and production which arise from the patient watchfulness of those on the spot who have a direct economic interest in improvement and economy of effort. [2]

The exaggeration of the benefits to be derived from mechanisation is due also to the failure to recognise that machines do not grow on trees, they have to be made with labour ; that heavy capital investment means that consumers must make immediate sacrifices and that the economies to be

---

[1] There is a fascinating, and I believe largely unexplored, relation between economic revolution and electricity. At the centre of nearly every overall plan is to be found a vast scheme of electrification, although the use of coal for the making of electricity is a relatively inefficient method of consuming this mineral.

[2] See Jerome, *Mechanisation of Industry* ; and Terborgh, *The Bogey of Economic Maturity.*

derived from bigger units in industry are limited.[1]

The average planner finds it hard to grasp the almost stupefying variety of the products of the economic system. One coal-field may produce three or four thousand different kinds of coal suitable for different purposes. There are several thousand kinds of sewing thread, hundreds of different kinds of textile products each produced to meet a special need.[2] Despite all this he still instinctively thinks of the economic system in terms of a few homogeneous ' basic ' products. He looks upon the economic system as a group of industries each of which can be identified, separated and handled independently, instead of as an intertwined mass of economic activities linked together inextricably by technical, production and commercial relations. He regards an industry as something essentially homogeneous. ' This industry is efficient, that industry is inefficient.' The truth is, of course, that an industry consists normally of a number of firms of very widely-varying efficiency, size and function. He picks out some industries as ' basic ', although in a highly wide-spread industrial system practically all industries are essential for efficient operation. His obsession with the spectacular leads him to regard as ' basic ' such industries as coal, iron and steel, chemicals and transport, but when shortage of production in some other industry threatens to hold up the system, then this industry automatically jumps into the list of ' basic ' industries. In the first two years of planning in Great Britain practically every industry at one time or another, with the exception of distribution, betting pools and amuse-

---

[1] See p. 38.

[2] No one should presume to discuss economic organisation who has not taken the trouble to examine at least one industry in all its detail. No publication gives a more vivid conception of the complexity of industry than Mr. Hubball's paper, *The Cotton Trades War Time Commodity Supplies*, read before the Manchester Statistical Society, December 11, 1946. He shows that hundreds of different minor products are used by the cotton industry and describes how shortages of such apparently remote materials as sodium and potassium bichromates, castor, linseed and other oils, farina, sago flour, glucose, antimony lactate, spermaceti wax and formaldehyde each threatened to hold up production at different times.

ments, was officially described as a ' basic ', ' vital ', ' essential '
or ' foundation ' industry. The process, therefore, of chasing
the shortages boils down to one of chasing the elusive basic
industries. The failure to understand the integration of all
industrial activity leads to the erroneous belief that the economy can be planned in successive stages, that one bit can
be put right whilst the rest is temporarily ignored. This, of
course, explains why the planner's work never seems to be
complete. He is always creating problems for himself.[1]

The planner usually has a strong predilection for tidiness
in the economic system. Loose ends and lack of uniformity
exasperate him and account often for his objection to a free
economy with its innumerable rivulets of enterprise taking
unexpected courses, its constant urge to expand and diversify,
and its endless multiplicity of activities, quite ungraspable in
their entirety by one mind.[2]

Of course, once the planner gets the opportunity to put
his scheme into action he quickly discovers his mistakes.
He then begins to realise the difficulties of increasing wealth
and to understand the extraordinary complexity of the system
he is trying to handle. So that until he gets into power the
planner complains that labour is sweated and the consumer

[1] Thus Sir Stafford Cripps, House of Commons, August 7, 1947 : " In order
to get this increased production we must carry out our planning in an orderly
way. We must secure raw materials and sources of power first of all for producing things like coal, steel, transport, agricultural production and those
primary things that are the basis of our industrial life . . . and then turn to
the semi-manufactured goods of importance and finally to the completely
manufactured goods."

[2] The neurotic anxiety for tidiness is perhaps best exemplified in the policy
of the British Government regarding the distribution of services such as
electricity and gas. A map showing Great Britain divided up into 14 areas for
the control of the distribution of electricity looks much tidier than one divided
in 450 areas. Within the larger areas uniform prices can be established even
though costs in different parts of the area are very different.

Another interesting case was provided in the *Statement on the Economic
Considerations affecting relations between Employers and Workers* issued by
the British Government in January 1947. This was a most gloomy review in
which it was admitted that " the position of Great Britain is extremely serious ",
that " there was a serious maldistribution of labour ". Yet the Statement
spoke approvingly of " the orderliness within our industrial system . . .
throughout . . . the transition from war to peace ".

under-supplied; after he gets into power he engages in constant exhortation for harder work and calls for an almost oriental patience from the impoverished consumer.[1] Unfortunately, owing to the exclusive nature of planning, only the very few in each generation can learn from experience in this way and those few will find it politically impossible, having once set out on their path, to retrace their steps in the light of their experience.

Consumption as a Crime

The failure to grasp the essential complexity of an advanced economic system derives from the lack of understanding of the purpose of economic activity. Scientists tell us that every ear of wheat in a field is different, ideally calling for different methods of cultivation and harvesting. Much more so is every consumer unique. The only rational purpose of an economic society is to strive to satisfy each peculiar bundle of tastes. The planner naturally finds his task easier if the consumer can be standardised, that is to say, deprived of those characteristics which make of him a consumer.

The consequence is that the planner reveals a certain impatience at the very existence of the consumer. He persuades himself, against all reliable physiological and psychological evidence, that equal shares are 'fair' shares.[2] He denies the 'sovereignty of the consumer';[3] he emphasises the losses which are suffered from 'excessive' variety in consumers' demand; he is instinctively attracted towards the standardisation of products; he approves of the creation

---

[1] It is, indeed, possible to identify the moment when, in the course of British planning, the crucial, age-long fact of scarcity was first recognised by the planners. In the *Economic Survey for 1947* is found this statement : " The central fact of 1947 is that we have not enough resources to do all that we want to do. We have barely enough to do all that we *must* do. . . . To get all that we want, production would have to be increased by at least 25 per cent."

[2] Dr. Widdowson, in his study of children's diets, has shown that equal rations for children in one age-group are grossly inequitable since individual requirements vary enormously.

[3] See Hobson, *Confessions of an Economic Heretic* ; and Dobb, *Political Economy and Capitalism.*

of ' utility ' models ; he looks upon ' design ' in industry as something which can best be imposed from above ; [1] he advocates the ' pooling ' of products ; he argues in favour of permanent rationing ; he believes that if any scheme is in the interests of a group of producers it must be in the interests of the community as a whole.[2]

Such measures as these are sometimes advocated on the grounds that one group of consumers is taking unfair advantage of another group and that it must be the function of the State to redress the injustice. But there is evidence to suggest that the objection is really to the interests of the consumers as a whole. It was the planners who first raised the cry that consumers were getting their goods at too low a price.[3] The growing practice of determining how well fed is the consumer by measuring his ' calorie intake ' is another indication that the consumer is increasingly looked upon as a part of the system of production into which must be shovelled a minimum quantity of fuel without too nice a regard for his own tastes or his own satisfactions. Consumer goods as a whole come to have two functions only : to keep the human machine efficient and to provide incentive to work. It is, therefore, not difficult to see why the planner is inclined to regard the consumer as a great inconvenience to his plans, and to look upon his interests as secondary. The ostensible reasons for keeping consumption screwed down have already been referred to : that we must sacrifice now for the sake of future gains, that we must work for our children and our

---

[1] Thus the Parliamentary Secretary to the Board of Trade boasted that the Design Panel for Utility Furniture included representatives of furniture manufacturers, designers, distributors and the furniture trade unions, and " a housewife is also included ". *One* housewife.

[2] Before the war, under the Milk Marketing Board, large milk distributors were allowed a rebate on surplus milk which had to be manufactured. Small distributors could not get this rebate. The latter laid a complaint with the Committee of Investigation, who found that the action of the Board was justified as it was in the interests of milk producers and milk manufacturers as a whole " and might therefore be said to be in the public interest ".

[3] Mr. Strachey, House of Commons, February 6, 1947: " Before the war . . . wheat was imported into this country at 49 cents a bushel. What was the effect ? . . . We imported two million unemployed along with them."

children's children, that consumption must temporarily give
way to the need for capital equipment.[1] But at the back of
all this is a confusion between the means and the ends of the
economic system.

The Fear of the Price System

Something has already been said of the morbid fears in
the minds of many planners about the free operation of the
price system.[2] In some cases this is due to ignorance of
the function of prices in bringing about the production of the
required goods and in distributing goods among consumers.
In others, the price mechanism is objected to by socialists
because it represents the traditional method of rationing
in a free economy and must, therefore, be suspect. Sometimes the objection is really to inequality in the distribution
of wealth or income.[3] Sometimes it is against the diversity
and complexity of prices : many planners are strongly in
favour of an extensive ' postalisation ' of prices by which,
irrespective of the cost of providing goods and services, all
consumers should be charged the same price or even no price
at all for gas, electricity, coal, transport, etc.[4] Sometimes it
arises from the failure to recognise that a price is a measure of
the satisfaction which a consumer derives from the goods or
services he is buying. The planner cannot be brought to
recognise, for example, that if a small shop charges more than

[1] It is perhaps superfluous to refer to any specific statement on this point.
But Sir Hartley Shawcross deserves mention. Speaking on September 28,
1946, he said, " While the Government held out no easy promises, if we tackled
the problems we had to face in the spirit of a free, energetic democracy, we
could achieve a golden age of freedom, happiness and prosperity ".

[2] See p. 99. Mr. Bevin has said (July 26, 1947), " We cannot go back
to the Cobdenite economy ". Mr. A. J. P. Taylor, *The Listener*, March 20,
1947, " This was the great revolutionary discovery of the nineteenth century :
that there were so-called natural economic laws ; everything, even human
beings, had to be subordinated to the ' price mechanism ', that terrible Moloch
to which old-fashioned economists still bow down ".

[3] Attempts to distort the price system in order to soak the rich often produce just the opposite result. Thus the policy of ' bringing electricity to the
countryside ' by charging low prices there, may well mean that a slum dweller
has to contribute to the cost of providing electricity for a country mansion.

[4] See Barbara Wootton, *Freedom under Planning*, p. 51.

a large for the same commodity that is not necessarily a proof that the former is less efficient than the latter but may be due to the fact that the consumer is prepared to pay the higher price for the greater convenience of the shop 'round the corner'.

In the last analysis, the planner's attitude towards the price mechanism may arise out of a feeling that such a mechanism deprives him of some part of the gratification of exercising control. To control an economic system through the so-called 'physical controls' — raw materials, labour, factory space, etc. — gives a direct and immediate sense of the use of power. There would be, indeed, something of an anti-climax to more than fifty years' struggle for socialism in Great Britain if, at this very last stage, the fruits of victory should be snatched away by employing for control the very price mechanism which, in one form or another, has been one of the major objects of attack in socialist propaganda.

The same distrust is naturally felt for all those processes and agencies by which prices perform their functions. Most planners are obsessed with the need for price stability. A price is essentially an indicator, by reference to which producers and consumers regulate their action. A price which cannot move cannot perform that function any more than a thermometer which cannot move can help us to decide when to put more coal on the furnace. It is true that there are substantial advantages in stability of a general price level, though there are times when an upward or downward movement is desirable. But the stability of general prices is impossible if specific prices cannot change in order to bring about readjustments within the economic system. Unfortunately the suspicion of price changes is addressed, by many planners, to specific prices. They feel, when such changes take place, that something is going on for which they are not responsible, that the economic system is playing queer tricks with them. The result is that the extraordinary measures are sanctioned to keep specific prices unchanged by the use of subsidies and other methods. The rate of interest, the price of capital, is specially suspect because of its close association in the public mind with the capitalist system, and normally efforts will be made first, to reduce it, and second, to keep it low. The consequence is that that particular price ceases to exercise its function in distributing capital to the different possible uses and in striking a balance between consumption and investment. Attempts will also nearly always be made to keep down that group of prices which enter into the cost-of-living index number by subsidising the commodities entering into the index and by preventing officially the upward move-ment of the cost of living, even though this may result in other prices rising abnormally.

British economic policy in 1946 and 1947 provides highly relevant illustrations of the serious consequences which may follow from planning which is operated in defiance of the price mechanism. Thus the fuel crisis which struck so serious a blow at British industry in early 1947 was made the worse because the consumption of electricity and gas was positively encouraged by the prices charged. In his 1946 Budget Mr. Dalton had withdrawn the purchase tax on electric fires, thus reducing their price ; the prices charged for gas and electricity had been kept abnormally low because they entered into the cost-of-living index number and the special pre-war tariffs which had been designed to encourage the consumption of electricity were still in operation.

More dangerous still is the belief that the price system is useless in abnormal times, that it is a fair-weather device. The truth is that the price mechanism is most valuable when serious readjustments are called for (the Russians recognised this when they established their New Economic Policy). The British planners have not been nearly so realistic. Thus Mr. Morrison, in the middle of 1947 when the British economy was rapidly approaching paralysis, said :

Any person or group who asks for more in the post-war circum-stances of Great Britain is, in fact, asking for more government.

The classical conditions in which more could be got by the free play of the market have ceased to operate for us for the time being.

More converts are brought to the planning fold through ignorance of the price system than through any other cause. For those who cannot, or will not, acquaint themselves with the principles of this system have no clue through which to reach an understanding of the intricate organisation operating around them. Tortured and bemused by the fear of the unknown, they finally come to believe that everything in the free economy is subject to ' the blind ravages of chance ' ; that what is produced, what work each man pursues, what price is fixed for commodities are isolated *ad hoc* decisions. Into this intellectual vacuum the idea of a planned economy rushes with all the force of a gospel of salvation.

The price system in a free economy is not without its defects. Prices can be manipulated. They fail on occasions to bring about necessary readjustments quickly enough. Inequality in the distribution of income may rob them of much of their social purpose. In some cases they fail to evoke services which the community urgently needs. There is no more need to conceal these defects than there would be to deny that a steam engine or an electricity generating station was not 100 per cent efficient. But no one has yet devised a better system for co-ordinating the work of very large groups of people, for shifting the emphasis of production as consumers' demands change, for enabling the consumer to distribute his income in the most convenient way between different products, or enabling the worker to choose his occupation freely, having regard to his relative assessment of work and leisure and his personal inclination towards one type of work or another.

Such a price system is of a remarkable ingenuity and simplicity. It is based upon the market and upon the firm. In the market the consumers, by their process of choosing, are engaged in a perpetual plebiscite as to the goods they want. The results of that constant and detailed voting are passed back to the firm, which must, in the light of its costs, decide what adjustments it should make to cater for the revised needs of the consumer. This is an old story, told in innumerable volumes. But the tragedy is that the vast majority of those who, in the name of planning, are now seeking to upset the economic systems of the world have never heard of it.

In a free economy prices must be linked to costs, indeed costs are but one special group of prices. The distrust of the price system is often attributable to an anxiety lest the control of costs over economic activity should prevent the community from following policies which it considers right. Now it has long been recognised that there are certain social costs, as distinct from private costs, which are not measured by the free economy and which therefore may well lead an individual, seeking his own interests, to pursue a given course to a point which is potently anti-social. If I reduce my factory costs by using a type of fuel which creates more smoke and incurs others in losses through having to wash their curtains more frequently, or through the general destruction of the amenities of the neighbourhood, then the price system is producing the wrong answers. The opponents of the price system have seized upon these defects and have sought to magnify them, although such social costs are small in relation to the total and can, in fact, be allowed for in a rough-and-ready way by State intervention within a free economy. Exceptions there must be : but unless the vast mass of economic decisions are made by reference to cost, and those methods for producing a given result chosen which yield the lowest cost, complete chaos will be the result. Yet this overriding criterion is increasingly being set on one side by those who make a nebulous appeal to 'the national interest'.[1]

[1] Thus Sir George Schuster, *The Observer*, December 8, 1946, speaking of the future of the cotton industry and re-equipment policy, points out that, in all the circumstances, " it may well be doubtful for an individual firm whether it will pay to put in new machinery ". He concludes that " if we could double the volume of production, *even with a slightly higher cost of manufacture* (my italics), it would be to the national interest to do so ".

Contempt for the Distributor

In a free economy the rapid equating of supply and demand through price changes goes on largely through the instrument of the merchant and the distributor. It is not, therefore, surprising to find that the merchant and distributor are regarded by most planners as impediments to the creation of wealth.

Nothing is more dangerous to economic progress in the long run than the view that a nation only grows richer by increasing the proportion of its population engaged in manufacturing industries, or that only those who are actually engaged in manufacture are contributing to the wealth of the community. Such a view cannot stand the test of facts. Even in the most highly industrialised countries only a minority of the workers are to be found in the so-called productive occupations. In the United States about 30 per cent of the occupied population is found in manufacturing industry, mining and building. The corresponding figure for Great Britain is 44 per cent. In both these countries, which represent instances of industrialisation carried practically to its limit, the larger part of the national income is derived, not from production in the narrow sense, but from other forms of economic activity.

Moreover, in nearly every advanced industrial country the proportion of the population which finds a livelihood in manufacture is falling. It has been falling in the United States for at least the last twenty years and in Great Britain for a much longer period. The outstanding feature of all rich economic communities is the very high proportion of workers who are to be found in the ' service ' occupations, *i.e.* in distribution, commerce, finance, transport and the other services. Both in Great Britain and the United States about one-half of the people at work are engaged in these service trades.

There are very good reasons for believing that this close

relation between the importance of the service trades and high standards of living is largely cause and effect, and that growing wealth is inseparably bound up with the extension of the services.

It is not difficult to understand why this should be so. Among the devices which men have conceived to increase wealth and to reduce the amount of work needed to reach a given end, the method of specialisation stands out as probably the most fruitful of all. Specialisation takes very many forms and runs through the whole of our economic life. Workers, by specialising, increase their skill and speed, and enormously extend production. Businesses, by specialising, increase their efficiency and reduce the complexity of their administration. Different parts of a country can with advantage specialise upon types of production which best suit the natural conditions and the type and quality of the existing labour force. And the history between the wars constitutes an irrefutable proof that unless the nations of the world are prepared to specialise in those forms of production in which they have the greatest economic advantage, then the world economy disintegrates in a futile beggar-my-neighbour struggle.

Without this specialisation in all its forms, the standard of living throughout the world would be considerably lower than it is today. If, on the other hand, it can be extended and developed, the prospect of a world set free from poverty is clearly within sight.

Specialisation, however, is only one side of the shield. It would be meaningless unless, at the same time, there were forces operating to integrate the separate parts and bind them up into a co-ordinated system. Specialisation and integration go together. Now the integrating forces in a specialised economy are just these services of distribution, commerce, finance and transport. It is through such services that the demands of the consumer are collected and passed back to the producer in order to avoid the waste of manufacturing what the consumer does not want ; that, before production can begin at all, raw materials in the right quantities and the right qualities are steered into the right channels ; that stocks can be accumulated at strategic points to dampen the effects of oscillations in the demands of the consumer and thus to keep production running smoothly ; that risks can be taken in opening up new markets and placing improved goods before the consumer ; that the multitudinous financial transactions involved in trading can be carried out expeditiously by experts ; that finally the finished products can be put into the hands of the consumer where and when he wants them.

The need for the parallel maintenance of those integrating and specialised elements in an efficient economy can be simply illustrated. Very large iron and steel plants have great technical advantages over small plants. This means that relatively few plants will normally be required in any country. But if the iron and steel plants are few and widely spaced it follows that the iron and steel industry must call increasingly upon transport and distribution services, since the wide spacing of the iron and steel industry means that raw materials — particularly coal and iron ore — must now be carried greater distances before they are turned into finished products. In this case, therefore, the gains of modern techniques and high outputs per head in the giant plants are dependent upon simultaneous increase in the activities of the services catering for the iron and steel industry.

Integration and specialisation go together. It is not an accident that those countries in the world, above all the United States, which have made the greatest use of the principle of specialisation to enhance output per worker and to raise the standard of living, have been compelled to employ an increasing part of their population in the service trades. We do not try to produce a faster and more efficient aeroplane simply by putting more powerful engines into it. We must, if catastrophe is to be avoided, at the same time render the system of controls stronger and more sensitive,

the supplementary aids to the pilot more adequate, the automatic stabilising devices more plentiful. We should not
expect to be able to enjoy the advantages of a more powerful
economic machine without a similar expansion of the guiding, controlling and ancillary economic functions which the
services provide.

These are economic truisms supported by both past
experience and logical analysis, which would not merit
repetition were it not for the frequency with which, in these
days, they are ignored or even disputed. There is, indeed,
one extreme school which appears to argue that the services
are largely unnecessary, that they are parasitic in the body
economic, and that by a ruthless removal of them the wealth
of a nation would be increased. There is one very simple
answer to the exponents of this type of millennium. It is to
invite them to try to lead their lives without using the services
which they regard as wasteful, to seek out a farmer to buy
wheat each time they want to eat, to make their own arrangement for the milling of the wheat and for the baking of the
flour, and so on through the whole range of the articles they
normally buy at retail ; to arrange for the transport of these
goods and their storage, to accumulate throughout the year
stocks of goods which they will need in specially large amounts
at certain periods, to search out a designer or inventor each
time they have a new want for which their existing goods
and equipment are not well suited.

Sometimes the argument is less extreme. It is admitted
that the services are necessary but it is claimed that they are
too extensive and, therefore, too costly.

Assertions of that kind are tantamount to a declaration
that producers do not know their jobs and consumers do not
know what is good for them. For no one compels a producer
to use the services of a merchant in the buying of his raw
materials. Broadly speaking, merchants have no monopoly
powers (in fact, it is sometimes urged that they compete too
much). Any producer at any time is free to carry out his

own distribution services. If he chooses not to do so, unless he is being charged with inefficiency, it must be assumed that he finds it more economical to allow an outside agency to carry out these services for him. Similarly with the final consumer, if he feels that he disposes of his income best by purchasing a loaf which is conveniently delivered to him, who has the right to say that he would really prefer to have two loaves which he must collect himself from the shop ? Those, in fact, who claim that our services are too extensive must take upon themselves the onus of laying down the principles by which they determine what constitutes ' too extensive ' and of explaining upon what grounds they have attained to the higher knowledge which enables them to judge more exactly of the best methods of production within business and the best methods of disposing of an individual income than can the individuals directly concerned.

The countries with a high proportion of their workers in the processes of distribution and transport are, without dispute, the richest countries of the world. But the planners cannot rid themselves of the feeling that such workers are essentially unproductive (it is indeed precisely in these essentially integrating services that the planned economies have broken down most seriously). Thus Sir Stafford Cripps has said :

Before the war we had been using a too large proportion of our labour in distribution and we must not allow that state of affairs to arise again. We must see to it that, beyond the reasonable minimum required for distribution, the best of our energy goes into production.[1]

Pre-war we had nearly three million people in distribution producing nothing.[2]

[Workers in distribution before the war] probably earned not far short of £500 millions per annum in wages and salaries, all of which had to be paid for by the consumer as an addition to the cost of production.[3]

[1] October 19, 1945.   [2] February 2, 1946.
[3] February 12, 1946.

Mr. Belcher has said :

We do not desire to encourage a return to the over-plus of labour in the distributive industry.[1]

These illogical views of ' productive ' and ' unproductive ' labour are so deeply implanted that they persist in the face of all evidence to the contrary. Thus in 1946, when Sir Stafford Cripps was making the statements quoted above, Great Britain was desperately short of labour largely because of the withdrawal of married women from industry. This withdrawal, in turn, was partly due to the shortage of workers in distribution which made the task of running a home quite incompatible with outside work. And whilst distributive workers were being classed as unproductive the Government was attempting to justify the retention of 2,000,000 workers in National and Local Government.[2]

Obscurity of Language

A remarkable consequence of the growth of planning ideas is the extensive use of vague and obscure terms which can mean very different things to different people. This helps to create a spurious sense of solidarity between different planners. For so long as they can conveniently ignore the different meanings they attach to the same word, conflict can be reduced to a minimum. On occasions these nebulous terms are deliberately adopted in order to mislead : more frequently they are the result of muddled thinking or are merely a substitute for thought itself.

Perhaps the most reprehensible tactics are those employed in the use of the term ' democratic society '. It is argued that a system of free enterprise cannot give us a democratic society and that only in a planned economy such as Russia does this condition exist.[3] Thus, by a violent inversion of

[1] House of Commons, July 8, 1947.

[2] It is also highly paradoxical that although the planners normally regard distributors as parasitic many of the planners' schemes increase distributors' margins. Thus before the war the setting up of the Milk Marketing Board tended to increase distributors' margins (R. Cohen, *Economic Journal*, March 1939).

[3] See Laski, *Manchester Guardian*, April 27, 1946.

meaning, a State which keeps millions of workers in slave camps, which ruthlessly transports large parts of its working population from one part of the country to another, which makes the holding of a ration card conditional upon the performance of prescribed work, has created economic democracy.   In the existing free economies, such as the United States, in which workers are free to leave their jobs, to move from one part of the country to another, to organise themselves for their own defence, to strike, to set up their own co-operative system of distribution or of factory production, to enforce in the courts their contracts with employers, it is alleged economic democracy does not exist.

It is also a common habit to insist that economic problems shall always be considered in terms of the ' broad interests of the community as a whole ' or of ' the general national interest '.   Now it is true that there are some decisions [1] which can only be made on public grounds and there the community must determine in a rough-and-ready fashion what constitutes the general interest.   The decision as to how far it would be justifiable to throw additional costs for smokeless fuel upon the householder in order to have cleaner cities would be one such case.   These decisions are extremely difficult to make, there is no systematic or scientific way of reaching them.   The public hullabaloo which precedes the location of a large electricity generating plant or a new town is adequate evidence that in all such matters we necessarily grope among the intangibles.

Yet the planners would invoke this test of ' national interest ' over the whole economic field, although in the vast range of economic decisions there are no criteria to decide what is the national interest.[2]   It is the outstanding merit of the free economy that such decisions are left to be made in

---

[1] See Chapter X, p. 195.

[2] Most planners would learn much, not least in clarity of exposition, from a careful reading of Adam Smith.   On this particular point he said (Book IV, chap. 2) : " I have never known much good done by those who affected to trade for the public good.   It is an affectation, indeed, not very common among merchants."

terms of individual interests, which can be measured, operating within a general framework through which individual and social interest will largely coincide.

This casual use of the ' national interest ' argument carries in its train many social dangers. First, it is a highly convenient device for justifying dictatorial action : so long as no one knows what the national interest is, an ingenious planner can make a good case for practically anything, however hard the policy may appear to bear on special groups in the community. Second, it means that many of our economic decisions must be made in the absence of concrete and objective criteria. Third, it leaves us open to the policies of cranks of every sort who will justify their case ' in the national interest '.

At bottom, of course, the attitude of mind which leads to the frequent use of this term is totalitarian. It is based upon the assumption that there is a communal interest which is above and independent of the interests of the individuals which constitute the community. Indeed there are recorded cases where a policy is advocated as in the national interest although it is admitted that that policy will run counter to the interests of every individual in the community.

The glossary of these misty planning terms is indeed a long one. At the head of the list stand ' co-ordination ' and ' integration ',[1] used mainly by those who have a vague sense that this or that service should be made more efficient but are not quite sure how. ' Stability ' and ' orderly progress ' are others in high repute. Recently the word ' balance ' has become extremely popular in discussions of social organisation. Thus we speak of a balanced distribution of industry, a healthy and well-balanced agriculture, a balanced population, a balanced community, and in each case the word carries a different meaning. At the moment in Great Britain,

---

[1] Mr. Barnes, the Minister of Transport, in introducing the Transport Bill in the House on December 16, 1946, said, " I expect that for processes of integration and co-ordination, country bus services will be more synchronised with railway services than they have been in the past ".

'balanced industry' seems to mean an arrangement by which each region has a wide range of industries, *i.e.* that all regions should ideally produce different goods in the same proportions. Balanced agriculture, however, does not mean that each farm should produce the same crops but just the opposite, *i.e.* that farmers should specialise in those crops in which they have the greatest comparative advantage so that the industry can be 'healthy' without having too large subsidies paid to it. A balanced community is one in which all social classes are proportionately represented.[1] A balanced population is one which is reproducing itself. A balanced region for the distribution of electricity is one in which one lot of consumers live in a populous area, where costs will be low, and another lot in a sparsely populated area where costs of distribution will be high. In fact the only thing common to all these different uses of the word is that they all involve the calling-in of the State to carry through, by ill-defined methods, obscurely conceived policies.

There is a wide range of terms employed by planners, or business men seeking to justify activities inconsistent with a free economy, all of which are really synonyms for the exercise of monopoly control: 'orderly marketing', 'concerted programmes', 'price management' (instead of the more brutal 'price control'), 'putting the house in order', 'cutting out the dead wood' and so on.

The ultimate effect of this use of slipshod language is to dilute, where it does not positively poison, the meaning of words to the point at which discussion could just as usefully be carried on in pure gibberish. Endless examples could be provided. The following may serve to illustrate the degree to which meaning can be bleached from words by a lavish employment of the planners' jargon.

(1) Before the war the British Government had conferred upon the iron and steel industry a large measure of

[1] Final Report of New Towns Committee (Cmd. 6876).

monopoly power. The interests of the consumer were supposed to be safeguarded by the Import Duties Advisory Committee. That Committee on page 47 of its ' Report on the Present Position and Future Development of the Iron and Steel Industry ' defined what it regarded as a proper price policy as follows :

> A sound and reasonable price policy, aiming at the maintenance on as stable a basis as possible of prices in times of good trade as low as consistent with the provision of adequate reserves for depreciation and obsolescence and a reasonable margin of reward to the efficient producer, and as high as consistent with an economic level of output in times of bad trade when demand is attenuated, whilst avoiding unfair discrimination, is then desirable in the interest both of the industry itself and the national economy of which it is so essential a part.

What is the meaning of sound, reasonable, stable, adequate, efficient, attenuated, unfair and national economy ?

(2) The State-appointed British Transport Advisory Council in its ' Report on Services and Rates ' gave the following definition of ' co-ordination ' :

> The Council considers that . . . coordination may be regarded as a state in which the various forms of transport, irrespective of ownership, can, under equitable conditions, function efficiently not only within their several spheres but also as a part of a comprehensive whole under a system, either imposed or reached by mutual agreement, conditioned by public interest.

What is the meaning of equitable, efficiently, comprehensive whole, public interest ?

(3) The Cotton Working Party, set up by the British Government in 1946, thought it worth while to define the objectives of the cotton industry in these terms :

> The Cotton industry must be operated in the national interest and play its proper part in the national economy. . . . Unless all those working in the separate units are prepared, when necessary, to take into account the interests not only of the industry as a whole but also the broad interests of

the nation, unless there is readiness both to agree and implement common policies when necessary for furthering such interests . . . there is little chance of a satisfactory outcome from any proposals.

What is the meaning of national interest, proper part in national economy, when necessary, the broad interests of the nation ?

(4) In the declaration of Labour Party policy in the 1945 election the following statement appeared :

> Each industry must have applied to it the test of national service. If it serves the nation, well and good ; if it is inefficient and falls down on its job, the nation must see that things are put right.

How does one determine whether an industry is serving the nation ? What is the test of national service ? How can a nation see that an industry is put right ?

In all these cases, of course, the authors vaguely state problems but use such language as to create the impression that they are answering them.

CHAPTER VII

PLANNING AS A SCIENTIFIC METHOD

Only an organising genius could produce a shortage of coal
and fish in Great Britain.—Mr. ANEURIN BEVAN, Labour
Party Conference, 1945.

I

THE comparative novelty of the idea of a centrally planned
economy goes far to explain the paradox that whilst British
socialists have been busy now for half a century in framing the
socialist commonwealth and whilst many millions of socialists are now clamouring for its establishment, those who
constitute the intellectual spearhead of the movement are
still disputing among themselves and with their opponents
whether planning will really work and, if so, how it can
best be made to work.

In the days of the Webbs, socialist intellectuals concerned
themselves largely with what may be described as administrative geometry. They sought to lay out, with hierarchical
precision, committees, councils, boards and tribunals, so that
the whole effect appeared tidy in an organisation diagram.
They sketched the ideal areas of operation of public services
so that everything would look neat and regular on a map.
Interest in this branch of socialism among the intellectuals
seems now largely to have evaporated. Instead they concern
themselves with the most fearsome algebra and calculus in the
hope that, through the higher mathematics, they may find
ways of introducing the price system into a socialist economy
and of bringing back competition as a benevolent game into
the economic mechanism.

The clash between those who believe that a plan must
consist of a quantitative determination by the State of pro-

duction and consumption and those who would employ a socialist price system has already been mentioned. But even in this second group there are fundamental differences of opinion as to the purposes for which the price system should be employed. If there is to be a socialist price system, some believe that it should be designed and operated to bring about the conditions which would emerge in a theoretical system of free competition; others argue in favour of the economic advantages of a substantial measure of monopoly. Many would advocate the general application of a rule whereby price would equal marginal cost; other writers have shown that, in practice, this might seriously undermine managerial efficiency. Is the consumer in a planned economy to be regarded as sovereign in the sense that he is likely to know what he wants and what is best for him, or are there cases where the State can act more wisely and with greater knowledge? By what devices will the State measure the 'social' costs which it is often alleged the individual ignores? Are there objective grounds for declaring that equality in the distribution of wealth is likely to maximise the welfare of the community, or must we move on such matters by instinct or intuition? In general, how are incentives to be maintained in a planned economy and, in particular, how is a high rate of taxation to be made consistent with maximum effort and production? [1]

All these speculations, which must be fascinating to the intellectual but depressingly abstract to the ordinary run of socialist who is anxious to get on with the planning, go to the very heart of the questions as to whether, in a planned economy, the planners will know what to do and whether, if they do agree what should be done, they will be able to do it.

[1] There is now a vast literature on this subject. For those who wish to pursue it reference may perhaps be made to the following: Lerner, *Economics of Control*, chap. 3; Schumpeter, *Capitalism, Socialism and Democracy*, chap. 8; Meade, 'Mr. Lerner on "The Economics of Control"', *Economic Journal*, April 1945; Wilson, 'Price and Outlay Policy of State Enterprise', *Economic Journal*, December 1945; A. M. Henderson, 'The Pricing of Public Utility Undertakings', *The Manchester School*, September 1947.

The present-day controversies, however, prompt three re-flections. First, it may be that the unsettled abstract problems will finally prove to be capable of resolution : on the other hand they may prove to be insoluble, either because of the logical difficulties, or because they call for the measurement of things which cannot, in the nature of things, be measured. It would be time enough to think about centrally planned economies if and when we knew which of these possibilities proved to be true.

Second, if these theoretical problems still remain un-solved, and if they are so fundamental as to justify the attention they are receiving, it may be asked what kind of a muddle we would have got into if we had socialised our economy when the great creators of socialist doctrine first advanced it. Nothing is clearer than that, if we had followed the Webbs' advice when it was first given, we should have embarked upon socialism at a time when, according to later discoveries, we did not even know what the more difficult problems of a planned economy would be. And if, as must now be admitted, our escape from the clumsy and unscientific manipulations of the early-day socialists was providential, is there not double reason to continue to exercise caution now whilst the latter-day socialists dispute among themselves ?

Third, those who are uninitiated into the mysteries of the more abstract economic analysis must not allow themselves to be so overwhelmed by the brilliance of these discussions as to assume that a planned economy is more scientific, and therefore preferable, to a free economy. For the most part these discussions are not devoted to the relative merits of the two systems. They are mainly concerned with the best way of running a planned economy if somebody else has already decided that there should be a planned economy. In other words (if the argument of this book is correct), of how one may make the best of a bad job.

II

Theoretically a price system could operate within a socialised state in such a way as to guide a given volume of production into those channels which best satisfy the consumer and to enable the consumer to distribute his income, among the goods produced, in such a way as to give him the greatest possible satisfaction. To take a simple illustration, suppose the community consists of one factory responsible for all production. Suppose that every producer is paid the same wage so that the total weekly wage bill is £1000. Suppose that the management fix such prices for the goods made each week that the total value of the goods is £1000. Then each week the workers draw their wages (£1000), buy the goods made (for £1000) and the £1000 pass back to the management and are ready to pay the next week's wages. The only possible snag is that some of the goods produced would not be sold because, at the price fixed, the workers did not want them. There is an easy way out of this. The price of the unwanted goods would be reduced and the price of the other goods increased — still keeping the total value of the output of the factory at £1000. Each separate commodity would be produced up to the point at which the money received for it in the shops was equal to what had to be paid in wages for its production (we are assuming everybody is paid the same wage). So the output of the commodities which were not wanted in the quantities originally produced would fall. Similarly the output of other goods would rise. Finally, a balancing point would be reached at which the goods produced each week at the prices fixed would all be bought each week. The only rules which would have to be observed would be, first, that total wages must equal the total value of sales, and second, that the wages paid in making each separate product should equal the money obtained by selling that product. When that position was reached no consumer would have any further interest in switching his income from

one commodity to another, the managers of the factory would
have no further interest in changing the proportions in which
the different commodities were produced.

Theoretically that argument is perfect. But the assumptions underlying it are often overlooked and the deductions
drawn from it are often fallacious. The important assumptions are these :

(a) The system described above provides no method of
determining objectively what part of the production
should go to consumer goods and what part should go to
making new equipment : that is to say, what part of their
total income the workers must save. It is, in fact, generally agreed that the volume of savings in a planned
economy must be an arbitrary political decision.[1] The
right of the individual to spread his spending between the
present and the future must be taken from him.

(b) Although the system will result in the correct distribution
of output among the various types of goods being produced, there seems to be no mechanism by which consumers can exercise a demand for a new product which is
not now being produced. Whether new products were
introduced would depend, presumably, upon the initiative
of the managers. It seems inevitable under such circumstances that economic progress, as represented by increasing variety of choice, would be endangered.

(c) The system would operate within a framework of major
economic decisions taken prior to the working of the
system. Thus a decision might be taken to pay all
workers equally. In that case compulsion would have to
be resorted to in order to get the right number of people

---

[1] Thus Schumpeter, *Capitalism, Socialism and Democracy*, p. 180, " The
vote on the investment item — at least on its amount — would involve a real
decision and stand on a par with the vote on army estimates and so on " ; and
Lerner, *Economics of Control*, p. 262, " The decision of how much investment
there should be is a political decision and cannot be otherwise. There is no
certain way, in a collectivist economy, of permitting the consumers to make
this decision via the price mechanism."

in the right jobs.   Alternatively, differential wages might
be paid to bring about the required distribution of labour.

III

But it is the deductions drawn from the discovery that a
price system can operate in a socialist State which are most
open to criticism.   Whilst many socialists squirm at the
unpleasant thought that modern planning theory involves the
use of a pricing mechanism so similar to that employed in a
free economy, many are now disposed to welcome the discovery as long-awaited proof that a planned economy will
' work '.   On that point two comments are relevant.

Every economic system may be said to ' work ', at least
until the last consumer drops dead from starvation.   What
one wants to know is whether the economy works well.

The presence or absence of a price system is not proof of
anything.   For the price system, in itself, is a neutral though
powerful weapon.   A knife may be used for social purposes,
like peeling potatoes, or anti-social purposes, like cutting other
people's throats.   So, too, the value of a price system for the
purpose of increasing economic welfare lies in the environment in which it is allowed to operate.   If it is allowed freely
to direct producers to the goods most needed and consumers
to the goods which provide the greatest satisfaction, for the
minimum of effort, it is doing its job properly.   But, of
course, a price system can be manipulated for bringing about
the most evil ends : for the destruction of a social group, for
the starvation of a whole community, for the gratification of
the sadistic influences of one man.   Or it may, through sheer
ignorance, be so mishandled as to produce spectacular and unnecessary shortages of goods — as the price-control system in
Great Britain and the United States did after the war.[1]

The vital questions are, therefore : Will those who wield

[1] No one should neglect to read the full story of how inept and timid price
control of agricultural products in the United States in 1945 brought privation to
millions of people all over the world.   It will be found in *Fortune* for May 1946.

supreme power in a planned economy be inclined to favour the use of a price system and, if they do so, will they allow it to operate with sufficient freedom, or can they be expected to manipulate it in order to control the lives of others and to withhold essential economic freedoms ? I submit that it is reasonable to expect the worst.

Every Economic Decision is potentially a Political Decision

There is, in the first place, the almost instinctive opposition of many planners to the price mechanism itself. The type of mind which is drawn towards central planning seems to be strongly attracted to quantitative, physical controls : they are simpler to understand, and convey to those who operate them a more immediate sense of the use of power over others. Even in time of war, when central planning had a purpose and was universally accepted as necessary, this reluctance to use the price mechanism to bring about the required results was much in evidence.

Assuming that these inhibitions could be removed, there still remains the major point that in a planned economy, however operated, no economic decision, however trivial and however intimately and peculiarly bound up with the circumstances of the individual consumer, will be safe from the possibility of interference from above.

It is, indeed, comically naïve to imagine that the political leaders in a planned economy will quietly allow a group of economic and statistical experts to operate, without question, an economic system according to the latest theoretical ideas as to how best goods can be produced and distributed in order to maximise total satisfaction. For the politicians can, will and must interfere in such a way as to make hay-wire of the scientifically devised plan. This issue cropped up in Great Britain when the Labour Government was pressed to establish a central Economic General Staff for the purpose of carrying out the planning. Mr. Morrison gave the inevitable answer in the House of Commons on February 28, 1946 :

Sometimes it is said — I think wrongly — that we need an economic general staff in the sense of a central body of economists and experts who would make the whole plan, get it approved, carry it through, administer it and execute it separately from the economic Departments of State. I think this is a mistaken conception. Such an organisation would become almost as big as the Government itself. The Departments of State which contribute to our economic affairs are very considerable in number. They spread over nearly the whole field of Government. It would not work, and there would be friction all round. . . . The problem is . . . to build up from the economic Departments of State, together with the common service sections of the Central Government, an efficient economic machine on the official level. . . . There are ministerial committees above, which of course determine issues of policy, to which the reports of the economic planners go, which determine what shall be done about the reports, which give instructions to the officers on the official level as to what they are to inquire into and what reports they are to produce. . . .

This puts the experts into their place with a vengeance. But it is important to recognise the true features of the alternative system of building up a plan as Mr. Morrison has outlined it.

A politician in power must be confident of his power to ' know what the people want '.[1] Everything conspires to create that confidence. He has the backing of at least a majority of the electorate. He regularly addresses large meetings of those who share his political views and can be expected to give him the popular applause which would strengthen the will of the most modest. His self-justification lies in this belief that he has a second sight in assessing public needs and demands. He probably recognises that in straight administration he is inferior to his civil servants. He may well accept his purely intellectual and academic inferiority to the numerous experts who are only too glad to advise him on any subject. Unless, therefore, he holds on grimly to the

---

[1] Mr. Bevin has put this point most clearly. Discussing in October 1947 the various cuts which were to be imposed upon the consumer, he said, " We are acting very much like a reasonable father and mother would act in managing a home ".

conviction that he is abnormally sensitive to the impulses, wishes and needs of the public, he would find no reason for being where he is.

In a free economy the opportunities of the ruling politician to interfere with the intimate economic life of the people is limited. By accepting the free economy he deprives himself, by a self-denying ordinance, of the power of intervention. But in a planned economy he is positively invited to fiddle about with such things. As a member of the Government he is personally responsible for every item in the national economic plan. Any other rule would mean that a body of expert economic planners, with no political responsibilities, were in fact placed outside his control and outside the control of the people. He may any day be attacked because there are not enough bicycles, or ice-cream, or because the bread is too brown or too white, or the equipment of industry is too new or too old. He cannot ignore the detail because it is the detail which might most easily catch him out.[1] He may naturally be disposed to play the politically attractive rôle of Father Christmas.[2]

Now a plan, by definition, is a highly integrated scheme in which every part of the programme is linked with every other part. The only way to criticise a plan rationally is, therefore, to criticise the whole of it — to argue that A should be altered and that, in consequence, B, C, D, E, F, etc. should be modified accordingly. But the statesman will never be in a position to do this. His time, knowledge and interests are limited. The scheme will be too vast in any case for him to

[1] Sir Stafford Cripps announced in the House of Commons on June 26, 1947, that his Department was receiving letters from the public at a rate of 1,225,000 a month.

[2] Thus Mr. Dalton, speaking at a Union Society debate at Cambridge, his old University, on June 3, 1947, recalled that the President of the Boat Club had told him that boats and oars were practically unavailable because of the export drive. He continued, " I am glad to say that, following a telephone conversation I had before leaving this evening, an exception is going to be made in the case of boats for the Olympic Games ". Dr. Summerskill announced in the House of Commons on June 17, 1947, that licences were to be issued to obtain wedding cakes free from price control for the celebration of golden weddings.

understand. He must confine himself to tinkering with those parts of the plan in which he has special interest.

In his tinkering he will be subject to powerful pressure groups. His own constituency must be closely watched. His own administrative duties, such as that of a Minister of Agriculture or of Fuel and Power, inevitably make him the guardian of some vested interests. His own political upbringing may have linked him with one group in the community whose troubles he understands and whose loyalties he esteems more than others. His activities, therefore, in relation to the whole of the plan, must essentially be irrational and disruptive. Since he is concerned directly with A (let us say the interests of the miners), and not with B, C, D, E, F, etc., he may insist that A be altered without B, C, D, E, F, etc. being modified. The logic of the plan is therefore endangered.

It is important to recognise that, in this analysis of what is likely to happen in a planned economy, nothing derogatory is implied regarding the statesman as such. He is simply the victim of a system which places upon him the impossible task of seeing everything at once and of forming a judgment, on highly conflicting matters, without allowing his own personal experiences to count or his own special knowledge to have weight. Indeed the greater the honesty and integrity of the Minister, the more difficult he must find it to put on one side his own beliefs in deference to the views of others which he cannot hope to comprehend so completely as his own.

So far we have discussed only the dilemma of one Minister, assuming that he were in fact an economic dictator. But, of course, in the early stages of a planned economy there will be many Ministers. Each one will have the same personal difficulties, but when they sit around a table to pool their common knowledge in approving or modifying the plan, other forces are set in train which further disrupt the integrated scheme. The Ministers will have somewhat conflicting interests, each is bound to have a group of special loyalties. What appears to one Minister to be his own special knowledge of a given subject, giving him the right to speak with authority on what he understands best, will be regarded as bias by other Ministers. Thus the Minister of Health, the Minister of Fuel and Power, the Minister of Agriculture, the Minister of Supply might, for example, make competing demands for labour. Each sincerely believes that, in the interests of the community, more houses, more coal, more food respectively are urgently needed. How are these differences to be resolved ?

They can only be resolved in committee. The outcome of the clash of rival views must then be settled, partly by the inherent strength of the case which each Minister has to make, but largely by the plausibility and knowledge of committee tactics which each Minister can bring to bear. An honest and zealous Minister must do his best in putting forward his own case. But in doing this, he creates the danger that the relative claims of consumers of houses, coal and food will be decided, not on the real merits of these claims, but by reference to the forensic skill of the different Ministers. This, in itself, is bad enough, even where Ministers are most scrupulously seeking to limit their demands to what they regard as reasonable. But it will be difficult, if not impossible, for a Minister to avoid some bias, particularly in the stress of argument. Then the whole basis of discussion degenerates. For if it comes to be considered that one Minister, for the purpose of bargaining, asks for more than he really needs, all Ministers must, in self-defence, adopt the same technique, and a scientific solution of the problem of distributing scarce resources is made even more impossible. Out of such an impasse the only escape routes are those which must inevitably destroy the integrated plan. There may be an Arithmetical Compromise. This, of course, is a confession of the impossibility of reaching a scientific answer to the problems of planning. Or, the discussion having exhausted itself, the final decision may be left to the Supreme Minister. In this case, of course, all the difficulties recur of one man making a sound decision in matters where personal bias cannot be eliminated.

In the hurly-burly of this kind of procedure the interests of the consumer must either be lost sight of altogether or relegated to a secondary place. The reactions upon millions of consumers of a compromise which has to be accepted or rejected forthwith in committee cannot be foreseen. And a compromise once reached in committee is difficult to modify, for all the parties to it are bound to defend it against outside attack. Moreover, in such a procedure, innovation and change will stand a poor chance of acceptance. For it will be the abnormal and unusual claims which will be most severely attacked and most readily relinquished. A committee nearing exhaustion will inevitably fall back, for agreement, upon what has happened in the past. Changes, therefore, will be at a discount.

So far we have discussed procedure in the making of the plan at the highest level. Ministers cannot be expected to follow slavishly the advice of experts, and British experience provides many illustrations of economic disorder following the refusal of Ministers to take politically unpopular courses.[1] But it by no means follows that if the experts were always obeyed (*i.e.* if the experts were made the real Ministers) that all would be well.

Preparatory discussions regarding the plan on an inter-departmental level will reveal the same features as those on the Ministerial level : conflicts of opinion in which there is no obvious right or wrong ; decisions which reflect the debating power of the various committee members ; a final resort to compromise to solve the insoluble. The presence of the official level of discussion, however, means further delay in reaching decisions. For the discussions at the Ministerial

[1] It seems clear, for instance, that the balance of payments crisis of Autumn 1947 was largely the result of the delay of Ministers in following the advice, given by their experts as early as February, to cut imports in order to reduce dollar expenditure. The consequence was that the world lost confidence in British recovery and a flight from sterling followed. The story is told in the *Manchester Guardian*, September 4, 1947.

level may get into such knots that the matter is passed down again for reconsideration at the official level. In such cases the real issues may well become more obscure. Each civil servant must, out of his professional and departmental loyalty, seek to find ways of defending the position taken up by his Minister and to establish a case which will give his Minister most help when the matter once again comes before Ministers. All this must, of course, take time.

Once the plan has been agreed and put forward by the Government it must, in a democratic community, be sent forward for discussion and amendment by the Representative Bodies. Here again the difficulty arises that an integrated scheme must inevitably be examined by those whose interests and knowledge are essentially local and piecemeal. The plan will be subjected to distortion through the activities of pressure groups. If amendments are made at this stage, it then becomes the task of the Government to determine what consequent changes in other parts of the plan will be required. Theoretically an endless process of shuttle-cocking would go on, only to be limited by the exercise of arbitrary power at some point.

Finally, in the operation of the integrated plan, reference must be made to the position of autonomous or semi-autonomous Boards. It has become the fashion, particularly in Great Britain, for a planning Government to seek to solve its problems by farming out different parts of its economic control to Boards which may have very wide powers in carrying on day-to-day work — such as the Coal Board or the Transport Board — or by creating organisations to exercise oversight in industries nominally still operating under free enterprise — such as the bodies to be set up under the Industrial Organisation Act. How would the plan affect these? It is sometimes argued that each Board could be given general directives and left free to operate within them. But in practice the Boards, in any one of their detailed activities, may conflict with the main plan or the detailed activities of other Boards. A very pertinent illustration has arisen in Great Britain regarding the siting of new electricity generating stations. Public discussion became so confusing and so acrid on this subject that the Chairman of the Central Board declared in December 1945 :

Today there seems to be a tendency for, perhaps, too many different planning authorities and they are planning our future from different points of view. They may be perfectly proper points of view but they are essentially different. What was wanted was . . . satisfactory machinery for dealing rapidly with any difference of views of those whose responsibility it was to plan from the point of view of economy and those whose responsibility it was to plan from the point of view of aesthetics.

If such difficulties can arise on one minor matter, it can easily be imagined that the activities of semi-autonomous Boards would create innumerable embarrassments in relation to a master plan covering all economic activities. A central plan cannot operate through semi-autonomous Boards. For so soon as such Boards exercise their autonomous powers they are likely to conflict in policy either with other Boards or the central plan itself.

To sum up. The purely logical and intellectual difficulties of running a planned economy have not yet been solved. It is not yet apparent that they can be solved. The use of a socialist price system, whilst theoretically possible, does not take us very far. There are still fundamental differences between the theoreticians as to how that price system would operate. It is far from certain that the economic rulers in a planned economy would favour the use of such a system. Even if they did, the socialist price system would probably be used for restricting, rather than maintaining, fundamental economic liberties. In the nature of things Supreme Economic Planners will be highly confident that they know what the people want and what is good for the people : their sense of duty will, therefore, lead them to usurp the individual rights of consumers. In a democracy, the procedure by which the plan is prepared and finally agreed must

tend to push the consumers' interests into the background
and to reflect, not the consumers' wishes, but the relative
dialectical skill of conflicting planners each pushing the vested
interests of a particular group. Under these conditions, if
there is a socialist price system, it will be not the impersonal
system of the competitive free economy but a price system
geared to implement the outcome of a shouting match.

Central Economic Planning is essentially Unscientific

There is one corollary of this. The idea that a central
economic plan can be drawn up with the precision or the
knowledge of ends or means that goes with (say) the building
of a bridge is false. Central economic planning cannot be
scientific. First, because the only proper target for such a
plan cannot be ascertained except through the operation of a
price system of a kind which is unacceptable to planners.
Second, because the planners must always be extremely
reluctant to admit mistakes, an attitude in itself unscientific.
Third, because in the planned economy scientifically controlled experiments in the field of industrial organisation will
always be difficult to carry out in an unbiased way. Fourth,
because in a planned economy there is no obvious objective
test of success or failure.

A central economic plan can only really have a scientific
purpose if it is designed to give the consumers what they
want and when they want it, and to provide freedom for the
consumer to decide whether he wishes to spend his money
now or in the future. But in the kind of planned economy
which is almost certain to emerge in practice, those who
possess the ultimate planning powers will have little to guide
them save their own prejudices of what others may want
or what is good for others. In extreme cases the consumer
may become simply a mechanism for the undiscriminating
absorption of the products of an industrial system which has
no rational objective but the observance of the planners'
behests.

Apart from this, the centrally planned economy is un-scientific in that those who take the final decisions must always avoid the confession of failure. For, to a politician, a public confession of failure is tantamount to political suicide. The aim must always be, therefore, to cover up mistakes at all costs.[1] A business man in a free economy must constantly submit himself to the test of the market. Unless he provides the kind of goods which the consumer wishes, then he will cease to make profits. The final test for him lies in the presence of the bankruptcy court. But there can, of course, be no such test for a statesman in whom is vested economic powers in a planned system. It is true that ultimately the planned economy may outrage public opinion and the statesman be swept out of office. But before that happens the politician will clearly strive to justify himself in public.[2] And that may be seductively easy. It is extremely difficult for the public to criticise State economic plans in any informed way. The public may feel that the shoe is pinching but the exact causes of the trouble may not be apparent. Only the State has in its possession the whole of the facts which would make a balanced judgment possible and which would enable blame to be properly placed on those responsible for mistakes. The politician, therefore, will not find it difficult to establish alibis where his plans have gone wrong. He can always argue that on particular economic matters there are many conflicting interests and that only the State can assess fairly between these conflicting interests. It will always be possible for him to point to certain acts of God, such as the failure of a harvest,

[1] Thus Mr. Shinwell, in speaking of the scheme for nationalising the Coal Industry, said on January 23, 1946, "The scheme would succeed because it must succeed".

[2] The simplest way of doing this is to make sweeping claims of success whatever the evidence. Thus Mr. Morrison on June 28, 1947, in the lull preceding the balance of payments crisis and widespread criticism of the National Coal Board and B.O.A.C., said : " It was up to both nationalisers and anti-nationalisers to show that their policies best served the public interest. We have satisfied the bulk of our fellow countrymen that our policy in this field is sound." Again, October 13, 1947, after admitting that " we are in a mess " and forecasting further grim and distasteful cuts in the standard of living, he claimed that the difficult transition from war " has been magnificently handled ".

or a strike, or the unreasonable attitude of some group in the community or of another government.   He may indeed seek to establish scapegoats.   Where the economy still contains some elements of private enterprise they would be the obvious targets for attack.   All centrally planned economies in the past have found it necessary from time to time to raise the cry of sabotage.   Or a planner who finds his schemes going astray may seek to cover up deficiencies by going further along the same road, much in the way that a clerk who has been robbing the till often finds it necessary to go from bad to worse.   For instance, if the State has nationalised the coal-mining industry and the alleged advantages of nationalisation in the way of increased efficiency, lower costs and lower prices do not eventuate, then the obvious next step is to declare that distribution costs are excessive and to move forward to the task of nationalising the distribution of coal.   There can, in brief, be no comparison whatsoever between a scientist in his laboratory objectively weighing evidence and systematically rejecting hypotheses which do not fit the facts, and a statesman committed by public utterance to a particular form of economic organisation and determined to justify his beliefs at any cost.

Indeed, under socialism, it is difficult to carry out restricted or controlled experiments in industrial organisation at all. It is true that lip-service is always paid by the socialist to the conception of controlled industrial experiments.[1]   Mr. Morrison, for instance, and other Labour Ministers in the British Government have argued that they intend to nationalise only those industries where it is clear that nationalisation will bring increased efficiency.   Where private enterprise can be assumed to be carrying out its functions reasonably well, then,

---

[1] Sir Stafford Cripps, *Democracy Alive*, p. 112, has said, " In the political, social and economic fields we need not be appalled by the uncertainty of the results of our experiments provided we enter upon them with an inquiring scientific mind rather than with a stubborn conviction that they must prove the accuracy of our theories ".   It would be interesting to know into what errors the central planners would have to fall and to what degree of poverty they would have to reduce the people of Great Britain, before Sir Stafford's stubborn conviction that central planning was the best form of economic organisation would be shaken.

according to this theory, nationalisation is not necessary. But the experience of the British Labour Government in the first years of office suggests that, in fact, no objective economic principles were being applied in choosing industries for nationalisation. The list of industries for nationalisation ran as follows : the Bank of England, Coal-mining, Iron and Steel, Cables and Wireless, Transport, Gas and Electricity, Civil Air Services. On that list are to be found industries new and old, allegedly efficient and inefficient, expanding and contracting, essentially export and essentially domestic, large scale and small scale. If there is a case for nationalising these industries, then there is a case for nationalising all industry. It seems clear that the choice was made not on economic but on political grounds. Similarly, whilst the operation of a world market in raw cotton was destroyed by the British Government by their taking over the Liverpool Cotton Market, other raw materials, such as wool and rubber, have been freed although it was impossible on economic grounds to distinguish between them. Take another illustration. There was no need on economic grounds to nationalise the whole of the British coal-mining industry at one step. It would have been much easier and much more convenient to carry out experiments in public ownership operating in one or more fields. Certain parts of the coal-mining industry were admittedly extremely efficient, others were notoriously inefficient. If the case of the Government for nationalisation was that the industry was inefficient, then it would have been sufficient for their purpose to take control of the poorer fields and determine by experiment whether any improvements could be effected through public ownership and control. That common-sense approach to the matter was clearly quite unacceptable to a Government which had already declared, despite the facts, that the whole of the industry was inefficient.

Finally, the planned economy cannot be scientific, because there is, in the long run, no way by which the public can decide whether it has succeeded or failed as a whole. To reach a conclusion on these matters would involve comparisons of some sort. The only satisfactory comparison which could be made would be, of course, that between the economic state of the community under a central plan and the economic conditions which would have existed if there had been no such plan and the free economy had been allowed to operate. In the nature of things that comparison cannot be made. The only possible comparisons are, first, that between conditions at the inception of the planned economy and conditions at some subsequent time, and, second, that between conditions in the planned economy and conditions in other parts of the world operating within a free economy. Both these comparisons, of course, are likely to lead to wrong conclusions. Nevertheless, it is significant that in all the centrally planned economies which have operated up to now the State has gone to very great trouble to falsify the progress being made and to prevent its citizens from comparing conditions within the country with conditions outside. It was perfectly logical for Russia or Germany to misinterpret the information about economic conditions in other countries and to prevent its own citizens from moving freely between its own country and other countries. For by these devices it was possible to stifle the only approximate tests that the members of the community could make regarding the success or failure of their planned economy.

The Misdirection of Production in Great Britain

Central planning is not a mature method of organising the economic system but, even at best, the benevolent but unscientific bungling of the few, striving vainly to decide for the many consumers what those consumers can only decide rationally for themselves. It is, therefore, to be expected that in the communities where attempts are made to impose a central plan there will be gross misdirection of production and widespread neglect of the needs of the consumer. That has certainly been the experience in Great Britain.

In the case of specific consumer goods, there were constant and widespread complaints in 1946 and 1947 that the things being made were not the things wanted. There were general shortages of sizes other than the average in personal articles such as clothing, boots and shoes. The need for special types of fuel adjusted to the equipment of the industrial or domestic user was widely ignored, which led to much waste of scarce resources. The principle of joint demand was neglected so that there were cups without saucers, cups without handles, lots of mugs but no vegetable dishes, egg-cups galore when there were few eggs, and so on throughout the whole range of domestic appliances.[1]

Despite the constant assertion that first things were to be produced first, it was patent to all that last things were often being produced first. Lots of trousers in the shops for women when men had the greatest difficulty in buying them.[2] The views expressed by one Labour M.P. well summarised what was obvious to all.

The amount of junk and unnecessary articles in our shops today is astonishing. On the ground floor (of one of our largest general stores in London) I found acres of floorspace and heaven knows how many assistants selling all kinds of expensive knick-knacks and all sorts of odds and ends — cigarette lighters at a guinea a time ; ladies' compacts, beautifully made ; every possible and conceivable shape of ash-tray and personal ornament.

The more general evidence of the maldistribution of economic effort was equally clear. The numerous production bottlenecks was one of the signs : a bottleneck is simply an indication that something which should not have been made has been made, and something which ought to have been made has not been made. Another sign was that although in Great Britain in 1947 there were more people at work than in 1938, and although the aggregate output had increased by 15–20 per cent, as measured by National Income figures, it was palpable that the people were worse off than

---

[1] See the debate in the House of Commons, June 26, 1947.
[2] House of Commons, July 8, 1947.

before the war. *The Economist* [1] put the point thus : " the country is producing in larger volume but the wrong things ". The correct way of looking at such a situation is to realise that producing the wrong things is not really producing at all.

The economic state of Great Britain in 1947 should have caused no surprise. The surprising thing would have been if conditions had been otherwise. For if productive resources are distributed through the decisions of a few planners, anxious to be our fathers and mothers, instead of through the expressed preferences of forty million consumers in the market, it is only by an infinitely tiny chance that the right distribution will be arrived at. It is an unscientific gamble with all the odds against success.

[1] August 16, 1947.

CHAPTER VIII

PLANNING AND PROSPERITY

If we were rich enough we would not want to have free medical services, we could pay the doctor.—MR. A. BEVAN, Labour Party Conference, 1945.

We have turned our backs on the economics of scarcity.— MR. H. MORRISON, Labour Party Conference, 1946.

Yes, I am pretty sure that we shall have a fine Autumn. There will be beautiful autumn tints of happiness in many a home and many people will say with increased conviction, " Labour gets things done ".—MR. DALTON, Labour Party Conference, 1946.

I

THE choice of the best type of economic organisation should not turn wholly on the material benefits arising from it. There are other relevant criteria : the extent to which the organisation commands the moral support of those who work in it ; the range of individual liberties it makes practicable for its members. But the poverty of the world is, and always has been, so appalling that it would be irresponsibility to ignore the crying need for a rapid increase in productive power. Without that it will be impossible, in the next one hundred years, to equip the whole world with those material things that westerners already consider the bare minimum for civilised living. Some inhabitants of those very restricted parts of the world — such as the United States and Great Britain — where there is comparative affluence, may be inclined to belittle the need for increased productivity. But in so doing they show a niggardly international attitude, for they ignore the claims of three-quarters of the globe where life is still nasty, brutish and short. Those in relative comfort in the great industrial countries who make a claim to too much leisure or who deliberately sacrifice efficient methods of production for inefficient, do so only at the expense of the less fortunate in other parts of the world.

On this question of productivity the collectivists fall into two groups. Some recognise that the free economy did deliver the goods in the past but believe that it is becoming progressively incapable of doing so in the future.[1] Others consider that the free economy might well continue to bring great material results but that the price in social and moral values is not worth while paying.

What are the facts ? In Great Britain in 1913 the ordinary person was four times as well off in real commodities as the person in the corresponding stage in the social scale at the beginning of the nineteenth century. The bulk of this advance was secured in the first part of the century.[2] In the half-century before 1913 real income per head of the occupied population increased by about 60 per cent. Between 1924 and 1937 there was a further increase of about 30 per cent in real income per head.[3] These are the bare bones of the story of economic progress in a century and a half of a free economy. With it went many other improvements in the normal lot which cannot be measured precisely in figures : a substantial reduction in weekly hours of work, a general fall in the proportion of those living below the poverty line, a steady improvement in the quality of consumer goods and services. No unbiased observer would wish to overlook the social blemishes of this turbulent period of expansion and increasing wealth. But he cannot deny the almost unbroken trend towards higher standards of living.

In the United States the progress is also spectacular — a 60 per cent increase in income per head in the thirty years before the first World War; a 20 per cent increase in the decade following this war;[4] a much more rapid reduction in hours

---

[1] This group differs in the date at which the decline of the free economy began. The Webbs date it from 1850 ; others would put it as late as 1930.
[2] Stamp, *Wealth and Taxable Capacity*, p. 95.
[3] Clark, *The Conditions of Economic Progress*, p. 83.
[4] S. Kuznets, *National Income : A Summary of Findings*, p. 32.

of work than in Great Britain. All this was bound up with swift improvements in agricultural and industrial technique [1] which almost doubled the output per man-hour in industry between 1923 and 1939, increased that in agriculture by about 40 per cent and generally made the law of diminishing returns look silly.

After 1930, indeed, there appeared to be one dark cloud on the American horizon. Economic progress seemed to have received a check, output was increasing less rapidly than population. So striking a reversal of previous trends naturally excited the interest of economists, some of whom found in it proof that the free economy was at last revealing its fundamental defect, the failure to maintain investment at a level sufficient to provide full employment and the maximum income of which the community was capable. The war temporarily set these doubts at rest. And the present position (1947) provides no foundation for pessimism of this kind. Industrial production is now about 80 per cent above the pre-war average, employment greater by 7 or 8 million workers and other indices are up in proportion. It is difficult to take seriously the theory of secular stagnation in the light of these conditions or to close one's eyes to the fact that the largest free economy has once again set the rest of the world targets to attain in the way of standards of living. For whilst on one side of the world Russia patiently plods towards its dialectical goal of a classless society in the shape of an impoverished proletariat, on the other side of the world the United States is moving swiftly towards the one-class society [2] by turning the whole community into a prosperous middle class.

[1] Arthur F. Burns, *Economic Research and the Keynesian Thinking of Our Times*.

[2] Schumpeter, *Capitalism, Socialism and Democracy*, p. 66, reaches the conclusion that " if capitalism repeated its past performance for another half-century starting with 1928, this would do away with anything that according to present standards could be called poverty, even in the lowest strata of the population, pathological cases alone excepted ".

II

In the light of this evidence of great and continuing economic achievement in the main centres of the free economy,
what solid grounds are there for the pessimism of the socialists
regarding its future potentialities ?

The overriding reason which they advance is that the free
economy has never been able to claim the respect of the
worker and can no longer enforce its iron laws of discipline
upon him. The system has ceased to be sustained by the
voluntary co-operation of the different sections of society.
In the nineteenth century, the argument runs, starvation and
fear drove men to work in factories. But the masses, with
their growing political power, have broken these whips : they
are not prepared any longer to collaborate with their former
slave-masters. The growing absence of voluntarily imposed
discipline rots the system at its roots. Socialism, with all its
works, is the only method of restoring discipline and recreating
the spirit of co-operation.[1] In the absence of it there can be
nothing but universal friction and perpetual ca' canny.

This is a spectacular and, it must be admitted, a widely
accepted view of the social processes at work. It certainly
records faithfully the view of many socialist intellectuals who
believe that they alone understand the relations between
employers and workers. And there are some cases in which
it fits the facts. For example, it had become patent by 1945
that the workers in the British coal-mining industry were not
prepared to go on working to effect unless they were granted
some measure of nationalisation. Whether their troubles really
arose from the capitalist system in which they worked and
whether these troubles will be removed by nationalisation is
another matter. But, assuming that Britain wishes the coal-
mining industry to survive and that these particular ideas
had taken hold firmly of the coal-mine workers, there was no

---

[1] See Tawney, *Acquisitive Society* ; and Webb, *Decay of Capitalist Civilisation.*

option but to experiment in nationalisation.

But how general is that attitude ?   It by no means follows from one or two illustrations that it is found universally.   If it really is universal, how has the free economy managed to produce its economic results in the past forty years ?   There are many industries in both the United States and Great Britain which have an unbroken record in the past twenty or thirty years of industrial peace, of confidence between employers and trade unionists.   Is this conceivable if the workers considered the employers as slave-masters now bereft of powers and the employers considered workers as emancipated slaves newly equipped with lethal weapons ?   Is it really irrelevant to point to numerous firms where employers and workers have a healthy respect for each other's functions or to suggest that this sense of collaboration might continue to grow throughout industry ?

Further, since the point we are discussing is that of economic efficiency, is it true that if the worker refuses to co-operate in a free economy he will automatically do so in a socialist State and a planned economy ?   If he will, why was it necessary in Russia to drive the workers on to increased efforts by terror, ballyhoo and appeal to cupidity ?   Why is it now necessary in Great Britain for Ministers to spend so much time urging the workers to work harder under nationalisation ?   Why the need of threats to push young British coal-miners into the Army who are not sufficiently assiduous ?   Why do British Ministers need to spend so much time in conducting abortive campaigns in favour of increased productivity ?

The other general argument by which it is sought to establish the superiority of a planned economy is that there are in competition certain wastes which would not exist under a plan.

There is one ' waste ' attributed to the free economy which can, for the moment, be set on one side, because what is true of the past need not be true of the future : the waste of unemployment. There are now methods available by which, within a framework of a free society, mass unemployment can be avoided. A fuller treatment of this point is given elsewhere.[1]

As regards the other charges of waste, it is important to be clear what this term means. All production, all progress, involves using up machines and materials. Ford once said that the greatest weapon in economic progress was the junk heap. Much of the ' waste ' attributed to the free economic system really represents efforts to go for long-distance results, to hurry on economic progress, to beat the clock. Thus, for instance, the ' waste ' of surplus capacity in industry may simply be a reflection of the speed at which newer and more efficient means of production are introduced. Much waste is the inevitable cost of experiment. The waste involved in the short life of many firms and the frequency of bankruptcy may be inevitable if an industry is to be kept efficient by the constant infusion of new blood and if sufficient new things are to be tried out on the consumer in order to pick a few winners which will ultimately heighten consumers' satisfaction. Much of the socialist complaint about competitive waste is as little justified as would be the complaint that thousands of different moulds are being examined and discarded in order to improve penicillin, or that researchers often must throw down the sink chemicals used in abortive experiments. The rapid, and apparently wasteful, exploitation of raw materials may well be justified if technical progress is going on rapidly enough to support the assumption that if these raw materials are not used up quickly they will become obsolete and valueless.

Other alleged wastes and weaknesses are arguable or, on closer examination, are found to be common to all systems of economic organisation. Thus it is argued that, in a free economy, there is both a private and a public sphere. Friction between these two spheres is inevitable. It is summed up by

[1] See Chapter IV.

the term *Government interference*.[1]   But is this ' waste ' any
greater than that created by friction between different
Government departments in a planned economy ?   Is not
everyone aware of the mixture of fear, exasperation and indignation with which any Government department approaches
the British Treasury ?   It is said that in the free economy
the friction between the public and private sections calls for
the work of groups of lawyers, work which would be unnecessary in a planned economy.   But is it not true that a
planned economy, in which the vested interests will work out
compromise by debate, will create a demand in every department for the lawyer type to put the case ? [2]   It is said that in a
planned economy the waste of the process of taxation would
be obviated ; taxes would vanish, since " it would clearly be
absurd for the central board to pay out incomes first and,
after having done so, to run after the recipients in order to
recover part of them ".[3]   In fact, of course, the centrally
planned economies up to date have adopted, for the purposes
of creating incentive, the most elaborate devices for giving
money to people and taking it from them again in other ways.
Moreover, if, in a socialist State, wages (ex-tax) are to be
fixed in a manner which conforms with socialist egalitarian
sentiment, it will be necessary, as Professor Schumpeter himself points out, to supplement the salaries of the higher strata
of officials by payment in kind, " official residences staffed at
public expense, allowances for official hospitality, the use of
Admiralty and other yachts, etc."   It is well known that the
administrative cost of checking the abuse of such facilities is
very heavy, perhaps heavier than the cost of taxing the same
individual.

[1] Schumpeter, *op. cit.* p. 197.
[2] One interesting instance of that was provided in the last war.   British
Government departments ranged round frantically to find statisticians when
they discovered that their case could be strengthened by the skilful deployment
of lots of figures.
[3] Schumpeter, *op. cit.* p. 199.

III

Even under the most favourable conditions, there are wastes and weaknesses in planning. The instinct of many planners to set their jaws and be prepared to pay for a planned economy in terms of increasing poverty, or to belittle the advantages of material wealth altogether, is a sound one.

There would probably be little dispute that, in the transition from a free economy to a planned system, there would be sufficient disorganisation and disruption to reduce the standard of living. For either the planned economy is introduced piecemeal or it is introduced suddenly as a whole. If the latter, then there would, at least for a time, inevitably be chaos and loss of effectiveness. If the former, then the private sector of industry becomes less efficient. No business man can foresee the future with certainty; he becomes less inclined to take risks, he refrains from embarking upon capital expenditure or changes in organisation which do not yield a quick return. He devotes a great part of his energy to so arranging his business affairs that he gains most under the Government's compensation scheme. Innumerable cases of this kind could be quoted from the experience of British industry in the first years of the Labour Government's socialisation programme. Indeed the socialist economy is, here, presented with a serious dilemma. It is often argued by socialists that the psychological moment for the introduction of socialism is when the free economy which is to be replaced is rich, ripe and prosperous : then the newly hatched chicken can live on the yolk it has already absorbed into its system. But, in practice, this will almost certainly be impossible. For a sudden and complete introduction of planning would give a shock to the system as a whole, not to mention the sabotage against the new system into which other countries might be precipitated by the sudden move. This paralysis would, in effect, prevent the revolutionaries from taking over a healthy and going concern. If the plan is introduced piecemeal, then the steady deterioration of incentive in what remains of the private sector will dissipate economic assets before they can be realised. In either case, the socialist State must take over a relatively enfeebled economy and, at least in the transition, the consumer must pay the price.

Among the long-distance wastages of the planned economy the obvious and clearly undeniable one is the cost of the bureaucracy set up to exercise control. A planned economy rightly calls for a large bureaucracy, but, in practice, the possibilities aie remote of restricting its demands for man-power to its vast and legitimate needs. Each Government department working within an integrated plan finds it needs advice on each part of the plan. It must, therefore, accumulate specialists on every conceivable subject under the sun.[1] The economic plan must not merely be drawn up, it must be enforced : the staff required for enforcement may be larger than that for preparing the plan. It is well known that, in private business, the larger the corporation the greater the proportion of administrative officials to workers. The planned economy pushes that process on much further. It is the natural inclination of any one department to double up on its staff : each director will hanker after a deputy director and so on : claims will be made for additional staff to cover the needs for holidays, for possibilities of sickness. All these are perfectly legitimate claims, difficult to resist. Meanwhile the State department controlling the employment of officials will be faced with a task of enforcing economy which, in any fair-sized country, would be insuperable. There are, for example, a million persons employed in National Government services in Great Britain, almost twice the corresponding number before the war. The task of weeding out the unnecessary officials from such a gigantic group, when no one

---

[1] The need for the ' doubling up ' of staff is particularly great where, as in Great Britain, the State hands over the operation of industries or services to Public Boards. For then the Boards must have their specialists. But the Central Government department which is ultimately responsible for the Board must also have its specialists. Otherwise its functions of maintaining general oversight of the working of the Board would become ineffective.

has any particular financial interest in weeding them out, is really hopeless. Indeed, the first step that the Treasury would have to take to try to do this would be to expand enormously its own staff. It is not an accident that all centrally planned economies find it necessary to wage steady war against bureaucracy, or that, despite such efforts, the number of Central Government officials steadily expands. There are now apparently over 800,000 economists and statisticians in Russia. And the British Government, in pursuing its policy, has been forced to tolerate over 2,000,000 workers in National and Local Government in a period of the most acute shortage of labour.

It is indeed doubtful whether serious attempts would be made to weed out the bureaucracy vigorously, for it has political advantages for the ruling powers. Each official represents a vested interest in planning : his political support can be relied upon. Each official must act with discretion and restraint in public discussion regarding the activities of the Government : free discussion is thereby blanketed.

The economic consequences of the existence of a large bureaucracy are obvious. Overhead costs are increased. Perhaps of equal importance, those overheads are in such a form that they cannot be properly or directly attributed to the specific items of production in which they are incurred.[1] Maldistribution of effort is consequently made likely. The costs of an industry fall into two parts : those incurred from the normal functions of an industry as it would operate under a free economy, and those incurred by the administration at the centre. It becomes possible to make transfers between these two sets of costs in a way which may deprive any socialist pricing system of its effectiveness.

[1] Thus Mr. Shinwell, in a reply in the House of Commons, January 25, 1946, in a question as to what the expenses of the process of nationalisation of the coal-mining industry would be and what effect they would have on the price of coal to the consumer, said : " It is not practicable at the present stage to estimate what the costs in question may amount to. The Bill provides that such costs are in general to be met out of monies provided by Parliament, and they will not, therefore, affect the price of coal in any way."

The losses associated with the essential instability of a
planned economy, even where the same planners remain in
power, are commented upon elsewhere.[1] But in the long
period two other forms of waste arising from instability are
to be expected. In the planned economy, the form and
direction of the economy are greatly influenced by the pre-
dilections of the Supreme Planners. If the personnel of the
supreme planning group changes, then disrupting and costly
changes in policy will follow.[2] Even greater dislocation is to be
expected where a socialist government, committed to planning, is replaced by a non-socialist government which favours
the free economy. So long as representative government is
maintained this possibility cannot be ruled out. Unless,
therefore, the highly undemocratic assumption is made that
the community will never change the political colour of its
government, it can expect, in the long run, to lose much
through subjection to periodical surgical operations upon its
economy. And the very possibility that these may occur will
tend to destroy confidence and the taking of long-distance
views so vital for steady economic progress.

There are other minor wastes associated with the planned
economy. It seems almost certain that technical progress
will be slower than it might be. This is not merely because a
planned economy tends to be destructive of the atmosphere
in which pure research can go on, but also because the very
size of the administrative machine, with its tendency to play
for safety, will inhibit the practical application of new
branches of knowledge. In 1907 Marshall concluded that " it
is notorious that, though departments of central and muni-
cipal governments employ many thousands of highly paid

[1] See Chapter IX.
[2] The Coalition Government in Great Britain had planned to produce a
very large number of small prefabricated houses after the end of the war. When
the Labour Party was returned to power at the end of the war Mr. Bevan, the
Minister of Health, was made responsible for housing. He attached great
importance to maintaining the standard for new housing. He was, therefore,
much less enthusiastic about the temporary prefabricated house than his pre-
decessors. The result was a muddle in the planning of such houses, much
greater than would otherwise have occurred.

servants in engineeering and other progressive industries, very few inventions of any importance are made by them, and nearly all those few are the work of men who had been thoroughly trained in free enterprise before they entered the government service ". That conclusion is still true. In the development of the internal combustion engine, the jet engine, the motor car, the aeroplane, wireless telegraphy, radar, television, domestic appliances of every kind, the design of houses and buildings, plastics, medical science, agricultural technique, the path has been blazed by independent workers, the part played by the State insignificant. In the two world wars many of the technical improvements have been forced upon the notice of an unreceptive bureaucracy, either military or civil.

A planned economy will tend to waste human effort in the holding of large stocks. The disinclination on the part of all to take risks, the elimination of the merchant, the distrust of the signals flown out to the economic system through price movements, the particularly great difficulties in obtaining statistics of stocks and of controlling stock policy : all these explain why in the centrally planned economies which have operated to date in peace-time and in the planned war economies, hoarding has been a quite ineradicable disease.

It must also waste through the uneconomic location of its production. Obsession with large units of production and the need, for political reasons, to cultivate the spectacular in economic reorganisation, will lead to the comparative neglect of the cost of such ancillary services as transport. It is not an accident that in Russia transport has always been a difficulty : that, in itself, is evidence of the break-down of the plan. Finally, of course, the ancillary services will be provided, but they remain a permanent cost incurred by the original location mistakes. In those planned economies where human beings have ceased to have rights the movement of labour to accord with the re-location of industry is a simple matter : political prisoners, the chain gang, the grant-

ing and withdrawal of ration cards, can easily settle the problem.   In communities seeking to graft a planned society
on to democratic customs, the tendency will be to ' take the
work to the worker ', in order to reduce the social costs of
transfer.   This may also lead to uneconomic production.
For those social costs cannot be measured and current location
policy becomes a game of blind-man's buff.[1]

IV

In the last analysis the answer to the question with which
we are concerned depends upon which type of economic
organisation will provide the greatest incentive to effort.
There the planners are most coy.   For although there are
vast libraries on such subjects as the constitution of the
socialist commonwealth, the preparation of plans, the enforcement of plans, planning and freedom, planning and
democracy, there is a significant absence of volumes upon
planning and incentive.

Whether, in fact, planning can evoke sufficiently powerful
incentives to enable it to match the economic results of a free
economy depends upon many physical, psychological and
even spiritual factors which are bound up with why men work
at all.   These factors are so complex and difficult to assess
that by far the wisest course would be to set on one side
general theoretical reasoning and to rely upon past experience.
Unfortunately that would involve an examination of the
Russian experiment, where apparently the spontaneous and
voluntary incentives aroused by participation in the plan have
proved so inadequate that they have had to be supplemented
by the most monstrous State dragooning of labour.   That type
of evidence, however, is not likely to affect the views of the
latter-day planners.   There is, therefore, no choice but to

[1] There seems to be little doubt, for instance, that the plans drawn up in
1946 for the modernisation of the British steel industry made such concessions
to the claims of the established centres of production that economic loss was
the inevitable result.

consumers, of two statesmen for a post of special responsibility and distinction, of two politicians for the support of the electorate — all these are normally agreeable to watch, bracing to take part in and conducive to the progress of the community.

If, however, this rivalry is to operate to maximum effect it must satisfy certain criteria. It must take place on roughly equal terms. The rivals must start level and run under roughly similar conditions. The results of the competition must confer status and reputation which is related to the character of the test. It would be futile, for example, to choose Cabinet Ministers by submitting the candidates to a 100-yards race. And the rivalry must take such a form that the maximum number of people have a chance of winning some sort of a race : otherwise interest and incentive is destroyed. This last condition is the most important. It implies that lots of different kinds of races should be run, with freedom for each person to take part in a race of his own choosing according to his interests and aptitudes.

It is not to be supposed that any free economy of which we have had experience has satisfied these conditions perfectly. Inequality of wealth has meant inequality of opportunity. Monopolies always deprive somebody of a chance to compete on equal terms. In every democracy there have, however, been great improvements in recent years, and at least it can be said that a free economy is not inherently inconsistent with the broad satisfaction of the ideal conditions.

Nor can it be doubted that a planned economy is not entirely lacking in beneficial rivalry. The worker may slave for the title of ' Hero of Socialist Toil ', the Commissar for power against his colleagues, the better to serve the socialist State.

The planned economy, however, will find it more difficult to satisfy these required conditions and will find less room for stimulating rivalry. It must exclude, openly or covertly, one group of people, the politically unreliable, from all the competitions. It must cut out a group of races, all those where men are at work with their own tools and their own property. It must limit by edict the number of entrants for each race — for the moment a plan is made to produce a given quantity of a commodity it must find some way (probably labour compulsion) of restricting the number of workers producing that commodity. Most important of all, it must so cut down the number of different types of races that most of the participants are so inherently unsuitable for that type of test that they have no opportunity of success and, therefore, no interest in the competition. In a free economy there are many ways of seeking to satisfy ambition — business, law, politics, religion, the services, medicine, the stage and so on. In Great Britain politics is perhaps the main attraction, in the United States business. But other walks of life hold out almost equal ways of gaining the respect of one's fellows. In the planned economy, ambition must be more narrowly channelled. The overwhelming preoccupation of the ambitious person is to be one of the planners, to be in a position to exercise power over others, since otherwise power will be exercised over him. The real work of the world — the patient fostering of the efficient organisation of a factory, the cultivation of craftsmanship, the extending of scientific knowledge, the teaching of the young, the healing of the sick — falls in public esteem. The glittering prizes are for those who stand above such humdrum tasks controlling the work of others. To this end attention must be devoted to skilful committee work, to steady progress upwards through the hierarchy of control. Those who find such a life disagreeable, or who find it impossible to divorce themselves sufficiently from their craft or intellectual interests to devote themselves wholeheartedly to scaling the hierarchical ladder, must be prepared to find that their own activities are controlled by others whom they consider technically and scientifically inferior. For the race must inevitably go to the weak.

Reward has a close relation to rivalry, but it touches another mainspring of effort for it leads the individual to look in upon himself rather than outwards to his neighbour. One may grow carnations to beat the man next door, one may grow them for delight in their intrinsic beauty.

No one, I fancy, would doubt that an economic system in which reward and effort were completely divorced, in which everybody received the same weekly wage, would destroy much incentive and lower the standard of living. Such an arrangement would be universally felt to be unfair, it would be considered as tantamount to an official belittling of effort. It would certainly reduce the effort of the great mass of people who are drawn on to do more work or more onerous or difficult work, by the prospect of being able, in consequence, to educate their children more adequately and surround themselves with more ample means of material satisfaction.

It by no means follows that all these rewards need come in terms of money. The respect of one's profession, whether it is expressed in the form of public declaration or not, can partly, but, I believe, not wholly, replace the money incentive. If there is to be inequality in income, reflecting the varying abilities of different people and their devotion to work, it does not follow that great inequality is necessary. The ideal arrangement, difficult as it is to establish in practice, would be one which the able and energetic members of the community, those who drive the system on, would never be paid less or more than was necessary to evoke their full efforts. Over a long period smaller income differentials than we have had in Great Britain and the United States in the past may well serve to evoke full effort.

Now the socialist is in a very difficult logical position on this question of rewards. His social philosophy is strongly based upon the principle of equality. The recent writings of socialist economists seem to provide a strong logical presumption in favour of equality in the distribution of income. But, in practice, all socialist systems seem to be driven to

accept differential economic rewards as an inevitable incentive. The range of money incomes among the wage
earners is probably greater in Russia than elsewhere. The
higher officials in a socialist State invariably draw a substantial
part of their real income from perquisites of one kind or
another. We can, therefore, safely assume that in both the
planned and the free economies some differentials in reward
will be found.

The differentials in the planned economy are, however,
likely to be less effective than in the free economy :

(a) In the planned economy the range of consumer goods
will almost inevitably be narrower than in the free economy.
The restriction of variety must reduce the attraction in
the possession and consumption of goods and, consequently, in the inclination to work to acquire them. The
socialist slogan ' bread before circuses ' illustrates this
point to perfection. The application by the State of this
principle, at first sight unexceptionable, may lead to
serious loss. If, for instance, the people who can best
make bread are not prepared to do so unless they are
allowed to attend circuses, then it may result in ' no bread
because no circuses '. Or if, for instance, those who are
interested in acting as circus performers cannot make
bread, or make it indifferently, the principle may boil
down to ' no circuses but no more bread in consequence '.
The greatest difficulty in applying the principle is, however, that one man's bread is another man's circus.
Individual tastes varying as they do, it is impossible, after
the most primitive needs have been met, to divide goods
into bread and circuses. And in seeking to do so the
planned economy will inevitably deprive the economic
system of some part of its internal driving force.

(b) In the planned economy the ownership of the means of
production by the State will rob personal possessions of
much of their interest. The commonest form of private

property is a house, a garden, household equipment. House property would probably be denied in the socialist state. But even if it is not it will no longer be possible to get small constructional changes carried out to suit one's conveniences. For the small jobbing carpenter and builder can hardly have a place in the planned state. Ownership will be deprived of some of its deepest satisfaction and may therefore be expected to provide weaker incentives.

(c) The socialist state will, at least for a time, underpay and therefore discourage the bourgeoisie — the class which is most responsible for the higher tasks of administration, organisation and research in any wealthy society. For, to the socialist, the bourgeois is the real enemy. It is hardly likely that, with the socialist state achieved, those in power will feel it incumbent upon them to reward adequately the class which the socialist has always intended to remove.[1] Ultimately, of course, this mistake may be remedied, or the socialist group may build up a ' bourgeoisie ' of its own. But the loss in the transition may well be great.

(d) More generally, the planned society will lessen the obvious connection between reward and effort and thereby reduce incentive. Under existing conditions each trade union conducts its own wage negotiations with employers. One consequence is that each worker is conscious of a certain degree of control over, and responsibility for, his own affairs. The reasons which lead him to demand higher wages or resist a wage reduction are always complex, but he is at least brought up against such questions as what the employer can afford to pay, what competition the goods in the industry must meet, etc. which are bound up with his own productivity. In a

---

[1] The penalising by the Labour Government of the middle classes, to the point at which their incentives are being seriously weakened, is already obvious in Great Britain. The crippling war rates of taxation have been maintained. House-building for the middle classes has been virtually prohibited.

planned economy, however, a planned distribution of labour is prescribed. This involves a planned national wages policy. Unless compulsion of labour is to be imposed, wage rates must be moved up and down by central action to encourage workers to move into this industry, to avoid that industry. All this would operate high up above the heads of the workers. Their responsibility for wage changes would become remote. At times they would receive windfalls, wages would be moved up because, in conformity with the plan, that industry needed to be expanded. At others, wages would be moved down to bring some necessary retraction. All this would weaken, in the mind of the worker, the connection between personal effort and reward and, thereby, weaken incentive.

Destruction of the Sense of Responsibility

The planned economy can never produce a widespread feeling of personal responsibility. It may for a time, provided the state propaganda is powerful enough, create a sense of participation in common effort, of being one of the crowd, which can be so exhilarating for the timid, the confused and the adolescent. In the long run it must deaden individual effort just as participation in any too large and too centralised an organisation will deaden it. The plan is itself an anodyne. When each has his prescribed place in a vast system, effort devoted to anything but the performance of an allotted task is futile and dangerous. The plan provides a place for every man, it breeds the feeling that far away up in the hierarchy are exceptionally able and exceptionally powerful Supreme Planners who can take the worries and carry the burdens of all. And, almost inevitably, the system moves round in a vicious circle. For the lack of a sense of responsibility weakens incentive ; the state is then called upon to try to create new incentives ranging from propaganda to the firing-squad. The propaganda may be ignored, even joked about. But safety from the firing-squad is best obtained by complete anonymity ; it is upon managers and bosses that the penalties are likely to fall. So that the average man finds it best to burrow deep down into the mass in which he can no longer be identified by character, by personality or by function.

There is no evidence to be derived, either from history or from an examination of the motives which underlie effort, to suggest that the centrally planned economy will give us greater economic wealth than the free economy. The case for the planned economy must be based on other grounds.[1]

[1] It is only fair to point out that many socialists would admit this. Thus Mr. Wilmot, Minister of Supply, is reported as saying, " as a member of the Labour Government he was first and foremost interested in the question of social justice. As Minister of Supply he was concerned with production. There was an apparent conflict between these two things. If their criterion was merely production — the amount of goods which could be produced in a given time — then the answer would be something which he regarded as profoundly anti-social " (*The Times*, September 11, 1946). Or Sir Stafford Cripps, House of Commons, June 26, 1947 : " It really is no use comparing this country with America, either before or after the war. Our standards have never been the same as those of America. We do not expect them to be so today." The point Sir Stafford misses is that the margin between the standards of living in the two countries has much widened since Great Britain became a planned economy.

CHAPTER IX

PLANNING AND ECONOMIC STABILITY

> You really cannot run a complicated modern civilisation
> on a basis where the whole machine is crazily accelerated
> for a few months and then has to swerve violently or be
> braked almost to a standstill because some perfectly foresee-
> able snag or fluctuation has not been foreseen and tackled
> in time.—MR. MORRISON, *Economic Planning*, p. 13.

I

THE causes of the growing faith throughout the world in
the benefits of a centrally directed economic system are
numerous and complex, but one is undoubtedly the belief
that only through detailed central planning can stability and
security be provided. The lure of balance and order in our
economic arrangements is proving irresistible even to many
people of deep liberal instincts who recognise some of the
social and political dangers of regimentation but who are so
desperately anxious that men should be masters of their
economic destiny that they are prepared to delegate to politicians control over the means of production and over the
freedom of consumers. They may have doubts as to
whether the State will be a competent receiver but, shudder-
ing at the bogy of chaotic competition and ignorant of the
working of the price system in a free economy, they close
their eyes and plunge for the plan.

Many writers, notably A. G. B. Fisher in his *Economic
Progress and Social Security*, have shown conclusively that
rapid economic expansion cannot be expected if the claims
for individual security are pressed unduly and that some
economic untidiness is the price we must pay for the
general gains of economic progress. The thesis of this
chapter is a rather different one. It is that the centrally

directed economy must inevitably tend to wasteful dis-
continuity and disruption in the process of production.
The outward manifestations of such waste can often be
concealed. The waste of labour need not result in open
unemployment. It may simply mean under-employment,
hoarding of labour and the performance of useless tasks. Or
it may be cloaked by imposing slavery on the individual
worker, by savagely bustling him about from one occupation
to another with little regard for his convenience, aptitudes
and inclinations. On other occasions, however, the disloca-
tions may be so great as to defy concealment. Planning
' crises ' supervene in which violent upheavals are called for
in order to ' re-balance ' the economy, and in which the
enthusiasm of the Supreme Planners to discover and punish
the scapegoats is matched only by their anxiety to find
alibis for themselves.

What does the planner mean by economic stability ?
What is it that is to be stabilised : income, prices, profits,
money wages, real wages, employment, output, the distribution of income, the technical methods of production or all or
some combination of these ? And what is implied by stability :
a complete absence of change, a constant rate of change
upwards, or simply the absence of any change which the community itself has not arranged and ordered ? One striking
paradox is evident at the outset. When the planner demands
a stable economy he is not asking for a stationary society.
He wants wealth to increase, industries to be progressive,
population and the labour force to grow. He wants rapid
change and progress as well as stability. He wants his bread
buttered on both sides. Unfortunately for him, and for the
rest of the world, the methods he proposes to employ must
prevent him from having it even on one side.

II

Why must a centrally directed economy inevitably prove
highly unstable ? First for political reasons. So long as the

community claims to be democratic then it must retain its powers to change its government. When a government pledged to planning is superseded by one which favours the free economy, the change-over will involve surgical operations on industry, the actual performance of which must weaken, and the very prospect of which must partially paralyse, the process of risk-taking and the exercise of forethought in industrial operations. The present position in Great Britain provides a good illustration of this. The Conservative Party is committed to the reversal of certain schemes of nationalisation already carried out by the Labour Government in their first term of office. The Conservatives would almost certainly be compelled, if they ultimately came back to power, to restore the free economy in those further sectors which the Labour Party has in mind for nationalisation if given a second term of office. Long-term industrial projects cannot flourish in such an environment of political uncertainty any more than can sober living among those persons who expect every day to be their last.

Even where one planning government is succeeded by another, sudden switches of policy are to be expected. For where the rival parties all subscribe to the idea of a directed economy they will compete for the claims of the electorate by offering plans with different sets of figures embodying the different views of the would-be Supreme Planners as to the correct distribution of national production between consumption and investment, home consumption and export, essential and inessential industries. The prospect is thus opened up of chaotic competition between rival plans.[1] There is no escape from such a dilemma unless one party has the courage of its convictions and, in the interests of the

---

[1] This is no fanciful suggestion. *The Times* has already declared itself in favour of it. In its leader of October 3, 1946, after declaring that laissez-faire was dead, it asserted, " if the opposition is to perform its constitutional function there must be a choice between two national plans ". And in some countries in Europe in the past two years several rival plans have competed for the support of the public.

continuity of its economic programmes, deprives the electorate of the right to change the government.

A centrally directed economy is subject to the full impact of political instabilities. But these are no more dangerous than its inherent tendency to create confusions for itself and to pass from one production crisis to another. The point can be most easily explained by considering the nature of the production programmes which, in the planned economy, must be laid down for each industry and each firm. The absence, in such a system, of the more normal incentives makes the achievement of the programme one of the main incentives — it is upon the comparison of actual output with planned output that workers and managers must be rewarded or punished. So long as the Supreme Planners are pressing for the maximum industrial production they are bound to raise all the integrated programmes of the different industries to a level which will keep the system as a whole at full stretch. The carrot must be dangled so nicely in front of the nose of the donkey that he will never lose hope of reward, but never be allowed to attain it without putting forth his maximum effort.

In a system in which there are many thousands of programmes this inevitably means that some of the programmes will not be achieved. Since they are, in any case, guesses which are just as likely to be wrong as right, and since, in addition, they are infused with a strong element of wishful thinking, only by a miracle could they all be just achieved and no more than achieved.[1] If one programme is not achieved all other programmes are thrown out of balance and waste and unemployment result. If the steel output is not achieved, then some machine tools which should have been produced cannot be made for lack of raw materials. Some labour in the machine-tool industry will then be unemployed.

---

[1] It must be borne in mind that to exceed a programme in an integrated plan is just as wasteful as to fall short of it. Just as if, when a bridge is planned, the workers on one of the piers exceed their programme and build their particular pier 5 feet higher than the other piers.

If the machine-tool programme is not achieved then some industries will be short of machine tools and their production will fall short of the target. General disequilibrium will result. If the programme for railway-wagon wheels is not reached then there will be a shortage of wagons with the consequent effect throughout industry. There are only two possible ways out of this dilemma. The first would be to change the whole of the detailed industrial programmes the moment one of them is not achieved or is recognised to be unachievable. That, however, is never practicable. For the preparation of the Master Plan is a mighty work taking much time and labour in a bureaucracy which, in the nature of things, must move slowly. The plan itself is the enemy of readjustment. The second would be to keep very large stocks so that mistakes could be rectified before crucial shortages occur. These stocks, however, would have to be stocks of everything — since no one can forecast where the planning mistakes will be made. If the mistakes could be foreseen, they could be avoided. The maintenance of such stocks is itself a confession of weakness, goods in store are temporarily lost to the community. Moreover, when technical progress is rapid, a large stocking policy may lead to sheer waste since the goods may become obsolete. But the crucial objection to stocking is that the most important factor of production, labour, cannot be stocked : unemployment means that effort is lost beyond recall. If, as a result of bad planning, labour is found to be badly distributed, either there will be under-employment or the workers must be switched around like cattle.

If the plan and all its constituent parts were capable of rapid day-to-day readjustments, original failures would be of little moment. That, it is argued above, is impossible because of the intricate nature of the plan. But even if this were theoretically possible, it would still remain impossible in practice because impending break-downs will be concealed up to the last moment and suddenly revealed only when it is too late for the economic system to turn the corner smoothly. It is characteristic of all planned economies that policy changes come as bolts from the blue.

This concealment will go on at many points in the State hierarchy. A production chief who fears that he is likely to fall short of the target set him will tend, for a time, to hope for the best. He will not wish to confess failure, with all its possible penalties, until he is quite sure of it. He may hope that something will occur at some other point in the planned economy, as for instance a failure of raw material supplies, which may provide him with a good alibi to cover the deficiencies for which he is responsible. Hope makes for confused planning and hope can never be stifled. When, however, the deficiencies can no longer be concealed from the Supreme Planners their first reaction also will be to avoid the unpopularity which comes in the train of an admission of defects in the plan and of unpleasantly disturbing upsets to workers. If, finally, the defect is too grave to be hushed up then there is a production ' crisis '. Charges of sabotage may be levelled against the production chiefs involved. They will probably be dismissed, new blood will be brought in and given a free hand to fill the gaps in production.

So long as the vast economic blunders of a centrally directed economy are not accepted for what they in fact are — the logical results of the planning process — then the remedies applied are likely to magnify the original errors. For the Supreme Planners will strive, as a first line of defence, to make a positive virtue of their failures and to welcome the economic vicissitudes to which they have exposed the people.[1] They then argue that the best way to keep the economic system moving smartly along is to adhere to the plan, watch for shortages as they arise and deal with these shortages as

---

[1] Thus Mr. Morrison, speaking on November 30, 1946, when universal shortages were already threatening a break-down of the economy, which came two months later, said, " it is not at all my view that this array of bottlenecks is a cause for gloom or discouragement. On the contrary, the fact that we see so many bottlenecks is evidence that we are expanding our economy."

quickly as possible. This is the policy popularly known as creating a vacuum, pushing hard all along the production line and hoping for the best. It explains why a planned economy is always in some sort of a crisis, why there is always a ' battle ' going on for something.[1] Special efforts are flung into the economic system at the point of weakness. This, however, can only heighten the confusion and waste of the system as a whole. For special efforts can only be efforts outside the plan, they really amount to scrapping the plan without openly admitting it. Frantic last-minute scrambles to repair the breaches naturally play havoc with the disposition of the other factors of production in the economy. The confusion is spread far and wide.

Planning crises are self-perpetuating, they set up disturbing reactions which persist over a long period. In the hysteria of combating unexpected shortages, steps will be taken which must, in the long run, be uneconomic.[2] When a shortage occurs, the tendency will be to put some new man in charge of the threatened section. He will be granted extraordinary powers for the purpose of overcoming the shortage as quickly as possible. New industrial capacity and more labour will be called for with a peak production sufficient not only to meet current requirements but also to make good past deficiencies. When these deficiencies have been met, therefore, the industry will have a potential output which is now too large for current needs. This industry must then be partially liquidated; workers who have been called upon to make special efforts in production must now be told that they

[1] We have already had ' The Battle for Coal ', ' The Battle for Output ' and ' The Battle for Dollars '. More battles are clearly in the offing.

[2] Mr. Bevan, the Minister of Health, has put this point very clearly. When his 1947 Housing Programme broke down, mainly because it was based on over-optimistic views about the supply of timber, and he was suddenly compelled to put a violent brake upon those from whom, a month before, he had been calling for a maximum effort, he made the comment, " Critics who say the programme was too big fail to appreciate that you cannot do two contradictory things at once. You cannot say to local authorities both ' Go ' and ' Stop '. Last year we said ' go ahead '. This year we say ' let us adjust the programme to the physical possibilities of the situation " (*Manchester Guardian*, May 5, 1947).

are redundant, and moved elsewhere. If the politicians jib at this unpleasant task, then unwanted goods must continue to be produced.

The constant preoccupation with day-to-day achievements and the unending and frantic struggles to make the plan work at all costs, forces everybody to think in terms of immediate results and ultimately destroys foresight.[1] Since the plan has constantly to be changed, it rapidly loses its sanction among those who bear the responsibility for carrying out the different parts of it. Each production manager keeps his eye on two things: his own performance and the chance that, if he fails to reach his own target, then the failure of some other part of the plan will provide him with a suitable alibi. Rumour and speculation as to impending changes in the plan run riot. The almost wistful hopes that sooner or later conditions will become orderly when the economic system has got ' round the corner ' are doomed to endless frustration, for the directed economy is inevitably creating corners more rapidly than they can be circumvented.

III

Recent history, particularly in Great Britain, provides many illustrations of the inner turbulence of the centrally directed economy. Between the wars many governments embarked upon restrictive practices, in the supposed interests of economic stability, which produced more disastrous fluctuations in output, prices and employment than had ever

[1] Maj.-Gen. J. R. Deane, who had a unique opportunity of watching the Russian bureaucracy at work during the war, brilliantly analyses this sense of confusion and insecurity associated with the directed economy in his *The Strange Alliance*. " The Soviet Administrative system results in waste and inefficiency. The watchful eye of the secret police promotes a feeling of personal insecurity which stifles initiative. Industry is hampered by outside interference. Charges of sabotage result from failure to meet the prescribed norms of production or from overburdening and destroying machinery in attempts to meet or exceed them. Continuity of management is lost in the upheaval of political purges and the full effectiveness of labour is lost by overtaxing its power. The urge to curry favour with those in authority and the fear of punishment induces padded reports of accomplishment and deception in covering mistakes. Immediate results are all that count, so the future suffers from lack of foresight."

been known before. If any reader doubts that, let him study the consequence of the policy of the British Government with regard to rubber, or the policy of the United States Government with regard to cotton. And anyone who had close contact with the working of the planned economies during the war will recognise the conditions summarised above : the logical and administrative futilities of a directed economy, the paralysing influence of orders and counter-orders from above, the jerks and jolts thus administered to the productive system, the waste that had necessarily to be tolerated in the form of unused resources, the sense of frustration created by the exhausting game of blind-man's buff in which one plan after another chased madly after the facts.

The most significant evidence, however, is to be found in the post-war experience of economic planning in Great Britain. There does not seem to be the slightest doubt that the Labour Ministers who came to power believed that, having equipped themselves with a few good statisticians and economists, they would be able to foresee economic events and make such timely preparations that serious economic disturbance would be avoided. Thus Mr. Morrison : [1]

When we went into the economic and financial smash of 1931 we did not know we were going there . . . because there was no proper machinery of the State to tell us, and when we got there we did not know fully what to do about it. . . . We are determined that we are not going to be caught unawares by blind economic forces under this Administration.

Clearly, there were shocks coming to those holding such naïve views about the nature of the economic system. They can be best illustrated by three major planning blunders in 1946 and 1947.

The Planning of Housing

The handling of housing exemplifies the fundamental dilemma of the planner in fixing his programmes, his anxiety

[1] Labour Party Conference, 1946.

to press forward and hold back at the same time, and the waste of resources incurred when the inevitable planning mistakes come home to roost. During 1946 the Minister of Health had resolutely refused to provide a housing programme [1] although, since the whole of the production of houses and building materials was under his control, it is difficult to understand how, without a programme, the industry knew what to do or the Minister knew how rapidly he should push forward in the training of labour for the building industry, or what claims he should make on the import programme for the import of such raw materials as timber. On January 29, 1947, the Minister published his *Housing Programme for 1947* which gave a figure of 240,000 houses to be completed in 1947. Warnings were given that the rate of building would be reduced if it proved impracticable to obtain increased imports of soft-wood timber. Then comes the vital confession, " It has not been thought right, however, to lower the estimate on account of uncertainty in regard to a single factor ". But what was happening to the other factors? Were they being programmed and pushed forward on the basis of the programme or were they not? It soon became clear that in the case of the vital factor, labour, the whole plan was falling out of phase. Less than a month after the issue of the Housing Programme, on February 21, the Government admitted in its *Economic Survey for 1947* that timber supplies would be only 75 per cent of minimum requirements. They were not yet, however, prepared to make an open confession of the implications of these facts.

It is not yet clear how far this will prevent attainment of the housing target, but the Government proposes to meet the situation if it arises by moderating the further immediate expansion of the building labour force and by taking up any slack which may develop by relaxing restrictions on work which uses little scarce material, including maintenance and repair.

[1] In the House of Commons on July 30, 1946, Mr. Bevan said, " I refuse to give a target because I am content rather to rest upon performance than promise ".

On May 8, 1947, when the industrial stoppage of February and March could be used as an effective alibi, the Minister of Health announced that " there seems now no possibility of securing this year the 240,000 houses ". There were, indeed, last-minute attempts to put a gloss on the breakdown of the plan. The Minister of Health, as late as July 28, 1947, was prepared to argue—

I resist the suggestion that has been made in some quarters that it is necessary for us to reduce our housing programme. I believe that if we did that, we would gravely jeopardise national progress. There is nothing which creates a sense of alarm and despondency more than not to see new houses springing up all over the country.

But the economic tide was running too strongly to be checked by Ministerial eloquence. The Government had at last recognised, and was to admit a few days later, that it had embarked upon a fantastically high capital investment programme which would have to be cut. Building labour, which had been the item in short supply in 1946, had now become the surplus item. As a result of the drive for building labour the force had risen to 943,000 by the end of 1946, although the target was only 970,000 for the middle of 1947. In September 1947 it was announced that the Government training schemes for building labour were to be discontinued. In October the Minister of Works was engaged in organising the transfer of building workers to other trades.

The consequences of the planning of house building therefore could, by the autumn of 1947, be summarised thus :

(1) In a period of acute general shortage of labour, waste of building labour had to be tolerated. The building force was first increased swiftly by expensive training schemes and then, having reached its peak, had immediately to be reduced.

(2) Raw materials were wasted by being embodied for abnormally long periods in semi-finished houses. Due to the failure to achieve smooth-flowing production, a sub-

stantial proportion of the houses set in hand in 1946 were destined to remain unfinished for two winters.

(3) Raw materials and labour were wasted in the building-material industries as a result of these miscalculations. As Mr. Bevan himself said :

> We are having to close down brickyards because they cannot get orders, and the reason they cannot get orders is because the rate of bricklaying is not what we are entitled to expect it to be. . . . There will be found on sites all round London, wherever one likes to look, stacks of bricks.[1]

The Fuel Crisis of February 1947

It is, however, to fuel and power to which we must turn for what will surely prove to be the classic example of a planning crisis. On February 7, 1947, late on a Friday afternoon when many members of Parliament had gone off to their constituencies and when it was far too late for the news to be spread quickly enough to enable factory managers to inform their workers, Mr. Shinwell, the Minister of Fuel and Power, announced almost as an aside to a dumbfounded House of Commons that, as from the following Monday, electricity supplies to industry were to be cut off completely in London and the South-East, the Midlands and the North-West. A Government pledged to planning and economic stability was compelled to order, at a moment's notice, the closing down of about two-thirds of British industry. At the time the Minister, clinging to his false optimism to the last, declared that the stoppage would " not last for longer than three or four days, or at the most for a week ", whilst " as regards the Lancashire area, it may be possible to avoid the cut — at any rate after the first day or so ". In the event the ban on the use of electricity lasted for about three weeks. No country has ever suffered from a more sudden or catastrophic economic seizure. Unemployment rose temporarily to over 2,000,000. The crisis probably lost Great Britain

[1] House of Commons, July 28, 1947.

£200 millions of exports.[1]   The overall loss of production
cannot be estimated with any precision.   It is sufficient
to say that Great Britain had suffered a crippling blow, the
effects of which were largely instrumental in precipitating
the balance of payments crisis suffered later in the year.

Looking back, it seems incredible that the whole system
could have been brought to a standstill in this way.   In 1946
the average weekly consumption of coal in Great Britain was
3,567,000 tons.   In the period 1935–39 the average weekly
internal consumption was 3,473,000 tons.   Yet there was no
fuel crisis, no closing down of British industry in 1935–39.
To put it in another way.   In September 1946 Mr. Shinwell
said :

> What stands between us and success this winter ?   A matter
> of 5,000,000 tons [2] of coal.   That is what all the fuss is about.

But if that was the case, why did it prove impracticable for
the national economic plan to adjust itself to such a tiny
margin?   Is it to be assumed that, under the planned regime,
if the British annual output of coal is 194 million tons, then
all is well, but that if the output is 189 million tons, then
a catastrophe of the kind suffered by Great Britain in early
1947 is inevitable and that the only rôle which then remains
for the planner is to close his eyes, wait for the crash and
then, when it comes, plead as did Mr. Shinwell that

> The Government took due warning of the position and exer-
> cised the greatest care and foresight in the preparation of a scheme
> which would ward off the difficulty.   We are not responsible for
> the weather conditions or the short fall.

The fuel crisis brought a full crop of alibis.   Some said
it was due to a shortage of coal.   Some said it was due to a
deficiency of capacity at the power plants, though it is not
easy to see how such a shortage can be ameliorated by closing down the power plants altogether.   Some said it was due

---

[1] Sir Stafford Cripps, May 4, 1947.
[2] In fact, as it proved, an extra 2 million tons of coal would have enabled us
to avoid the industrial crisis.

to the bad weather. Some said it was due to a shortage of transport. Some said it was due to the rejection by the Conservatives in 1942 of the suggestion for fuel rationing. Some said it was due to responsibility being divided among three Ministers — the Minister of Fuel and Power, the President of the Board of Trade and the Minister of Supply. Some said it was due to low output, others said it was due to bad administration. Some said it was due to sinister business men making frantic and exaggerated claims for more fuel in order to throw political discredit upon the Government. Mr. Dalton thought it was " entirely the responsibility of private enterprise in the mining industry who flitted (*i.e.* after the nationalisation of the industry) with stocks of coal lower than ever before in our history ".[1]

Undoubtedly the Government contributed to its own difficulties by permitting inflation to persist and by using the price system to stimulate instead of restrict the consumption of fuel.[2] But the proximate cause of the trouble was that Ministers gambled in the hope of avoiding measures which were politically unpopular. The warnings of a probable fuel crisis had flowed in from every quarter from the summer of 1946 onwards. Indeed the Minister of Fuel and Power himself had said, on October 24 :

Everybody knows that there is going to be a serious crisis in the coal industry — except the Minister of Fuel and Power. There is not going to be a crisis in coal, if by a crisis you mean that industrial organisation is going to be seriously dislocated.

But even the Minister of Fuel and Power really knew the facts. On January 6, 1947, he declared, " We must do the best we can, but somebody must go short ". Somebody did not go short enough because that would have been unpopular. The economy, like a ship, rudderless because of the absence of a price system, and in charge of a crew not prepared either to get the stokers to raise more steam or to put the

---

[1] *Manchester Guardian*, February 3, 1947.
[2] See p. 74 *et seq.*

passengers to the tedium of taking to the boats, went smashing helplessly on to the rocks.

The Ministers gambled, on a mild winter, on an increase in output, on voluntary austerity. Ministers will perhaps always gamble for popularity and the support of the people. But, unfortunately, in a planned economy they have it within their power to gamble not only with their own political future but with the economic fortunes and happiness of the people.

And so, in the middle of 1947, the British economy, enfeebled by the collapse earlier in the year, was still struggling with its coal crisis and still caught up in the coils of the fundamental lack of logic in a planned economy. The *Economic Survey for 1947* had laid down a target of 200 million tons of coal for the year. " Production of 200 million tons is an indispensable minimum. It will be a hard target for the miners to reach but it will meet only our minimum requirements." But no one was asking : what happens if, as seems more than likely, this target is not achieved? No planning was being done on the basis of a lower figure, for the Government could not do that without the knowledge leaking out. The very fact that the Government was prepared to conceive of that situation would of itself have been regarded as defeatism. And if a plan had been based on an output of (say) 180 million tons, that would inevitably have involved steps which would have made it the more likely that the higher target would not be achieved. So a rigid attitude had to be taken up. Two hundred million tons or bust. Great Britain cannot have a plan unless its miners produce 200 million tons of coal. It is precisely this need for pinning the whole system to one figure that turns the running of the economy into a vast speculation in which security and stability are at an end.

The Balance of Payments Crisis

The British balance of payments crisis which came to a head in Mr. Attlee's speech in the House of Commons on

August 6, 1947, could be used to illustrate many of the characteristic features of a planning crisis — how one planning crisis generates others, how Ministers will seek to minimise the consequences to the people of the sudden change of plan, how the disaster when it comes will be attributed to forces outside the control of the Government, how the failure of State authorities to use intelligently what powers they already have will lead them to take on extended powers. But it is, above all, a clear-cut example of the bolts-from-the-blue which are to be expected under central planning and of how a change from one plan to another cannot be gradual but must always be sharp and disruptive. The price system brings about gradual and continuous readjustment in a changing economic world; the central planning technique means that, from time to time, the economic system must be kicked downstairs. Mr. Dalton put the point succinctly.[1] "This storm . . . has sprung up very swiftly but it has been brewing for a long time." The storm, of course, sprang up swiftly precisely because it had been allowed to brew for a very long time.

When Mr. Attlee spoke in the House on August 6 it was in effect to announce a new economic plan. The nation, he explained, had been trying to do too much and to live at too high a standard. Capital investment would have to be reduced, imports would have to be cut (particularly of food); higher export targets would have to be set; the country would need to become more self-sufficient agriculturally, more controls would have to be imposed for carrying out the new plan.

This involved a violent reversal of old plans. And yet the old plans had to be defended and advocated in public up to the last. The contrast between Mr. Attlee's speech and those of some of his Ministers immediately before the day the plan was changed is very striking.

Mr. Attlee made it clear (August 6) that imports of food would have to be cut and more austerity imposed. But the

[1] House of Commons, August 6, 1947.

following statements had also been made on official occasions by the Ministers named within five weeks of this date.

June 30, Mr. Dalton in the House of Commons:

Whilst, therefore, we shall not be able to afford all the imports of foodstuffs for which we had hoped, H.M. Government have decided to maintain, and, indeed, in some directions slightly to increase, the volume of these imports as compared with the year which ends today. Owing to the unexpectedly large rise in prices this means that a substantially larger sum, in terms of foreign exchange, will have to be found for food imports in the next twelve months.

July 1, Mr. Strachey in the House of Commons:

There is no need whatever for the housewives or the people of this country to feel that they will find it difficult or impossible, as is sometimes suggested, to obtain, partly from at home and partly from abroad, the food they need.

July 8, Mr. Dalton in the House of Commons:

I was asked: Why did I make a statement last week at all? The answer is very short and simple. It is, that each year . . . we make an import programme to the best of our power and foresight. . . . In that sense, therefore, my statement was a routine statement. . . . I maintain that at this moment it was the right thing not to cut into our import programme.

Mr. Attlee made it clear that there would have to be a substantial cut in domestic investment.

July 3, Mr. Hall, Parliamentary Secretary to the Treasury, in the House of Commons:

We are asking every type of legitimate business to plough back its profits.

July 28, Mr. Bevan in the House of Commons:

I resist the suggestion that has been made in some quarters that it is necessary for us to reduce our housing programme.

It is easy to understand how this dilemma arises and how when a decision has finally been made and announced to the community it gives the impression of a sudden landslide which throws everything into confusion. It is more than likely that all through the summer of 1947 some Ministers believed that the programme finally outlined by Mr. Attlee on August 6 was inevitable. Other Ministers perhaps disagreed. But all Ministers necessarily continued to advocate in public the old plan. This was inevitable since, until the final decision was made, no one could be sure that the old plan would not be continued. The only alternative would have been for Ministers, in their public utterances, to admit that, for the time being, there was no plan at all, it was being argued out in Cabinet. Most members of the community would still be actively engaged in trying to carry out the old plan. At the higher levels of the Civil Service, however, there would be paralysis. For the higher civil servants would know of the growing doubts of Ministers as to the practicability of the old plan. They would naturally hold back on too vigorous a prosecution of the old plan, making it all the more certain that it could not be achieved. But they could do very little in preparation for the new plan, for this would involve inter-departmental discussions on assumptions which had not yet been accepted as Ministerial policy.

The period, therefore, preceding a change of plan will be one of stagnation among the planners. The period which follows must be one of feverish activity. The lost time has to be made up, all the implications of the new plan worked out at double-quick time. All those unsuspecting people who go to bed one night, after a conscientious day working for the fulfilment of the old plan, and who wake up in the morning to find a new plan awaiting them, will want to know immediately what precisely the new plan means to them. However energetically the planners work, these answers will not be quickly forthcoming.[1] The result is a period of stagnation now among those who are being planned. This is the period when snap decisions will be likely to lead to further gross errors in which will be sown the seeds of the next planning crisis.

---

[1] Thus Mr. Attlee announced the cuts in capital investment on August 6, 1947. The White Paper on Capital Investment was not published until December 1.

CHAPTER X

PLANNING AND FREEDOM

I

WHEN Sir Stafford Cripps declared in the House of Commons on February 28, 1946, that no country in the world has yet succeeded in carrying through a planned economy without compulsion of labour, he might, with equal truth, have gone much further and admitted that no planned economy has yet operated without suppressing free speech, destroying representative government, robbing the consumer of free choice and virtually abolishing private property. This is no accident. It cannot be attributed to fortuitous events such as the wickedness of the men in whom the economic power came to be vested or the absence of an instinct for freedom on the part of the people who were the victims of the plan. It is due to the logical incompatibility of a planned economy and freedom for the individual.[1] For the various strands of personal liberty — economic, political and social — are bound together. Weaken or destroy one and the whole rope inevitably snaps.

What are the essentials of a free society, what conditions must be satisfied if we are to be able to say that, despite anomalies and exceptions, a community has set itself upon a course which makes for the fullest expression of personality? This is the crucial question of our times to which no short answer can be given. But one thing is certain. The answer

---

[1] If Britain ever slides, by insensible degrees, into a regimented economy it will not be for lack of warnings. Professor Hayek in his *The Road to Serfdom* portrayed the connection between planning and slavery in an analysis which has never been confuted. And Mr. Churchill, in his opening broadcast in the General Election of 1946, uttered a sincere warning which was received with the same kind of indignant incredulity as his warnings, before 1939, that Germany was bent upon world domination.

cannot be given purely in terms of institutions, of administrative and representative machinery. We cannot sum up, in terms of social organisation, the arrangements which will guarantee that men shall not be slaves. A free society cannot exist unless people want to be free. Without this, the whole paraphernalia of democratic organisation becomes a dreary mockery.

We can, however, point to certain vital pre-requisites in the social machinery which must be present if failure is not to be certain and absolute. Because of its organic nature, the essence of a free community can never be fully described in terms of a simple set of rules : the conditions for success are too complicated for that. But we can say, in a negative sense, that there are some types of society in which, merely because they fail to provide certain minimum conditions, freedom would rot away however inherently liberty-loving the people in that society might be.

The fundamental forms of freedom are these :

(1) Freedom of expression in all its forms.
(2) Freedom to choose and to change the members of the governing body of the community.
(3) Freedom in the choice of occupation.
(4) Freedom in the disposal of incomes.
(5) Freedom to acquire and to hold property.

II

It is important to recognise what is meant by the last three of these, the so-called ' economic ' freedoms, for there is, in contemporary discussions, great confusion regarding their content.

Freedom in the choice of occupation means the right to make the financial sacrifices necessary to order one's working life as one wishes. It means the right to choose between work and leisure, the right to choose what work one shall do, when it shall be done, where it shall be done and for whom it shall be done. It means the right of the individual to hold on to his own assessment of the inherent worth-whileness of his work whatever valuation may be placed upon it by others. Such freedom has, of course, like all other freedoms, to be paid for. It may be that the products of the work a man chooses are not highly esteemed by the consumer, that little will be paid for them. In that case the worker has no right to insist that the consumer shall pay more. Similarly the consumer, or anyone else in the community, has no right to insist that the worker must do other work. The fundamental economic right is the right to sacrifice income either for leisure or for the advantages of working at a self-chosen occupation. It is a form of slavery to insist that a man must work ' for the sake of the community ' or that a man must be a baker, instead of a carpenter or a circus performer, in ' the interests of the nation '. For, in forcing such sacrifices upon the worker, the State is disposing of the person of the worker in a wholly arbitrary and irresponsible fashion, since the State cannot assess the values involved in the decision.

Freedom for the consumer in the disposal of his income means that the individual has the right to make an offer to other members of the community to work for him. It is the converse of the worker's right to turn to any job he thinks fit. The consumer has no right to insist that goods shall be provided for him below their cost, *i.e.* below the price at which the worker is prepared to make them. The consumer distributes his income between the different possible uses according to a set of valuations which no one else can possibly measure or balance. It must, therefore, be both unscientific, if not irrelevant and impertinent, for the State to countermand or frustrate these subtle and intangible valuations on the part of the consumer. The consumer's freedom can be infringed by a direct control over his income — *e.g.* by rationing. But it can be just as effectively, and anti-socially, restricted by so controlling the productive resources of the community that they can no longer move and adjust themselves to satisfying the consumer's declared preferences.

Freedom to own property consists partly of the right of the individual to decide when he shall spend his income and partly of his right to surround himself with durable goods best fitted, according to his own valuations, to his own personality. In a general sense this right must be all-embracing. In particular the distinction which socialists make between the ownership of personal property — clothes, furniture, houses, etc. — which they regard as harmless,[1] and ownership of property in the means of production — factories, machines, tools, taxis, barber's scissors, etc. — which they consider immoral,[2] is a distinction which is both logically meaningless and socially dangerous because it leads to policies which destroy the functions of property. The distinction between personal property and property in the means of production is logically without content. First, because some goods are both personal property and the means of production. If I own a pair of overalls or a kit of tools suitable for my work, or a set of law books, or a house and garden which provides leisure and recreation and thus increases my economic efficiency, these goods are both personal property and a part of the means of production. If an employer now provides my overalls or my tools, can it really be said that the economic system has suddenly been debauched? Second, those who own the means of production do not necessarily make a contract of service with those who use them and, in such cases, no exploitation can possibly arise. If I hire out a building or a machine to another man I am not necessarily exploiting him, he may be exploiting me. Third, contracts of service may involve exploitation although property in the means of production does not enter into the matter. Whether I make a hard bargain

[1] The Webbs, however, consider the unequal ownership of personal property as immoral. See *Decay of Capitalist Civilisation*, p. 30.
[2] Sir Stafford Cripps, *Towards Christian Democracy*, p. 53.

with a lawyer, a doctor or a private singer does not turn on who owns the means of production.

The ownership of the means of production is not necessarily an instrument of exploitation. There was slavery before machines made their appearance. The machine age indeed has, on the whole, been one in which individual freedom was lifted to new levels. A contract between two free agents involving the use by the one of the property of the other is perfectly consistent with freedom and dignity. On the other hand, the potent form of exploitation has always been that of the State where, as in the planned economy, the few have been able to use the power of government against the many.

The association of exploitation with ownership of the means of production, and hence with the employing class, has been one of the most successful red herrings employed by the socialist. For it has enabled him to avoid the unpalatable truth that, in a free economy, where monopoly is kept in check, it is the consumer who determines the contracts of service between employers and workers. The remedy for exploitation is for competition to be enforced between employers, and for the workers to use those methods which for a long time have been open to them to equalise their bargaining power with the employer. Beyond that, to argue that the consumer is exploiting the producer is tantamount to a declaration that the producer should be allowed to exploit the consumer.

The social function of property as a bulwark of freedom inheres in all forms of property. These functions have long been well understood. The institution of property is the device, and indeed the only known device, by which an individual can freely make his choice as to how he will spend his resources, when he will consume, when save. Property is the means by which the individual creates independence for himself against the powers of the State and the powers of organised opinion in the community. It is fundamentally bound up with freedom of occupation, freedom to choose between work and leisure.

Property of the type commonly known as personal property would of itself be quite inadequate to serve these important purposes. It is an unsuitable form in which to save. The essence and value of personal property to the individual lies in its peculiar adaptation to his own personality which in itself reduces its value in the market. The more exactly my suit fits me the more certain it is that it will fit no one else, that its market value will be low. Personal property, by its nature, is largely non-transferable. It is not an appropriate means whereby one can save now so that one may spend in the future. Transferable property must largely consist of land, of the means of production directly, of rights in those means in the form of shares or of State loans. If only State loans are available, to the exclusion of the first three, then the whole community is placed, as in Russia, under the direct thumb of the State, thereby destroying the atmosphere of independence by the individual without which State power must inevitably run riot.

The abolition of private ownership of the means of production would constitute the abolition of the institution of property itself, and that in turn would involve the destruction of all forms of freedom. It would wipe out the one-man show and with it the solid core of independence and nonconformity which has traditionally been bred in such surroundings, not to mention the steady flow of enterprise and variety which it has infused into the economic system. It would wipe out the merchant. It would impose cramping restrictions on those who are temperamentally attracted by the task of taking risks, organising or innovating. It would restrict all choice of occupation except that approved by the State. It would deprive people of the right to save except under conditions which make them more completely subservient to the State. And, by preventing the creation of a class with a measure of financial independence, it would

enfeeble the expression of unpopular minority views which
represent the salt and savour of any society and so often
constitute, in one generation, what comes to be accepted as
the wisdom of the following.

III

In society none of these three economic freedoms can be
absolute. It is that fact which renders so difficult and subtle
the task of creating a society which is stable and which
also gives the maximum play to individual personality. The
freedom of expression must be limited by rules regarding
obscenity and libel. The democratic choice of governors is
subject to the rule of the majority. The choice of occupation
may be legitimately restricted in the interest of the worker, as
by legislation concerning hours and conditions of work. The
consumer cannot be allowed to spend his income on proscribed goods, such as narcotics. It may be perfectly reasonable to encourage him to spend his income on desirable foods
— such as milk for children — by using subsidies. In any
case, a part of this income must be taken away by the State
in taxation to pay for public services. Property is a bundle of
rights the use of any one of which may need to be narrowed
down as to time, place and circumstance.

Here then is the baffling riddle. Individual freedom and
rules for controlling the individual are different aspects of the
same thing. Freedom for all and restraint for all are two
ways of expressing the same answer. Is there, in fact, any
solution of it? I suggest there are four working precepts that
contribute to a solution.

First, the restrictions imposed by the State on the fundamental freedoms must be strictly limited, they must be the
exceptions, they must be marginal. Each degree of restraint
imposed by the State multiplies the danger of taking a next
restrictive step. There is a critical point beyond which,
although the shadow of liberty remains, the substance has

disappeared. It is not necessary for all our actions to be centrally regulated in order to produce a degree of regimentation which is virtually absolute. If freedom of expression is permitted, except for the right to criticise the Government, that is tantamount to the complete suppression of free speech. Freedom to change the Government only once every twenty years would constitute the effective abolition of representative government. Freedom to spend one's income but only on the goods which the State has decided to produce destroys the consumer's rights completely. Freedom to choose one's occupation but only within the range prescribed by authority is slavery.

Second, negative restraints, narrowly defining what men cannot do, are less dangerous than restraints which prescribe exactly what they may do. For the former still leaves the possibility of growth and development, however contorted it may be. The latter forbids it entirely.

Third, restraints should, as far as possible, be impersonal, applying to all men of similar condition equally. Repression most swiftly springs up when some men perceive the opportunity of restricting others without being themselves subject to the rules.

Fourth, and most important for the present argument, the restriction of one of these freedoms almost invariably reduces others. The freedoms hang together, the living social tissue of which they are a part can be destroyed by an attack on them jointly or severally. It is futile to try to distinguish between them on the grounds of their essentiality. It is, in particular, vital to recognise that the economic freedoms cannot be whittled away without destroying social and political freedoms. One can begin at any point and trace through the circle of dependence.

If the State, for example, forbids someone from working as a writer — perhaps on the score that man-power is short, that first things must come first and that bakers are more urgently needed — the restriction of the choice of occupation undermines all other freedoms. The consumer is deprived of the right of reading the works of that particular author. At least one member of the community is prevented from expressing his opinions in the manner he would have chosen. Further, if the State is logical and is to enforce its restrictions, it must prevent the writer from perversely following his own bent and living upon any property he may have whilst continuing to write. This can only be done by the State drastically restricting the right to own and dispose of property. It must do its best to prevent him from gaining access to writing materials, from using the resources of the community in publishing his work once it has been written.

It is just as dangerous to cramp the choice of occupation of the carpenter, the mechanic, the jockey, the football-pool operator, the small shopkeeper. Directly or indirectly the freedom of choice of work is bound up with freedom of expression, freedom for the consumer, freedom for the holder of property.

The same vicious circle of restriction is created where the State makes its immediate attack on the consumer — by laying down social priorities which declare that certain goods shall not be made until certain other goods are produced. This may seem at first sight unexceptionable. But it involves the State in matters of definition and enforcement which will throw their shadow across every aspect of social living.

This then is the reason why the free society always appears so precarious, so pitifully defenceless against the inroads of tyranny. Its position can be assaulted, sapped or undermined from any angle. It can be destroyed simply by denying free speech or by forbidding representative government or by an authoritarian distribution of workers between jobs, or by regimenting the consumer or by abolishing private property. It can be defended only by a robust defence at every point of the precious minimum circle of individual rights.

IV

The planned and centrally directed economy must inevitably undermine the economic freedoms and, with them, the whole fabric of a free society.

Freedom of Occupation

If there is a plan in the sense of a closely integrated set of controls to bring about a predetermined economic end, then clearly there must be no recalcitrant element. For that would upset the whole of the plan. Labour is one of the resources which must be forced to fit into the scheme as a whole. Some forms of State restriction, such as those on raw materials, on consumer's income, on the use of property, can often be imposed without creating, at least at the outset, the sense of servitude. But direction of labour is one control which, to most minds, stands out so grossly as slavery that the battle for freedom will probably be lost or won at this point. It is not, of course, true that a society is free so long as there is, legally, no direction of labour. Other forms of coercion may render the legal freedom of the worker meaningless. But if the worker is told what to do and when to do it, then clearly nothing remains to defend.

Now direction of labour is inevitably bound up with a plan courageously followed to its logical conclusion. How powerful are the forces driving in that direction can be well exemplified by the story of how the British planners, against all their best instincts, were driven to the restoration of conscription of labour in 1947.

At that time, largely due to the Plan, labour was seriously maldistributed in the sense that consumers were being offered the goods of one type of industry — notably engineering — when they would have much preferred the goods of other industries — such as the textile industries. This problem was variously, and misleadingly, described as ' the problem of the undermanned industries ' or ' the problem of

the overall shortage of man-power '. The fantastic position
in which the economic system was making the wrong things
was clear to everybody. It was also clear that redistribution of
labour was required to avoid the enormous real economic
waste involved. What was to be done about it?

Every route appeared to be blocked. Mr. Attlee, than
whom there could be no sturdier democrat, tried to find his
way out of the dilemma by making a moral appeal, by throw-
ing the insoluble problem back on the worker. In a broadcast
appeal to the nation on March 18, 1947, he said:

> Ask yourself whether you are doing the kind of work which
> the nation needs in view of the shortage of labour. Your job
> may bring you in more money but be quite useless to the com-
> munity. You may complain of the shortage of coal or houses . . .
> towels and underclothing . . . but have you any right to com-
> plain if you are content to do some better-paid but quite useless
> work?

But, clearly, to ask the individual to decide what is socially
useful work, outside the price system, leads straight to chaos.
In the event few, if any, members of the public seem to have
taken any notice of the appeal. It is clear also that some
members of the Government were in favour of a ' national '
wage policy, that is central control of wage rates by the State
in order to create the necessary attraction towards the undermanned industries without increasing the existing inflationary
pressure. It was never clear just how that policy could have
been operated. But, in any case, the trade unions were firmly
opposed to any domination of their functions in the sphere of
wage-fixing whether this meant direction of labour or not.[1]

At the beginning of 1947 no public figure would have
dared to declare himself in favour of labour conscription in
peace-time. By the autumn of that year it was the law of the

---

[1] Thus Mr. Deakin, Secretary of the Transport and General Workers'
Union, said at the Annual Conference on July 15, 1947, " trade unions must
be ready to accept a limited measure of direction to meet the nation's pressing
economic needs ". At the Labour Conference earlier in the year he said, " under
no circumstances is the regulation of wages a matter for the Government. The
people that I represent are not prepared to play second fiddle."

land that (with the exception of a small proportion of the working population) no man between the ages of 18 and 50 years and no woman between the ages of 18 and 40 years could change his or her occupation at will. Every such change had to be registered at the Employment Exchange, and the Minister of Labour had the power to direct workers changing their jobs to the employment he considered best in the national interest.

It is extremely significant, and indeed sinister, to watch how, by the logic of events, the ardent planner, still retaining his respect for individual freedom acquired from his up-bringing in another type of society, was driven to hedge, to temporise, to qualify and finally to capitulate before the inexorable demands of the Plan. This can, perhaps, best be seen through the speeches of Sir Stafford Cripps.

In February 1946 he had said :

Our objective is to carry through a planned economy without compulsion of labour.

In the debate in the House of Commons on the *Economic Survey for 1947* in March 1947, when the fuel crisis had given us a foretaste of what was to come, he had said :

We are attempting to make a success of democratic planning and, save for emergency measures such as are necessitated by war, *or may be necessitated by some urgent economic crisis*, we have decided not to employ, *as a normal matter*, methods of direction or compulsion of man-power outside the necessities of defence. (My italics.)

On August 7, 1947, during the debate on the State of the Nation, and one day after Mr. Attlee had indicated that it was intended to resume powers of direction of labour, Sir Stafford made this statement :

It has been decided to stop, by negative control, further people from going into the less necessary industries. If, at some future date, further and more stringent measures become necessary, we can then consider the question of the direction of labour, but my right hon. friend the Prime Minister said it was only in a marginal case connected with the negative control that that power might possibly be used under existing circumstances, not as a general proposition.

On September 12, 1947, still refusing to face the fact that the Government had been forced to choose between planning and freedom of occupation and had plumped for planning, he said:

We do not propose to introduce industrial conscription unless it is proved there is no other way out.

Attempts were made to minimise the significance of what had happened. The power of direction was to be employed ' to a limited extent '. The control was to be ' negative ' and ' marginal '. Direction was not to be used as ' an instrument in itself '. It was argued that we had never really been without direction of labour because, in the past, it had come through starvation.[1]

The barriers, however, were down. For the first time Great Britain had accepted labour conscription in time of peace. It was evident from the start that if the direction of labour was ' limited ' then it would not serve the purpose of the Plan. Although it had been indicated that workers would not be expected to leave jobs they were already in, Mr. Isaacs, by the middle of September, was saying:

If more extensive direction were found necessary, the Government would not hesitate to use it.

Although it had originally been understood that workers would not be moved from their own districts, it was soon announced that single men and women and married men ' in special cases ' would be liable to be sent away from home. Although it had been originally stated that direction would be applied only to unemployed persons refusing to take essential work, it quickly became evident that the Government intended to take full advantage of its slightly nauseating campaign against ' spivs and drones ' by including within this term

[1] Mr. Bevin, addressing the Trade Union Congress on September 3, 1947.

workers who were making ' no contribution to the national well-being ' as well as persons not gainfully employed who were capable of work.

So long as the aim is a planned economy there can be no doubt of the trend of social pressures : it will be towards a progressive restriction in the choice of occupation. The path can be cleared by very obvious devices : by imposing additional restrictions during the periodic planning crises when sacrifices can be called for in the national interest ; by claiming that the control will be applied sympathetically ; by falling severely on the less well-organised workers who cannot resist effectively ; by running heresy hunts against the ' drones ' in society who happen to be doing jobs of which the State does not approve ; by public belittlement of some kinds of work as against others.

This further narrows the circle of choice of occupation, which is, in any case, inevitably restricted with growing socialisation. For, as the bureaucracy grows, the economic horizon for the individual is cut down. What remains of private enterprise is under a cloud. The big opportunities are to be found as administrators in the State organisation.

It is safer to be a bureaucrat than a maker, and the young men know it. As the ceiling of opportunity comes down, they will be forced to stoop lower and lower over their official desks to think of nothing but their subordination. It takes the heart out of young men, and out of every woman who runs a home and not an office. It is not only politically false but morally destructive.[1]

The Freedom of the Consumer

It has already been indicated[2] that the free consumer will always stand between the planned economy and the achievement of its targets, and that every planned economy has called for sacrifices on the part of the consumer and has used up no little part of the resources of the community in devising ways of curbing the total and minimising the variety of consumer

[1] Charles Morgan, *Sunday Times*, July 7, 1946.
[2] See Chapter VI.

goods. The real economic waste of a system in which goods
are not being produced in the proportions in which consumers
would freely choose to buy them can never be measured.
But it may be enormous and it is likely to grow. For the
longer the system operates without consulting the consumer
the more at sea the whole economy becomes. In the early
stages of a planned economy the pre-plan preferences of the
consumer act as some sort of rational guide, but, gradually,
this indicator loses its validity.

The curbing of the consumer carries with it threats to
other forms of freedom. For when the shortages become so
acute that they cannot be wholly denied, opportunities are
provided for that strident State propaganda which is so un-
pleasing a feature of the planned economy. The propaganda
may be employed for the relatively innocuous purpose of
extolling the virtues of austerity. But it must mainly be
devoted to identifying and denouncing the enemies who are
threatening national survival. The culprit may be the person
who asks for something different from the standardised
article ; [1] this helps to condition the public to the belief that
to be different is to be wrong. Or the culprit may be found in
the people of another country [2] who are blamed for eating too
much, or for not being generous enough, or for letting their
prices rise too high, and so on. This helps to deaden the sense
of individual responsibility without which respect for the
rights of others is impossible.

If the consumer is to have only limited rights in the home
market, then he must be carefully watched and controlled if
he attempts to travel to countries where the consumer is
permitted the license of spending what income he has on

[1] Thus the Parliamentary Secretary to the Ministry of Food declared on
February 25, 1947, when urged to provide a greater variety of cheese, " the
function of the Ministry of Food is not to pander to an acquired taste but to
ensure that people who have never had the time to acquire these tastes are
suitably fed ".

[2] Thus in 1947 a very large number of people in Great Britain (which had
within the previous eighteen months spent £1000 millions loaned by the
United States) sincerely believed that their troubles were largely due to the
actions of the American people.

what goods he wishes. Such travellers may bring back to the home country stories which throw doubts on the case for planned production. So that exchange restrictions, currency controls, postal censorship and elaborate passport arrangements became a normal part of the planned system.

The Destruction of Free Enterprise

In some planned economies an attempt is made, at least for a period, to retain some of the value of free economic enterprise by leaving a certain field open for such enterprise. In Great Britain, for example, the Labour Government declared its intention of leaving 80 per cent of the economy ' free '.[1] This, in itself, was proof that the Government did not understand what constitutes a free economy. Free enterprise is impossible where the State controls certain fundamental processes. Thus it can control the whole economy through the control of investment, or the control of imports, or the control of coal, or the control of transport. Even where it actually owns no industry it can destroy the operation of free enterprise by a set of controls which purport to replace the price system.[2] In a ' mixed ' economy of this kind each industry will necessarily organise itself to fulfil the general orders of the Government; monopoly must be the order of the day. Moreover, the constant threat of impending nationalisation will not only destroy incentive and lead to a failure to take risks. It will also result in policies being pushed upon industries which they recognise as uneconomical and which they accept under duress of one kind or another. Once the productive processes and their organisation become, in this way, irrational to the managers, then cynicism and indifference creep in. A striking illustration of this is provided by the policy of the British Government in seeking to force the Lancashire spinning industry to form very large amal-

[1] See M. Young, *Labour's Plan for Plenty*, p. 81.
[2] Anyone interested in a detailed account of the manner of operating one such ' free ' industry should read a letter, ' Chocolate Circus ', in *The Economist*, August 9, 1947.

gamations. In the innumerable public and private enquiries which have been made into that industry there has never been any shred of evidence put forward to support the claim that large amalgamations have any advantage over spinning mills of about 100,000 spindles. The Cotton Working Party was unable to discover any such advantages, and indeed one-half of the members of the Working Party set forth sound reasons why the amalgamations might well be less efficient.[1] Despite this the Government sought to impose amalgamation on the industry by offering large subsidies to them and by granting to them priorities for the delivery of new machinery. Even these bribes were insufficient to lead the greater part of the industry to adopt methods of organisation which it knew to be uneconomical.

The Destruction of Independent Thought and Criticism

In the long run the planned economy destroys the independent habits and attitudes through which alone freedom can be preserved. As private property diminishes in importance through penal taxation, the lowering of the rate of interest and the growing relative importance of State property, fewer and fewer people are in the independent position in which they can fearlessly criticise Government policy without risking their livelihood and the security of their family. The number of people grows whose incomes wholly or partly depend upon keeping their mouths shut and their thoughts private. The planned economy always involves a great increase in the number of Government officials who can hardly criticise their employer without risking their chances of promotion.[2] Business men operating in what is left of the

[1] See Cotton Working Party Report, p. 220.
[2] In January 1947 the General Manager of the North-Eastern Division of the National Coal Board sent out instructions that, in regard to their officials, " all council work such as R.D.C., D.C., etc., must cease within three months from today ". Only as a result of public outcry was an undertaking extracted from the Government that " the vast majority of those employed in nationalised industries will be as free as those employed in other industries to participate without restriction in political activities whether national or local ". Mr.

free economy know only too well that there are innumerable ways in which outspoken critics of official muddles can be penalised. They may tell in private their stories of planning inefficiency but, in self-defence, they dare go no further.[1] And some professional classes, such as accountants and lawyers, often stand to gain, at least for a time, out of the conditions which exist under extensive Government intervention.

Independence is further undermined by the deliberate destruction or the progressive atrophy of voluntary organisations and associations. These forms of co-operation are not ' plannable instruments ' and must, therefore, be frowned upon in the planned system. Voluntary associations are the life-blood of free society ; they have in the past led to much of our progress in education, social insurance and health services because they have left the way open for groups of like-minded people to experiment with new ideas and to criticise existing methods by showing the way to do better.[2] They are hardly likely to survive in an environment in which it is assumed that the State has taken upon itself the responsibility, often to the deliberate exclusion of private effort, for all social services.

The planned economy must finally destroy the very instruments of free speech. The burden thrown upon the legislature by the enormous mass of work involved in a planned economy inevitably drives the executive to restrict the freedom of debate in the Houses of Representatives.[3]

Shinwell had been guilty of the following outburst, " I am bound to say that for a mine manager to contest a seat in the Tory interest against a Labour man in a mining constituency is a first-class piece of impudence " (*Sunday Times*, February 2, 1947).

[1] There was an interesting discussion in the House of Commons on June 23, 1947, as to whether officials of electricity supply companies who had opposed nationalisation would be eligible for posts in the industry after nationalisation. Mr. Shinwell, on that occasion, said, " I say quite frankly that . . . if I have to appoint electricity boards it would be quite improper to appoint to such boards a person who was definitely opposed to the nationalisation of the industry ".

[2] See Braithwaite, *The Voluntary Citizen.*

[3] The classic instance is the manner in which the Transport Bill was rushed through the House of Commons.

When resources have to be allocated between rival uses, the claims of the instruments of free speech will be relegated to second or third place.[1] Harassed by the interminable complexities of their own system, the planners must finally be driven, in order to keep economic life in operation at all, to cut through their knots by making arbitrary decisions and stifling unwelcome criticism.

Perhaps, however, for the mass of the people the whole atmosphere of independence and freedom is most insidiously destroyed by the proliferation of minor officials, essential for the working of the plan, each of whom is charged with certain powers over our everyday actions. These officials are no better or worse than any of us. Most of them may be conscientiously anxious to carry out their duties and to use their powers with discretion and understanding. But the system which brings them into existence is dangerous. They are conscious of their power, they (and those who are subject to them) recognise the inconvenience of recourse to appeal against the exercise of that power. These are the conditions which may multiply petty tyranny of the most obnoxious kind. The network of power may extend quietly without it being remarked. The Prime Minister revealed in February 1947 that seventeen Ministries have power to authorise inspections involving the entry into private houses and premises without a search warrant. It later was admitted that 10,916 Government officials were authorised to carry out inspections and investigations without a search warrant.[2] The ' snooping ' called for in enforcing regulations leads to the creation of a new body of plain-clothed police whose work may differ little from that of the *agent provocateur*.[3] This is

---

[1] During the fuel crisis of early 1947 Mr. Shinwell forbade the publication of periodicals even though, as it emerged subsequently, he had no power to do so. During the growing economic crisis over the balance of payments in the middle of 1947 the first really serious cut in imports was made in newsprint.

[2] House of Commons, March 11, 1947.

[3] The *Evening News* reported such a case on December 31, 1946 :

Mr. John Flowers, K.C., defending at East Sussex Quarter Sessions, Lewes, a Hove restaurant proprietor accused of supplying meals over the five-the sordid atmosphere which breeds the anonymous informer and everywhere sets one man against another.[1]

V

The modern planning movement sets out, with good will and noble intentions, to control things and invariably ends up by controlling men.

It is precisely because the centrally directed economy breeds crises that it always brings about a continuous narrowing of the rights of the individual. The errors in the plan and the mistakes of the planners can be covered up if they can be disguised as natural misfortunes, which strong nations should meet manfully by accepting lower standards of living and more personal restrictions. It often arises, therefore, that economic disasters which are themselves due to the absence of individual economic initiative result in even tighter State control and less room for such initiative. There is no end to this process of seeking to cure the evils of planning by more planning except a totalitarian economy of the Russian type.

Such a prospect is terrifying unless one believes in the

shilling maximum, submitted that it was a shocking thing that people employed by the Government should go into restaurants and deliberately attempt to bring about an offence. . . .

He was commenting on the fact that a Food Ministry enforcement officer, Henry James Reed, and a Miss Dickerson, his typist, went into Tommy Tucker's Larder at Hove, on June 25th, and ordered meals costing a total of 14 shillings.

Reed agreed that he had tried to get the restaurant people to go over the five shillings. When he asked the waitress, Mrs. Pelham, for trifle, she said : " I'm not supposed to, but I'll try to get you one."

Mr. Flowers : " Did it occur to you to say ' If you are not supposed to, don't ' ? " — " No."

Mrs. Pelham said Reed pestered her for trifle and she got one to get rid of him.

At Carmarthen on December 30th Mr. Lewis was fined £2 for buying rabbits at a price exceeding the maximum. The divisional enforcement officer of the Ministry of Food admitted that, on the instructions of the Ministry, he had taken a dozen rabbits to the market. The defendant approached him and offered and paid him 2s. 6d. each for the rabbits. (*The Times*, December 31, 1946.)

[1] The Board of Trade receives 200 anonymous letters monthly about rationing offences being committed by named individuals. The corresponding figure for the Ministry of Food does not seem to have been made public.

creation of a society in which the economic status and functions of the individual are determined by the State. And there are people who would argue that the economic freedoms are unimportant and are not wanted. They may be right. But the evidence is still strongly against them. The Army provides security, status and an opportunity of service, but when, in peace-time, did men flock in unlimited numbers voluntarily into the forces? Can there ever have been a more costly and futile experiment than that of the ' Bevin ' boys, an attempt to apply war-time conscription in the coal-mines, with its absenteeism and wholesale desertions? There would be one way to test the truth of this monstrous slander on the human race. It would be to throw open the frontiers of all countries and to observe whether the movement of population was outwards from or towards the totalitarian States.[1] Until we are quite sure that people would flock away from the countries which provided opportunities for economic independence we must go on believing that people can only be deprived of their freedom, either by their own intellectual errors concerning the economic organisation of society, or through the deceptions of their rulers.

[1] It is not without significance that in August 1947, according to a statement by Mr. Churchill, half a million British people had applied to emigrate to the Dominions, and several hundred thousand more wanted to go to the United States or South America.

CHAPTER XI

THE MORAL SICKNESS OF A PLANNED SOCIETY

> The prime principle of the Socialism for which we stand
> lies not in the methods of organisation of our society
> that we adopt but in the high purpose at which we aim.
> SIR STAFFORD CRIPPS, *Democracy Alive.*

SOCIALISTS have always held that, apart from its other
deficiencies, the market economy is fundamentally immoral.
The profit motive, it is argued, is unchristian since it breeds
selfishness, acquisitiveness and the idolatry of wealth. Inequality of income divides communities into non-sympathetic
classes and leads to exploitation. Competition puts a premium
upon dishonesty and deception and forces producers to make
shoddy and adulterated goods. The growth of big business
debauches public life and corrupts the legislature. The
ostentatious display of wealth by the rich destroys taste and
judgment in the arts. The rich become a ruling class to whom
the rest are subject through economic necessity.[1] The in-
justices which men create for themselves can only be removed
by the State, " which is, in fact, accepted as the nearest we
can get to an impartial judge in any matter ".[2]

Now the centrally directed economy is the ultimate
manifestation of State activity. Does the experience of
planning in Great Britain suggest that this form of economic
organisation stimulates the life of the spirit and fosters those
simple, upright human associations which are universally
regarded as the test of civilised living?

---

[1] Those who feel that this summary of the socialist attitude is overdrawn
should read the Webbs' *The Decay of Capitalist Civilisation* ; R. H. Tawney,
The Sickness of an Acquisitive Society ; Sir Stafford Cripps, *Towards Christian
Democracy.*
[2] Sir Stafford Cripps, *Towards Christian Democracy*, p. 55.

The answer can be given very briefly. Since 1945 the Supreme Planners have been increasingly engaged in searching for alibis, in hunting for scapegoats and in trailing red herrings. The public have increasingly devoted themselves to the evasion of the law and to operations upon the black markets. Contempt for authority has increased; class consciousness has become more acute; cynicism regarding corruption in public life more prevalent; personal and class irresponsibility more in evidence; gambling practices more widespread. Liberal society in all its aspects is being eaten away.

This, of course, is not the fault of any individual or group of individuals. It is the fault of an economic system which multiplies unenforceable laws and hence the opportunities of breaking them, and which places upon the materialistic conception of life so great an importance that the spiritual values are weakened or stamped out. Under it, men of integrity and good will may just as easily be dragged down to lower moral standards as are the crooks and the law-breakers.

Alibis, Scapegoats and Red Herrings

In the centrally directed economy the Supreme Planners take the crucial economic decisions; they must, therefore, take responsibility for the consequences of those decisions. They will be inclined to put the best possible gloss upon their economic achievements and, since they alone are in the possession of all the facts, this is not a difficult matter. But when the inevitable mistakes are made they will be tempted to conceal their errors, or to attribute them to forces over which no one can have control or to ascribe them to the wrongdoing of others. On such occasions the public, lost in the labyrinth of highly technical questions and confused by masses of statistics, is robbed of the power to judge either of the competence of the planners or of the efficiency of the system they are trying to operate.

British experience since 1945 provides many illustrations

of attempts on the part of planners to shift from their own shoulders the blame which rightly belongs there. The discussion in late 1946 and early 1947 on the consumption of food is an excellent example of the attempt to confuse the issue. In May 1946 Sir Ben Smith [1] said frankly :

The food situation [of 1939–44] prevails substantially today and its continuance imposes an increasing strain on the patience and the good will of the public.

On November 13, 1946, Mr. Dalton [2] made this striking statement :

Most of our people (my italics) are better fed under present rationing than before the war under Tory rule.

Mr. Attlee had, on November 12, 1946, made a similar statement :

Broadly speaking, the mass of the people (my italics) are better fed than in the days of peace.

These statements raised a storm of protest among the public, who were acutely conscious, whatever might be said about their calorie intake, that they were short of nearly all the more appetising and popular staple foods and that they were compelled to meet their physical needs by filling up with larger quantities of the bulky and less attractive cereal foodstuffs. The Government were finally forced to moderate their claims to Mr. Strachey's statement on February 25, 1947, that—

The bottom third of the population (my italics) is better fed now than before the war.

The truth was that, before the war, about one-third of the population was below the ' poverty-line ' standard of food consumption and two-thirds at or above that standard. In 1946 the whole of the population was at the poverty-line standard : one-third had gained, two-thirds had suffered. Mr. Strachey, even whilst ultimately admitting this, sought

---

[1] *How Britain Was Fed in War-Time.*
[2] In a lecture before the Fabian Society.

to evade the issue by declaring that even if the people had not sufficient food they had plenty of money : [1]

It was a splendid thing that the British people for the first time were getting enough money to buy all the food they ought to have.

In brief, the Government, finding it impossible to boast about the supplies of food, sought to confuse the issue by boasting that they had allowed an inflationary position to develop.

The fuel crisis in the winter of 1947 also produced its crop of alibis. For a time in 1946 the shortages of heat, light and power had been met by declaring that " people were getting more coal now and will get more coal during the winter than they got before the war. One of the reasons, strangely enough, is that they can afford to buy it." [2] Fears that a real shortage of coal would develop and affect electricity supplies were brushed aside. " The shortage of coal had nothing to do with the interruption of electricity supplies." [3] When the crash came early in 1947 and the power stations and industry had to be closed down, Ministers dodged about from one explanation to another as it fitted their purpose : the bad weather, the shortage of coal, the inadequacy of the equipment of the power stations, limited transport facilities, the plentiful purchasing power of the public, the earlier mis-doings of private enterprise. Later Mr. Dalton sought to lay part of the blame on the whole community. The breakdown of the electricity supply had been made the more certain by the failure of the plan to check the rapid growth in production of electric fires. Mr. Dalton had contributed to this by taking the Purchase Tax off them in his 1946 Budget. In his 1947 Budget he re-imposed the tax and said : [4]

The gift of foresight is sometimes denied, not only to Ministers of the Crown and Members of Parliament but to the whole

---

[1] October 16, 1946.
[2] Mr. Shinwell, September 15, 1946.
[3] Mr. Shinwell, October 28, 1946.
[4] House of Commons, April 15, 1947.

community. . . . It is quite clear we were all wrong — all of us — about these electrical appliances.

As the errors of the planned economy piled up, and the balance of payments crisis of August 1947 supervened, the excuses widened. Planning apologists argued that our troubles were due to two hundred years of Tory misrule, to the loss of man-power during the war of 1914–18, to the failure to raise the school-leaving age and to reorganise industry between the wars, to the economic policy pursued between 1919 and 1939. The Government in the debate on the State of the Nation on August 6 and August 7 explained the crisis on four grounds.

First, without openly saying so, they sought to lay blame upon the United States. The rise in prices in America had reduced the value of the loan, but no one mentioned that when the loan had been granted all socialists believed that the United States, with its unplanned economy, was certain to go into a depression with a consequent fall in prices. There was a universal ' dollar starvation ', but no Minister pointed out that this was not due to any backsliding on the part of the Americans but simply to the desire of other countries to buy from the United States more than they could really afford to buy.

Second, they pleaded the serious consequences to the British economy of the fuel crisis earlier in the year. This is the first recorded attempt to explain away one planning crisis by reference to an earlier crisis.

Third, they made what they appear to believe is an entirely novel discovery about the place of Great Britain in the world economy. Our position from 1914 onwards, by which we exported manufactured goods and imported food and raw materials, was ' artificial '.[1] Something mysterious had gone wrong with the ' balance ' between the Old World and the New.

[1] Mr. Attlee.

The world dollar-shortage is fundamentally a problem of under-productivity outside the Western Hemisphere. . . . The only permanent remedy is the restoration of the balance between production in the Old World and production in the New.[1]

This Government had at last probed to the heart of things.

The economic relationships of the world have vastly changed since before the first world war. . . . On the present basis of world production and consumption there is a balance of production in the United States of 12–13 billion dollars a year which must, however, be transferred somehow to the rest of the world. . . .[2]

The truth up to now had been concealed from us.

The period of living on our 19th-century investments is over. . . . This fundamental change in conditions of our national life has been cloaked in recent years by many factors.[3]

It is almost impossible to disentangle this appalling jumble of false statistics, inaccurate economic history and bad economics by which tired Ministers, worn out in the pursuit of their unattainable aim of planning the economy, sought in a new crisis to convince themselves and others that what had happened could not be laid at their door. But it will suffice to make three comments. The loss of British overseas investment was not the cause of the economic malaise. Great Britain has not disposed of the whole of her investments. In 1946 the income from overseas investment was £150 millions; in 1938 it was £205 millions. The difference of £55 millions is insignificant in relation to the real difficulties of the nation. It is not true that it is artificial for a country to live by selling some things and buying others. This is precisely how everybody in the world does live. It is not true that there are any special difficulties involved in poor countries trading with rich, this kind of international trade went on throughout the nineteenth century. It was the basis of the industrial emergence of Great Britain and of the benefits which our free trade policy brought to the world.

[1] Mr. Attlee.   [2] Sir Stafford Cripps.   [3] Mr. Dalton.

Prevarication may be the first line of defence of the planner but it is rarely regarded as sufficient in itself, and planned economies have always resulted in much talk of sabotage by which the war can be carried into the enemies' camp. It is beginning in Great Britain. Mr. Shinwell has accused the mine-owners of a lack of patriotism.[1] Mr. Bevan has indicted the private house builders for his own failures.[2] Mr. Morrison[3] and Mr. Shinwell[4] have not even scrupled to impugn the patriotism of Mr. Churchill. Sir Hartley Shawcross attacked the Housewives League because they expressed dismay at " the collapse of our standard of living ". These " were not the women of Great Britain at all ".[5] Sir Stafford Cripps described their activities as " unpatriotic propaganda ".[6]

But perhaps the most sinister manifestation of this defensive head-hunting was the hysterical drive that was made in the middle of 1947 against ' spivs and drones '. The Government declared that increasing war was to be waged upon these enemies of society.[7] No one quite knew who or what they were except that they frequented the Riviera, Ascot or Soho, and got their photographs in the *Tatler and Bystander*.[8] So elusive, indeed, was the concept that Mr. Isaacs described them as ' eels and butterflies '.[9] This was a hunt in which the quarry was unidentifiable and the crime

[1] " I have a suspicion — not without solid basis — that some mine-owners are more concerned about picking the eyes out of the pits while they are in their possession than they are about the future " (October 3, 1946).

[2] " If . . . the completion of houses has not been as rapid as we expected . . . then the indictment is an indictment of private economic adventure in house building " (October 21, 1946).

[3] " [Mr. Churchill] chose to make a party political speech calculated to weaken our solidarity and the will to win through and to damage us abroad " (August 23, 1947).

[4] " It is shocking that in this critical situation the Tory Party, led by Mr. Churchill, are promoting the maximum amount of mischief."

[5] June 8, 1947.

[6] June 16, 1947.

[7] Lord Pakenham, House of Lords, August 6, 1947 ; Mr. Attlee, House of Commons, August 6, 1947.

[8] Mr. Driberg, August 7, 1947.

[9] September 2, 1947.

undefinable. But the trail was good enough to divert attention from the real architects of the economic chaos.

The Petty Restrictions

Whilst the major blunders of the planners can, at least for a time, be concealed or passed off as acts of God so that the public come to accept them patiently as they would changes in the weather, the minor restrictions necessarily imposed upon individuals by the smaller fry of the bureaucracy are more immediately vexatious and more easily traceable to their source. It is here that the public become most acutely aware of the personal restriction and the waste of the administrative controls.

No pen could fully describe and no mind could wholly grasp the vast mesh of controls in Great Britain that now circumscribe everyday action. But a casual reading of newspapers over a few months throws up sufficient cases to provide some notion of the extraordinarily fine network of restraints and hindrances that surround us.

A market gardener requires a new shaft for a wheelbarrow, a piece of wood costing perhaps ninepence. A licence must be applied for from the surveyor of the district council on the appropriate form. The licence has to be registered and filed by the district surveyor and then presented to, registered and filed by the timber merchant.[1] A local authority for roads wishes to improve visibility at a dangerous junction by substituting some twenty yards of iron fence for the existing hedge. To obtain permission to do this five enormous forms and nine maps, some of them coloured, have to be prepared and submitted.[2] The despatch of a small shipment of six drums of lubricating oil involves the filling in of forty-six forms, requiring forty-two signatures, not including the customer's invoice or delivery notes.[3] A local authority

---

[1] *Daily Telegraph*, February 3, 1947.
[2] *Daily Telegraph*, February 3, 1947.
[3] *Manchester Guardian*, June 26, 1947.

cannot increase the pocket-money of a child under its care without first obtaining sanction from the Home Office.[1] Newspapers are fined for exceeding more than 55 per cent of advertising matter.[2] A firm is fined for making 60,000 frying-pans for the home market, although it is established by evidence that the firm had done this only because of long delays by the Board of Trade in providing an export licence, a licence which in fact had been received after the fine had been imposed.[3] A provincial corn merchant operates under fourteen licences and 160 fixed prices. His books have been minutely investigated five times since control began; inspectors drop in at least four times a year to see if they can catch him; the Costings Department of his Ministry require his trading accounts and balance sheets; he is expected to remember the salient points of hundreds of Orders and Regulations.[4] Orders are couched in language open to all sorts of meanings so that the public could not know whether they were acting legally or not unless they took counsel's opinion or a solicitor's advice.[5] Four Lincolnshire farmers are fined £1200 for growing canary seed.[6] Mrs. Shenton, aged 79, is fined £10 for growing too few potatoes;[7] she said she had responded to a Ministry broadcast appeal to grow more wheat.

Producers struggle to work through a coil of regulations that must defeat all but the hardiest or the most unscrupulous. One authenticated case of this must suffice.[8]

We apply to the Timber Control on a large form, in triplicate, measuring $16\frac{3}{8}$ in. by $8\frac{1}{4}$ in., stating our requirements. We use timber (hardwood) for a great number of lines, but as there is

[1] *Manchester Guardian*, July 2, 1947.
[2] *Manchester Guardian*, November 8, 1946.
[3] *Manchester Guardian*, November 9, 1946.
[4] *Sunday Times*, January 19, 1947.
[5] The Lord Chief Justice, discussing the Eggs (Control and Prices) Order as amended by an Order dated June 1, 1945 (S.R. and O. 1945, No. 645).
[6] *The Times*, January 6, 1947.
[7] *Manchester Guardian*, December 6, 1946.
[8] *Manchester Guardian*, February 24, 1947.

little room on the form we give a representative few. The Timber Control returns the application stating that we must apply to the Ministry of Supply for one line, to the Board of Trade for another, and to the Ministry of Education for another.

We prepare new sets of the application forms, in triplicate, for each Ministry mentioned and send them despondently to London. After some weeks replies come from the Ministries. One says that we are not permitted to make such articles without a permit, though we have been making them for forty years and they are essential to every business. Another Ministry says we must apply to another section of the Ministry at another address, though we sent it to the address given by the Timber Control. We try to enlighten the first Ministry and we send a further application to the second one.

But the third, the Ministry of Education, asks us to furnish the actual orders from the schools which are going to use the articles we wish to make. This is impossible as the schools do not send their orders to us but to their own local education authority. Neither do the local education authorities send us orders — the business is not done that way, but the Ministry seems singularly unaware of the manner in which schools get their supplies.

The Ministry wants the actual orders to make sure that we make only the actual quantities needed and leave none over for stock. But we cannot make such things in ones and twos as they are required, or the cost would be prohibitive. All this has to be explained to the Ministry, and much correspondence follows ; on our part, we reply by return, but the Ministry takes several weeks to reply.

Eventually we may get a licence for part of our needs in one or two cases, and in the others we give up in despair. Meanwhile our woodworking department is desperately needing the timber, and in one case it took seven months to get the licence through.

Even then, our timber merchants tell us we are only at the beginning of the struggle, as the merchant has to battle with the Timber Control to get an allocation even when he has our licence.

When we want further supplies for the same purpose it is quite useless referring to previous correspondence ; the whole business of detailed explanations has to be gone through again. Apparently the Civil Service does not possess any filing system. With a first-rate filing system the Civil Service would probably save thousands of clerks — but that is not the bureaucrats' way.

Criticisms of this kind are met by statements such as those of Mr. Attlee at the 45th Annual Conference of the Labour

Party. " The demand for the abolition of controls is practically confined to the lunatic fringe."

The detail of the control is incredible. The *Board of
Trade Journal* warns retailers that it is illegal to embellish
utility furniture.[1] The women of Pangbourne wanted to
run a bazaar to raise funds for a village hall; they were
informed by the Board of Trade that a pair of boy's trousers
made out of an adult's skirt or trousers are regarded as new
and, therefore, coupons must be charged.[2] The Board of
Trade finds time to fix maximum prices for haircuts.[3]
Churchers College, Peterfield, receives a form from the
Ministry of Fuel and Power informing them that their previous allocation of coke had been cancelled and that their
basic allocation for the twelve months to April 30, 1948, was
nil tons, that it was possible only to allocate nil tons, divided
as to nil tons a month in the summer and nil tons a month
in the winter, and that the name of the supplier was also
indicated.[4] Boxes containing fragments of wedding-cake sent
to friends abroad are emptied and sent on empty because the
export of confectionery is prohibited.[5] The Government seeks
to impose an Order preventing a householder from decorating
his own house, without getting a licence, if the cost of the
raw materials plus the estimated cost of his own labour comes
to more than £10. Strong protests forced the Government
to exclude the cost of labour but not to drop the control.[6]
The owners of private gardens are prohibited, except under
licence, to bottle fruit and sell it to the public.[7] A householder cannot obtain a replacement for a cracked wash-bowl
without getting a licence from the local authority and having
the bowl examined to prove it is unusable.

The list of futile, harassing and costly prohibitions could

---

[1] *Manchester Guardian*, November 30, 1946.
[2] *Time and Tide*, March 22, 1947.
[3] *Manchester Guardian*, June 23, 1947.
[4] House of Commons, June 19, 1947.
[5] *Manchester Guardian*, November 25, 1946.
[6] House of Commons, February 27, 1947.
[7] House of Commons, June 18, 1947.

be expanded almost indefinitely. It represents the inevitable outcome of a planned economy where the exceptional cases can never be allowed for and the regulations are drawn up for the average man who does not exist. This state of affairs has two serious consequences on the morale of the people. It breeds a feeling that the law is brutally inept and leads sensible people to seek its circumvention. And it creates in the minds of the public a contempt for the, quite innocent, minor civil servant who is the instrument through which the Supreme Planners seek to impose their will.

Law-breaking and the Black Markets

As the planned economy unfolds its consequences the ordinary member of the public is conscious of a group of Supreme Planners making large errors, and a host of minor planners who are enforcing regulations in which there seems to be neither rhyme nor reason. It is in this atmosphere that disregard for the law grows apace and the black markets flourish.

Great Britain is not naturally a fertile field for black marketing. The people are law-abiding by habit and tradition. There is no large agricultural population from which, as in many other countries, food can be acquired illegally or by barter. But there can be little doubt that, by the middle of 1947, a large part of the British population were breaking some of the laws of which they were aware, a greater part were breaking laws of which they were not aware, and a still greater part would have been prepared to break the laws if they had had the opportunity.

The anxiety of the Government regarding 'spivs and drones' was, in itself, good evidence of this. Responsible and independent public men, not given to exaggeration, were warning us of the decay of morals.[1] Thieving and petty

[1] Thus Sir John Anderson in the House of Commons, April 16, 1947: "A proportion — I fear a growing proportion — are yielding to the temptation to enter the black market . . . or to resort to various devices doubtfully within the law". Or the head master of Clifton College, June 28, 1947: "In some

pilfering abounded. Barter, for those who had scarce commodities to exchange, became common. The use of pound
notes for the settlement of debts was employed as a method
of tax evasion. The black markets were particularly prevalent
in house repairing, food and clothing. A Minister lamented,
" we cannot have a policeman behind every hedge ".

The Decline in the Quality of Production

By the middle of 1947 it was a matter of common observa-
tion that a high proportion of the goods in the shops were
of bad design and poor quality. One indignant housewife
spoke the thoughts of many : " Enamelled store cupboards
and refuse bins, chromium ladles and fish slices that flake and
rust within a few weeks ; knicker elastic that gives in after a
couple of weeks' washings ; slippers and children's sandals
that part from their uppers after a little wear ; scrubbing
brushes that moult ; toys never intended for use by children ;
aluminium saucepans that rust." She might have added
rubber hose which cracks within the first week, domestic
tools which fracture under strain, paint which cracks and peels
within the month, — and a mass of other equipment pitiful
in its ineffectiveness, heart-breaking in its wastefulness.

The trend towards the production of rubbish was undeniable, the causes of it obscure and diverse. In part it
was undoubtedly attributable to the existing inflationary condition, for when manufacturers are certain that whatever
they produce can be sold, their anxiety to maintain the good
will of the consumer evaporates. In part it was due to the
shortages arising out of the bad distribution of raw materials
under planning which compelled producers to do their best
with the materials that came to them. In part it was a
reflection of the emphasis, common among planners, placed
on mass production and standardisation. The upshot was a
declining sense of service by the producer to the consumer,

homes the old English strict views on honesty and right dealing have been
allowed to go by the board. Transactions under the counter and in black
markets . . . are referred to by some parents in front of their boys."

contributing to the dreariness of existence and representing a real waste of economic satisfaction.[1]

The Growth of Class Consciousness

All real progress in society consists of the growth of charity, freely and spontaneously expressed, through which the material distinctions between individuals are smoothed away in the consciousness of their common human heritage. This was the philosophy providing the foundation for the growing humanitarianism of the nineteenth century. At best, it implied a classless society. At worst, it presumed that if classes were created through differences in income, in occupation, in taste or in ability, the class distinctions should be secondary in the sense that movement between the classes should be unimpeded by privilege and that no class should have it in its power to dominate another. The socialist attacks on the social rigidities and privileges of Victorian England were sound and, being sound, were successful in paving the way for a greater measure of economic equality and the break-down of many vested interests.

But it is becoming clear that the centrally directed economy germinates a new crop of privileged groups and thus weakens social cohesion based upon consent.

There is, first, the clash between the planners and the planned, between those who wield the power and those who must submit to it. The planner is confronted with the baffling administrative problems raised by the diversity of individual needs and individual circumstances. He must simplify and standardise, frame his rules in relation to the average, aim at dealing with masses. By definition, therefore, the rules will not fit individual cases. The planned, recog-

[1] It is true that the Government sought to encourage Design in Industry by setting up Councils and holding exhibitions. In this, however, they were pushing against the grain of the economic organisation which they had created. It is significant that the standards of design set before the British manufacturer by the State were frequently those already achieved in the United States where they had no such Councils and where competition was sufficient to bring about steady improvements in design.

nising the arbitrariness of the general rule and perceiving how badly it fits his special case, strive to evade regulations apparently neither just nor rational. The more widespread the evasion the more stringent and repressive must be the laws. The vicious circle is then complete. For whilst the planner always sees the solution of his problems in just one more set of controls to block some new form of evasion, each member of the planned class sees his salvation in more skilful evasion or the sweeping away of controls altogether. The circle of mutual distrust can grow almost indefinitely. This is why the British Civil Service, probably the least corruptible and the most hard-working and able cadre that has ever operated, is so popularly derided that Ministers must come to its defence in public. This is why the civil servant must constantly add to his unpopularity by seeking for fresh powers of repression if he is to try to carry out the behests of his masters, and why planners in all countries have ultimately found it necessary to raise cries against the recalcitrant classes — be they capitalists, Jews, kulaks, the middle classes or merely spivs and drones.

Secondly, there are the jealousies and envies created between the greater part of the public and those groups which, for the moment, enjoy economic privileges. When planning blunders are made, compulsion can be used to patch up the broken system. But economic incentives are also useful. So that when coal is short the coal-miner will be granted special rations and other perquisites. But other groups in the community will think that their work is as hard, as unpleasant or as necessary as that of the coal-miner and feel a sense of injustice. Each group, therefore, will have a direct interest in keeping down its production, in making its product the crucial bottleneck in the economy. For in that way the power of the group will be increased and the bounty of the planners' largesse made more certain.

Thirdly, in an atmosphere of black markets and lawlessness each man's hand is set against another's. Those who have inherited habits of honesty from life in a liberal society become first indignant at, and ultimately covetous of, the profits going to the law-breakers. The common informer comes into his own [1] and the free-and-easy contacts between individuals are spoilt.

Fourthly, vested interests must organise themselves and clash because, once the market economy is destroyed, that is the form taken by social competition. In allocating the national resources the planners can follow no guiding principles. Since the price system can no longer pass back messages concerning the proper allocation of goods and services, the planners must either organise production without regard for consumers' needs or turn themselves into a gigantic listening-post through which they seek to record in other ways the demands of the people. If the Government is listening, it clearly pays organised groups to shout hard to establish their claims to some sort of priority and to belittle the claims of others. New class rivalries are, thereby, created.

Finally, comprehensive national planning sets one nation against another and engenders frictions which result in the disintegration of the world economy and the danger of war. This subject will be referred to in the next chapter.

The Obsession with Material Ends

At some periods throughout the vicissitudinous history of socialist ideas, spiritual values have been highly rated and at all times the solid support for socialist policy has come from men of good will who dreamed of a finer and more humane society. It is the more tragic that the contemporary efforts to fulfil the socialist purpose through the central direction of the economy is destined to drag down these fine aspirations to an over-preoccupation with material things and physical satisfactions.

The symptoms are always the same. Public discussion

[1] See pp. 207-8.

centres almost wholly on economic affairs; the community lives in a distracting hullabaloo, momentarily stimulating but ultimately exhausting; the leaders harangue and exhort in ever more strident tones in an effort to picture economic effort as a struggle for survival in which luxuries and refinements must be cut off and individual liberty must temporarily go to the wall; there is an anxious straining for more and more effort, higher and higher targets; the public sadly yearns for the promised land which steadily recedes.

This immitigable struggle leaves less room for the refinements of life such as the delights of leisure, the pleasures of solitude, the search for knowledge, the satisfaction of craftsmanship. So the local soviets in Russia gather together to applaud last month's steel output and pledge themselves to ever greater effort. So the British citizen submits to bombardment from cinema, newspaper, radio and hoarding urging him to work harder and accept more sacrifices. In this there is nothing which satisfies the spirit. The harvest festivals of the past did at least confer a sense of a task well done, a purpose fulfilled. But the industrial festivals of the planning age seem to provide nothing but the occasion for once again laying the lash on the backs of workers with the endless cry for more. The keen and stimulating buoyancy of an expanding free economy may at times be fretful and wearing but, at least, it leaves wide individual horizons, opportunity and the right to withdraw from the race at any time. In the planned economy the anxiety neurosis is that of individuals who watch the circle of their initiative slowly shrinking.

The absence of an inner tranquillity in the planned economy is commonly observed but the many and variable reasons for it are perhaps not so well understood. The first is that since planned economies will be poverty-stricken, the minds of the people are much taken up with meeting elementary physical needs. The second is that the planners, in order to cover up the deficiencies of the system and to achieve this target or that programme, will seek to attach some mystical value to work for its own sake and will overlook the elementary truth that work is for leisure and the means to make leisure purposeful. The choice between work and leisure is not a choice between good and evil but between different ways of gaining satisfaction. The third is that the planning crises tend to be sharper, more unpredictable and more catastrophic than any known in other economic systems, and the sense of ever-impending disaster is as crippling as the prospects, to an invalid, of the onset of some dread disease, such as thrombosis or haemophilia.

But the most deep-rooted sickness of the planned economy is that it seeks to bind together the community by an appeal to an end which cannot provide any lasting social cohesion — the pursuit of wealth. It is ultimately disastrous to expect men to enjoy the communion of their common brotherhood, their sense of playing their part in some satisfying joint effort, their feeling of the unfolding of the full potentialities of their personality by putting before them a target (incidentally fixed by someone else) for the output of steel, coal, electrical switches or paper bags. Yet this is precisely the religion that is preached. Thus Lenin: [1]

We need a plan at once to give the masses a shining unimpeded example to work for.

So Sir Oliver Franks: [2]

The plans must become the plans of the nation and animate the constructive endeavour of the managements and workers. . . . Import and Export programmes must become symbols of the life the people wills to achieve. . . . It is at once the task and the miracle of statesmanship to translate them into terms which have meaning and inspiration to ordinary men in ordinary circumstances.

So Sir Stafford Cripps: [3]

We have got to engender in the people the same spirit of determination to see this programme through that they have displayed in winning victory in the war.

[1] See p. 3.   [2] *Central Planning and Control in War and Peace*, p. 37.
[3] Labour Party Conference, 1945.

The planners seem to dig themselves out of one pit only by digging themselves into another. They recognise, and rightly, that the plan stands no chance of success unless the economic affairs of the community are placed in the very forefront of every mind in the group. Work, sacrifice and the achievement of targets must be hammered into the public sleeping and waking, eating and drinking. The statesman must adopt every trick and device to mould the ideal economic man for the purpose. Cupidity ('the golden age is just round the corner'); narrow patriotism ('our community must stand on its own feet'); fear ('the struggle is one for survival') and hatred ('the laggards must be run to earth'); the use of all these are now well-established methods of the planned economy.

Let us assume that the miracle of statesmanship is performed (which I submit is impossible in a free society) and the life of the people is firmly centred on material objectives. Let us further assume that the economic objectives are reached (which I submit are unachievable). Then the community must disintegrate. For the pursuit of wealth cannot bind men together, it is a centrifugal not a centripetal force. The vow of poverty can bring social cohesion. Trappists, Hindus, Christians, Buddhists — history is full of cases where groups have voluntarily and willingly submitted themselves to deprivation because they believed their cause was good. But not so the vow of plenty. There is never in this the threads out of which can be woven the mutual respect and comradeship constituting the stuff of stable and effective communities.

So is destroyed the last hope of the philosophers of planning. For when all else fails — when the promise of plenty is not fulfilled, when security and stability is not achieved, when the claims of the plan to be scientific prove hollow, when the effective employment of the resources of the community is not reached, when the targets prove to be will-o'-the-wisps — it is still argued that the plan justifies itself because, woeful as may be its economic consequences, it still makes it possible for each member of the group to feel himself " part of a united community . . . moving purposefully towards known objectives ".[1]   But in the last analysis the spiritual content of planning proves to be a sham.

These, of course, are precisely the charges which have been laid against the free market economy. But in that economy no one need ever claim that economic activity is the highest form of activity or that the first aim of an individual or a community is to become rich. The market economy is simply a device for creating automatic regulations which will enable us to provide for physical needs by the most economical route, of pushing economic problems into a corner to be forgotten, like the thermostat in a house, so that we can get on as uninterruptedly as possible with the development of the real art of living and the discovery of those forms of human relations which will bring us the ideal society.

[1] *The Times*, September 1, 1947.

CHAPTER XII

NATIONAL PLANNING AND THE WORLD ECONOMY

IT has long been known that planning by individual nations must lead to international chaos, the degree of the chaos being in direct proportion to the number, the completeness and the efficiency of the separate national plans. The manner in which the socialist State, beginning often with high aspirations of international harmony, will contribute to the breakdown of the world economy has frequently been described.[1] National planning reduces international trade. It stifles the free movement of capital and labour and thus undermines the international specialisation of effort. International economic relations become highly unstable because of the recurrence of national planning crises and because trading is a matter of high politics and thereby suffers from every twist and turn in political relations. As each planned economy is driven towards autarchy the problem of the ' have ' and the ' have not ' nations emerges and may well make for war. With the sordid experience behind us of the inter-war years these are axioms. This chapter is a postscript showing how Great Britain under planning is, in international economic affairs, being driven along a path which will damage her own economic prospects and contribute to the impoverishment of the whole world.

I

The illustration is apt. For the Labour Government when it came into power firmly believed in freer world trading

[1] See, in particular, L. Robbins, *International Planning and Economic Order.*

and showed considerable courage in seeking to foster it. It is true that immediate British interests coincided with this policy. The traditional dependence of Great Britain upon exports had been increased by the loss of some investments during the war. The conditions attached to the American Loan pledged Britain to multilateralism willy-nilly. But no one could doubt the high motives of the British Government when they opted for freer world trading. Thus Sir Stafford Cripps : [1]

If, on a basis of self-defence and timidity, trade and financial restrictions of every kind are to spring up again, we shall all be the sufferers however much we try by economic and financial devices to protect our own people. The cumulative despair of restrictionism has proved itself the worst friend of the masses . . . and has been a powerful factor in bringing about the crisis of war. We must do something better, more courageous and more imaginative after this war than was done after the last.

This was in October 1946. By August 1947 the tune had changed. The Prime Minister had announced an expensive scheme for bringing Great Britain nearer to agricultural self-sufficiency; imports were to be cut and a new drive for exports begun. Stricter control of the migration of capital and of persons was to be instituted. Mr. Wilson, then Parliamentary Secretary to the Board of Trade, in language which recalled the funeral orations over the world economy of pre-war conferences, had said, at the closing session of the International Trade Conference at Geneva :

We must face the fact that methods might have to be used in the intervening months and years which might appear to be opposed to the principles and methods of the draft charter. We will certainly have to assist our position by agreements with particular countries.

Why had the high hopes been dashed? The immediate cause was, of course, the British balance of payments crisis in August 1947. The American Loan had run out more quickly than anticipated. The adverse trade balance had reached a

[1] October 3, 1946.

level of £600 millions per annum. The measures to meet
the immediate crisis included the abandonment of the convertibility of sterling and a substantial cut in imports discriminating against the hard currency areas. It may well
be true that administrative ineptitude in the British Treasury
and the insistence upon the part of the Americans on too
early a return to convertibility had precipitated the crisis prematurely. But there was something much more fundamentally wrong. The doctors might have kept the patient going
a little longer, but the collapse was inevitable.

The collapse was inevitable because of a series of grave
errors in the British planning strategy.

The first of these lay in the fixing of export targets and in
pursuing policies based upon the assumption that the targets
would be reached. The export targets were never achieved
and had constantly to be reduced. The first figure which
gained currency was that of a 75 per cent increase in the
volume of exports over the corresponding figure for 1938.
It represented a simple arithmetical calculation of the volume
of exports which would be needed, on certain highly arbitrary
assumptions, to maintain the pre-war British standard of
living.[1] This figure was nailed as a flag to the planning mast.
It was assumed that the pre-war standard of living could be
reached (no one knowing on what grounds the assumption
was made) and, therefore, assumed that the 75 per cent
increase in exports was imperative and attainable. But
periodically the flag had to be lowered. In February 1947
Mr. Dalton was still declaring "75 per cent as soon as
possible ". In the *Economic Survey for 1947* (March 1947)
the target was lowered to 40 per cent by the end of 1947.
In August 1947 Mr. Attlee, in the middle of the balance of
payments crisis, lowered the target to 40 per cent by the
middle of 1948 and 60 per cent by the end of 1948. Now

---

[1] The whole story of the slap-dash methods of planning could be written
around the history of this one figure and the consequence it had for the British
public. A part of that story is told by Mr. Snow in *The Times*, January 23,
1947.

a swollen and unachievable export target within a planned economy may easily reduce exports below the level which they might have achieved if there had been no plan at all. For when the export target is fixed, consequential allocations of raw materials and labour must be made. If the target is not achieved, these resources will have been wrongly placed. They might well have led to larger exports if they had been placed elsewhere. Just as a moderate runner, by establishing too high a standard, may take longer to run 100 yards if he tries to run it in 10 seconds than if he tries to run it in 12 seconds. Export planning reduces exports.

The second planning error was the setting of too high a domestic investment programme. For nearly two years the Government encouraged investment by precept and example. The cotton, coal-mining and iron and steel industries were pressed to install much new equipment. The principle was that, since Great Britain was short of man-power and since machines saved labour, every industry should re-equip as quickly as possible. It was overlooked that machines need labour to build them and that an increase in output per head in one factory may be obtained at the cost of a decrease in output per head over the system as a whole. It was not until the balance of payments crisis occurred that the Government discovered that some re-equipment was better deferred and that there is only a pint in a pint pot. The planning craze for investment reduced exports and worsened the balance of payments problem.

The third planning error was probably (it is impossible always to be certain in these economic might-have-beens) the maintenance of an inappropriate rate of exchange. The Government had pegged the exchange rate at 4·03 dollars to the pound. Whether that was the right rate or not was anybody's guess. No one could possibly know without leaving the rate free to be fixed by market forces. What was known was that sterling had deteriorated heavily in New York and the pound could only be kept at its fixed rate by the strictest exchange control. In the event, since the rest of the world believed that sterling would have to be devalued, speculation contributed to such a drain on the dollars of the American Loan that convertibility of sterling had to be abandoned although the plugged rate was maintained.

It was these three errors, combined with the domestic inflation which increased imports and, as a consequence of the physical anti-inflationary controls, reduced exports, which finally produced the balance of payments crisis and forced Great Britain, against all the best instincts of the Government, into bilateralism.

What would have happened in the free economy? The State would have confined itself to its legitimate rôle of restricting the volume of money sufficiently to prevent domestic inflation. Exports would have been stimulated because that would have been the only outlet for goods. The cramping effect upon industry of physical controls would have been avoided. No export targets would have been fixed, exports would have been left to find their own level. The long-period exchange rate would have been left to determine itself. A deficit in the balance of payments would have been met by a fall in the exchange rate, thus increasing exports and reducing imports. If the nation was living at a level beyond its means, the fact would have been immediately signalled to all and the increase in domestic prices would have pressed down the standard of living to what was possible.

It is futile to argue that this is a theoretical model which would not have worked in the peculiar circumstances of the time. Help from America by way of the loan, the blocking of post-war debts, these would still have been practicable whilst leaving the international price mechanism to decide what standard of living Great Britain could enjoy and what level of exports was consistent with that standard of living.

This was not a choice for the British between taking their medicine or not taking it. It was a choice between making the readjustments gradually and in a fashion which did not disrupt the organic nature of the economic system or taking it in the form of the balance of payments crisis with the Government chopping hysterically at food supplies and, incidentally, following courses which destroyed the chance, which seemed so great at one time, that Great Britain and America together would recreate a new world economy after a quarter of a century's restriction.

How little the planners realised the consequences of their own actions in the international sphere can easily be seen from their conception of international economics as revealed in the crucial debate on the State of the Nation on August 6 and 7, 1947, in the House of Commons. Reference has already been made [1] to the smoke-screen of dubious argument by which the Government sought to conceal the real causes of the international break-down. It led inevitably to the oldest and the most deeply embedded fallacy in economic thinking: the belief that, whatever the cost, it is always a good thing for a country to produce its own food.

Mr. Attlee had announced that British agricultural output was to be increased by £100 millions (or 20 per cent), requiring an additional 100,000 workers and a large amount of capital equipment. A week later the Minister of Agriculture announced new and higher prices for farmers. The ostensible reason for this policy was that " agriculture was a great dollar saver ", and even that growing food was equivalent to " growing dollars on our own soil ".[2] At least four assumptions, all of them unfounded, were embodied in this line of reasoning. The first was that we could produce food domestically as cheaply as we could buy it from abroad: but the very fact that it was found necessary to subsidise British farmers disproves this. The second was that if an additional 100,000 workers and a large amount of capital is invested in agriculture this will put more food into British bellies than if this labour and capital were put into some manufacturing

---

[1] See Chapter XI, p. 186.
[2] Minister of Agriculture, *The Listener*, September 4, 1947.

industry, say textiles, the additional product being exported and food obtained from abroad in exchange. The third was that if we cut off imports from abroad our chance of developing our export trade will be unaffected. The fourth was that if our domestic food production is increased in value by 20 per cent it will be increased in volume by 20 per cent whatever happens to unit prices. But, of course, saving one dollar of imports by losing two dollars of exports is not good economics. Neither is growing dollars on your own land at two dollars a time.

II

By instinct the British planners favoured freer world trade. But the addicts to planning are not always masters of themselves and, in this case, certain of their preconceptions helped to frustrate their better purposes. Of these the most dangerous were the reliance upon bulk purchase and the habit of planning exports.

Bulk Purchase of Imports

In any over-simplified and mechanistic conception of economics, State trading in imports seems to have many advantages. Large-scale operations enable the one monopoly purchaser to make better bargains, price fluctuations can be levelled out, speculation can be obviated, merchants' margins can be abolished. In addition, a grip on imports provides a grip on every phase and aspect of the whole economy. It is, therefore, not surprising that the Socialist Government held on to the war-time system of State purchase which they found in their hands when they came to power in 1945.[1]

[1] In 1946 the following items were still being purchased in bulk by the British Government : Timber ; Raw Materials for Textiles ; Hides, Skins and Tanning Materials ; Paper, Board and Paper-making Materials ; Rubber (Natural and Synthetic) ; Materials for Fertilisers ; Chemicals ; Chromic Ore, Molybdenum Concentrates ; Tungsten Ore ; Lead ; Zinc ; Copper ; Tin Ore ; Aluminium ; Pig-Iron ; Steel ; Fruits and Vegetables ; Fish ; Meat and Bacon ; Tea, Coffee, Cocoa ; Cereals ; Pulses ; Starch ; Sugar ; Milk Products ; Eggs.

It is still too early to assess the full consequences upon world trade and the world economy of the British system of bulk purchase, but some items in the price that will undoubtedly have to be paid can already be listed.

Whilst small, short-period price fluctuations can clearly be avoided by bulk purchase, when an error is made by the State's purchasing agency very violent and disruptive price changes occur. The Ministry of Food increased the price overnight of linseed oil from £55 a ton to £135, subsequently the price rose to £200. In October 1946 the Cotton Control raised its prices suddenly by 5¾d. a pound, a rise unheard of when the world's futures markets were operating normally, and a rise all the more confusing when, on the same day, the price of cotton in America declined by 3½d. a pound. This confirms the pre-war lesson that large-scale intervention by the State in trading will mean serious upsets to world trade, due to the catastrophic nature of delayed price adjustments.

Uncertainty in the markets is increased by State trading. Prices are dependent upon the unforeseeable outcome of international negotiations in which political as well as economic forces are at play. Governments are free to impose price changes unilaterally. In early 1947 the Government of Ceylon threw over their bulk-purchase arrangements for tea and copra and raised their prices suddenly against us. Mr. Strachey was forced to admit " the Government of Ceylon has a perfect right to do this ".[1] In March 1946 the Argentine suddenly demanded an extra £7 millions on a meat contract for which prices had already been fixed. When the House of Commons protested, Dr. Summerskill replied, " I do not think it is necessary to explain . . . that today we have a sellers' market ".[2] Uncertainty of the future of prices is further increased by the growing secrecy which surrounds the international bargaining. Before the war the statistics of stocks of food and raw materials were generally

[1] House of Commons, February 6, 1947.
[2] March 7, 1947.

available. Trading governments must for obvious reasons now suppress these figures. The Minister of Food when pressed in the House of Commons to reveal British wheat stocks refused : " I have to go out into the world and buy in a sellers' market — and to come here and reveal stocks openly to the House makes my position very difficult unless I want to force the prices up to sky-high positions ".[1] But since, of course, a market is always a buyers' or a sellers' market, some government always has an interest in concealing the facts which must be public if markets are to be stable. Ministers have also refused to disclose stocks of tea (although in this case it was a very simple matter for anybody to calculate them with fair accuracy), edible oils, wheat, petroleum products, or to reveal prices paid for food. This growing obscurantism turns the world markets into a grim wrestling of giants in the dark. Uncertainty is finally increased by protracted negotiations. The squabble between Great Britain and Denmark over food prices had, in October 1947, already been going on for a year and a half, and had, on more than one occasion, resulted in a complete stoppage of vital food imports from Denmark.

Bulk purchasing by one country encourages retaliatory bulk sales by others. The Governments of Ceylon, Siam and the Argentine replied in this way to British efforts to gain the bargaining advantages of bulk purchase. These governments all followed the very obvious practice of charging the British Government a higher price than was allowed to the producer. So that the British consumer, in paying the higher price, did not even derive the benefit, automatic in a market economy, of increased output following from increased prices.

International frictions are exacerbated by bulk trading. Hard bargaining, country by country, means that some countries will receive a lower price from a bulk purchaser than others. There has already been grumbling by our Dominions that we are paying them lower prices than those

[1] February 6, 1946.

offered to other countries. Prolonged wrangling between governments makes for bad blood; one side always feels that the other has put on the screw. History may still have to record that Britain's high-handed attitude with Denmark over the prices of bacon and butter forced Denmark into economic dependence on Russia and pushed behind the iron curtain a country with a long tradition of democratic living.

Bulk purchase destroys the futures market, one of the most highly specialised weapons of a world economy. Perhaps the most disastrous case in Great Britain was the closing down, against the wishes of the vast majority of the manufacturing end of the cotton industry, of the Liverpool Cotton Futures Market on the grounds that large-scale buying by the State is " the modern method ", that " in future there will be no opportunity for outsiders to dabble in the fortunes of this great industry ", and that the State purchase and distribution of cotton would reduce employment by some 2500 persons.[1]

The Planning of Exports

Bulk purchase of imports by the State is, in the long run, destructive of a free world economy. So is the State planning of exports. Indeed the planning of exports does not seem to have any meaning except in terms either of bilateral bargaining or of a quite impracticable world economic plan in which all countries voluntarily agree upon some allocation of world markets. In all other circumstances what one country will export will be determined, not by the government of that country, but by the consumers in the importing country. Export targets then become either mere estimates of what the exporting government thinks will happen anyway or wishful longing for unattainable ends.

Up to the middle of 1947 British export planning took the form of estimates. No one could know, and perhaps least of all the Government, what volume of British goods would be taken by other countries. The officials of the

[1] Mr. Marquand, House of Commons, December 2, 1946.

Board of Trade went to the different industries to ask each what volume of goods it thought it could export. Business men did not find it easy to give an answer. The markets of the world were, in any case, highly disorganised. The domestic planned economy was equally unstable. No producer knew what supplies of raw materials and labour he could expect. Some business men, moved by patriotism or by the thought that a high export quota might give them a higher priority for raw materials and labour, were inclined to give optimistic estimates. Others, more cautious or more anxious to take advantage of the plentiful demand in the home market, were inclined to give lower estimates. The Government officials were in no real position to check or query these estimates, but out of them they had to frame an export plan. There was no particular reason why the plan should be right, very many reasons why it should be wrong. The second form of export planning was revealed during the balance of payments crisis of August 1947. Faced with a given deficit, the Government made what import cuts it thought practicable and then chose as the export target a figure large enough to cover the remainder of the deficit. It is not surprising that the British export targets proved so unreal as to become an object of derision.

There was, indeed, one legitimate purpose behind the British export targets — the counteracting of some of the effects of the domestic inflation. The purchasing power at home was so large and was so persistently seeking out the goods available that industry would have found it easy to sell most of its products internally. It was necessary, therefore, to force exports by cutting down quotas for the home market. But this, of course, was the clumsiest conceivable method of attaining the desired results. If there is inflation, the obvious remedy is for the State to withdraw purchasing power by taxation, in which case the demand of the home market is restricted. But to strive to reach the same end by fixing export quotas for each firm, and by allocating raw materials and labour on the basis of these quotas, is as devious a method as going to Glastonbury by way of Goodwin Sands.

Export plans in a multilateral world are a ludicrous waste of time. They can, however, be given real meaning if the State is prepared to make bilateral bargains. It is not surprising that those who begin with an article of faith that exports must be planned finish by discarding multilateralism.

The planned economy is driven remorselessly towards self-sufficiency. It is exasperating for planners who have established rigid controls in the home market, by allocating raw materials, factory space, machines and labour, by controlling investment and by rationing consumers, to contemplate the freedom of foreign consumers who can take or reject goods at their own wish. This, to their minds, is old chaos breaking out again. The license of the foreign consumer disturbs the best-laid domestic plans.

Moreover, the encouragement of exports involves the planner in what are, to him, highly distasteful practices and attitudes. Competition is immoral. Yet exports have to be gained through a fierce competitive struggle. The planner is never very happy at the thought that ' inessentials ' are being produced. Yet the exports of a manufacturing country must increasingly consist of high-quality and even luxury goods, since the agricultural countries are beginning to produce their own low-quality goods. Exporting calls for elaborate distributive and market organisations, good packaging, advertising, high-pressure statesmanship — all the practices which the planner has always frowned upon as evidence of the decay of capitalist civilisation. It was not some boosting advertising manager giving a pep talk to his salesmen but Sir Stafford Cripps himself who said :

We cannot afford . . . to adopt the old ' take it or leave it ' line. We have got to go out to get markets and make sales, and we must see that our products are reasonably competitive in every way.[1]

[1] *Democracy Alive*, p. 59.

A planner trying to adhere to multilateralism is, therefore, working to a double moral code.

Bilateralism is always at hand to solve his difficulties if he will only embrace it. Export trade then becomes a known, although of course a smaller, quantity. It need no longer disturb the domestic plan. The painful competitive struggle of the market can be transformed into calm discussion of officials round a table at an international conference. The country can feel that it is standing on its own feet. It is not surprising that the planner succumbs to the temptation.

III

One other way out is sometimes advocated : a world plan in which the determination of each country's exports and imports would fall into place as a part of the authoritative control of all the economic activities on the globe. This might come about either through wide political federation or through the planning nations retaining their political autonomy whilst voluntarily agreeing to make their different plans fit together.

World political federation has much to commend it, although it is not a subject that can be discussed here. But one thing is certain. If the nations ever agreed to merge their sovereign rights in a common Government, the life of that Government for many years would be precious but fragile, the political forces tending to pull it apart would be strong and unwearying. But the federation's chance of survival would be nil if, in addition to its other preoccupations, it were called upon to operate a world economic plan. For this plan would suffer, in an even more serious way, from all the defects which are inevitably attached to a national plan. A player who finds it difficult to play one game of chess does not make things easier for himself by undertaking to play one hundred games simultaneously. A world political federation could only survive if it delegated to the market and the price system the control and regulation of the economic system.

In any attempt, on the other hand, by planning bodies still retaining their sovereignty, to fit together their national plans, the world economy is doomed from the outset. For the plans will not fit and the attempts to make them fit will degenerate quickly into cynical and unscrupulous bargaining, in which the only men not allowed to speak at the conference —the ordinary customer and the free producer and merchant — will be squeezed flat against the wall. Each planned economy will be trying to do the same thing : to increase exports and reduce imports ; to invest heavily in capital equipment and in the basic industries, and, for this purpose, to borrow from the others ; to build up uneconomic industries so that it can bargain more effectively at the table of the international conference. The prolonged negotiations will always be outstripped by the economic facts of the time. So the conferences will break up in confusion with binding agreements, always subject to waiver, phrased in grandiloquent but meaningless terms,[1] and with arrangements to set up futile ' study groups ' which can only waste more time. And so the delegates will go home, wearied with their life on the treadmill, convinced of the unreasonableness of the foreigner, and more than ever certain that in the international babel their country must stand on its own feet, which means in effect that it must also stand on the economic jugular vein of some other country.

[1] Such as " the maintenance of supplies ample to the needs of consumers without creating a burden of unwanted surpluses and without uneconomic incentive to high cost producers ", or " orderly distribution at prices fair to both producers and consumers ".

INDEX

THE END